D1796366

FIRST
VINTAGE

Julie McIntyre

FIRST VINTAGE

Wine in colonial New South Wales

UNSW PRESS

A UNSW Press book

Published by
NewSouth Publishing
University of New South Wales Press Ltd
University of New South Wales
Sydney NSW 2052
AUSTRALIA
newsouthpublishing.com

© Julie McIntyre 2012
First published 2012

10 9 8 7 6 5 4 3 2 1

This book is copyright. Apart from any fair dealing for the purpose of private study, research, criticism or review, as permitted under the Copyright Act, no part may be reproduced by any process without written permission. Inquiries should be addressed to the publisher.

National Library of Australia Cataloguing-in-Publication entry
    Author: McIntyre, Julie.
    Title: First vintage: wine in colonial New South Wales/Julie McIntyre.
    ISBN: 9781742233444 (hbk.)
    ISBN: 9781742241241 (epub)
    ISBN: 9781742246147 (epdf)
    Subjects: Wine and wine making – New South Wales – History.
    Wineries – New South Wales – History.
    Dewey Number: 663.2009944

Design Di Quick
Cover images Sweetwater, later identified as the sherry grape, Palomino, was common in early colonial vineyards. George Brookshaw. *The Horticultural Repository, Containing Delineations of the Best Varieties of the Different Species of English Fruits*, Mitchell Library, State Library of NSW; Plants framing the pathway through the subsistence garden at the first Government House, Sydney, are thought to be the first grape vines planted in Australia. This 1791 painting by William Bradley depicts the 'coming in' of local Aboriginal people after the payback spearing of Governor Arthur Phillip the previous year at Manly, an event in which an offer of wine played a role in cross-cultural diplomacy. *Mitchell Library, State Library of NSW*; McWilliam's Mark View Wines at Junee. *McWilliam's Wines*
Printer Everbest, China

This book is printed on paper using fibre supplied from plantation or sustainably managed forests.

NEW SOUTH WALES
wine

Contents

A note on style and measurements

Where direct quotes from historical sources have contained capitalisation, spelling errors or symbols, as long as changes have not altered the meaning of the quotes, they have been modified for greater ease of reading.

Measurements are usually listed in their contemporary form and the following may assist with some of the unfamiliar terms used in wine trade. Measurements of wine quantity have historically been unreliable. As Jan Todd pointed out, the four different gallon measures in England were only standardised in 1824, after at least 800 years of confusion.[1]

The most frequently used quantity measures for wine in colonial New South Wales were gallons, pipes and hogsheads. Change from imperial to metric measurement in Australia is recent enough that only a conversion is provided on this page for the gallon, but pipe also requires explanation. According to an entry in the *Oxford Companion to Wine*, the pipe originated as a wine trade term from the Portuguese *pipa* or barrel.[2] Madeira and Marsala, common Portuguese fortified wine exports, were measured in pipes but measurements varied from 534 to 630 litres, depending on use and region. The shipping measure was usually closest to 534 litres, so that is used here to understand the quantities described by colonial growers. References to land use the contemporary colonial measurement of acres but the metric conversion is supplied below.

1 gallon = 4.55 litres 26.5 gallons = 1 hectolitre
1 gallon = six bottles of wine of 750mls
2 gallons = a case of 12 bottles of wine)
1 hogshead = 63 gallons of wine, 285 litres
1 hogshead = 2 barrels
1 pipe = (approx.) 534 litres, also equal to 117 gallons
1 pipe = (approx.) 712 bottles of wine of 750 ml or almost 60 cases
1 acre = 0.405 hectares
1 mile = 1.6 kilometres

Acknowledgments

This book owes an enormous debt to the accomplished and emerging scholars who have guided my research and writing, the unfailingly polite research staff and curators at dozens of libraries, public archives and historical societies; vignerons in the New South Wales wine industry who have been more than generous with time and knowledge; and the elegantly efficient and ever patient team at NewSouth/UNSW Press.

In particular, my appreciation to Richard Waterhouse, Grace Karskens, David Dunstan, John Germov, Catherine Oddie, Rebecca Mitchell, Philip Dwyer, Roger Markwick, Erik Eklund, Ivor Indyk, Carl Bridge, Frank Bongiorno, Ian Henderson, Robert Aldrich, David Roberts, Marian Quartly, Richard Broome, Penny Russell, Richard White, Kirsten McKenzie, Susie Khamis, Kate Darian-Smith, Victoria Haskins, John Tulloch, Jacqui Newling, Ian Cupit and Norrie Doyle, Tracy Bradford, James Halliday, Stephen Guilbaud-Oulton, Stuart McGrath-Kerr, Don Seton-Wilkinson, Brian McGuigan, Phil Ryan, Jay Tulloch, Hazel Murphy, Lucy Anderson, Julie Watt, Phil Ashley-Brown, Jo Upham, Craig Munro, Phillipa McGuinness, Elspeth Menzies, Uthpala Gunethilake, Heather Cam, Di Quick, Fiona Sim, John and Edwina Macarthur-Stanham, Rebecca Barrett and Michael Anderson, Nicola Ross and Pete Allsop, Virginia Newell and Mark Burslem, Jen and Andrew Denzin, Nicola Hensel and John Tourier, Katrin Gustafson and Ben Ewald, Sidsel Grimstad, Jane Smith, Chris Battle, Katrina Gordon, Maureen Beckett, Catherine Henry, Janine Bendit, Kylie Morris and Bharat Nalluri, Justin and Helen Morey, Angela Macpherson and Graham Calder-Smith, Sally Knox and Bill Frewen and the Argiris family.

Thanks to my grandparents, Mum and my stepdad, Dad and Rose-marie Morris, my brother Joe, Aunty Margaret, Aunty Kit, Marie and Ken Muir, Heather McIntyre, my step children Kylie, Zoë, Elizabeth, Alexander (their partners and multitude of progeny) who are in the folds of this story as well as in my heart, my offspring Isaac and Benny, who are the sunshine and above all, Phillip McIntyre who is a source of scaffolding, scholarship and the soul of the entire enterprise.

Substantial portions of this book were completed while I held the Rydon Fellowship at the Menzies Centre for Australian Studies, King's College, London in 2010 and thanks to generous funding from the Wine Industry Research Collaborative, Centre for Institutional and Organisational Studies, University of Newcastle.

Sections of material in this book have previously been published in the following articles and I am grateful to the editors of these journals for permission to reproduce them here:

McIntyre, J (2011) 'Adam Smith and Faith in the Transformative Qualities of Wine in Colonial New South Wales, *Australian Historical Studies*, 42, 2, pp. 194–211, at pages 51, 65, and 84–88.

McIntyre, J (2011) 'Resisting Ages-Old Fixity as a Factor in Wine Quality: Colonial wine tours and Australia's early wine industry', *Locale: The Australasian–Pacific Journal of Regional Food Studies*, 1, 1, pp. 1–19, at pages 64 and 172.

McIntyre, J (2009) 'Not Rich and Not British: Philip Schaeffer, "failed" farmer', *Journal of Australian Colonial History*, 11, p. 1–20, at pages 46–49.

McIntyre, J (2008) '"Bannelong Sat Down to Dinner with Governor Phillip, and Drank His Wine and Coffee as Usual": Aborigines and wine in early New South Wales', *History Australia*, 5, 2, pp. 39.1–39.14, at pages 37–42.

McIntyre, J (2007) 'Camden to London and Paris: The role of the Macarthur family in the early New South Wales Wine Industry', *History Compass*, 5, 2, pp. 427–38, at pages 56–59 and 165.

Contemporary wine regions of New South Wales

From Register of Protected Geographical Indications, Wine Australia

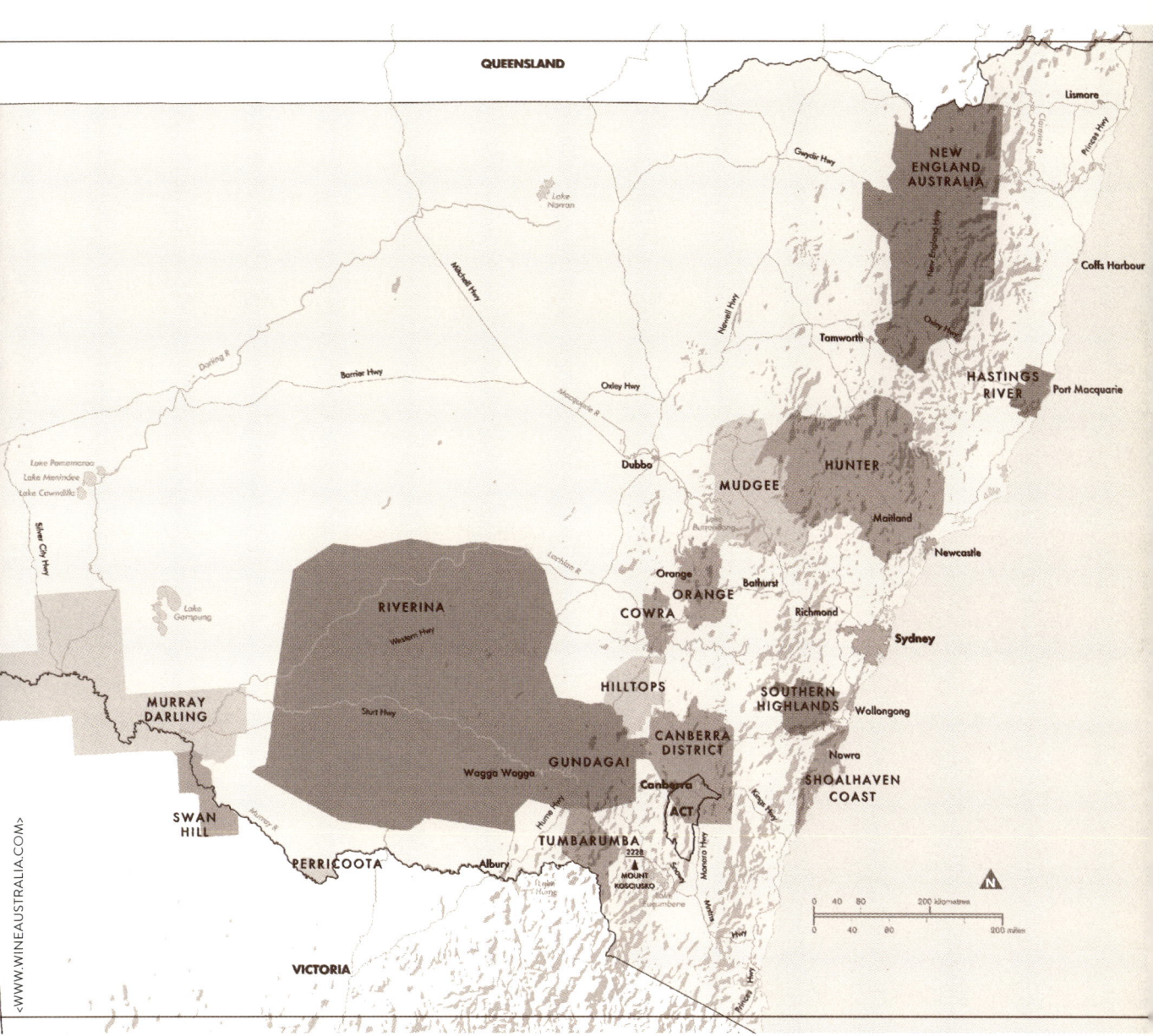

QUEENSLAND

Lismore

Clarence R.

Princes Hwy

NEW ENGLAND AUSTRALIA

New England Hwy

Coffs Harbour

Gwydir Hwy

Lake Narran

Mitchell Hwy

Newell Hwy

Oxley Hwy

Tamworth

HASTINGS RIVER

Port Macquarie

Oxley Hwy

Darling R.

Barrier Hwy

Macquarie R.

Dubbo

MUDGEE

HUNTER

Maitland

Newcastle

Lake Pamamaroo
Lake Menindee
Lake Cawndilla

Silver City Hwy

Lake Gumpung

Lachlan R.

Orange

ORANGE

Bathurst

Richmond

Sydney

RIVERINA

Western Hwy

COWRA

HILLTOPS

SOUTHERN HIGHLANDS

Wollongong

MURRAY DARLING

Sturt Hwy

GUNDAGAI

CANBERRA DISTRICT

Canberra

ACT

Nowra

SHOALHAVEN COAST

Kings Hwy

Wagga Wagga

SWAN HILL

Murray R.

Hume Hwy

TUMBARUMBA

2228
MOUNT KOSCIUSKO

Monaro Hwy

PERRICOOTA

Albury

Tumut R.
Tumut

Tumbarumba

VICTORIA

Princes Hwy

0 40 80   200 kilometres
0 40 80   200 miles

N

<WWW.WINEAUSTRALIA.COM>

Timeline of first plantings of wine grapes in districts across New South Wales

1787 The First Fleet sailed from Britain to establish the colony of New South Wales. Wine was purchased in the Spanish colony of the Canary Islands, the Portuguese colony of Rio and the (then) Dutch colony of the Cape of Good Hope. Wine grape stock was also obtained at the Cape.

1788 Australia's first grape vines were planted in the governor's garden at Sydney Cove and later at Norfolk Island. (New South Wales in its early years extended from the north east of the continent to the south-west including Van Diemen's Land, later Tasmania, and coastal islands.)

1791 Philip Schaeffer, a retired Hessian (German) soldier, was allocated 140 acres of land on the Parramatta riverfront which he called The Vineyard and trialled grain crops, tobacco and wine grapes.

1792 Governor Phillip returned to England with souvenirs and scientific specimens from New South Wales. There is some evidence that wine made in New South Wales may have been among this cargo.

1800–10 Vine plantings extended to Castle Hill, St Marys and Campbelltown outside Sydney.

1800 Arrival in the colony of two French prisoners of war from a British gaol; the two men were singled out for their skills in wine grape growing and paid to try to create successful vineyards.

1803 The first edition of the colony's first newspaper, the *Sydney Gazette and New South Wales Advertiser*, included translated French instructions on vine growing.

1810–20 Vine plantings extended throughout the Cumberland Plain (e.g. Richmond, Windsor, Eastwood, Emu Plains, banks of the Nepean and Hawkesbury rivers).

1815–16 John, James and William Macarthur took a walking tour through France to Switzerland and back; the first deliberate fact-finding journey through European wine lands. They observed the vintage at the winery of a Swiss vigneron who had vineyards in the former British colony of Kentucky and collected vine stock from renowned regions of France and, on the journey back to Sydney, from the Portuguese colony of Madeira where some of the world's finest wine was produced.

1819 Reverend Samuel Marsden took vine cuttings from New South Wales to New Zealand.

1820s Vine plantings extended to Camden, Bathurst and the Hunter Valley (along the banks of the Hunter, Williams and Paterson rivers).

1822 Gregory Blaxland took his colonial claret to London to be judged by the Society for the Arts.

1824 James Busby arrived in the colony after a short study tour of France to collect French wine manuals and observe wine growing. Once in Sydney he completed the manuscript for the first wine instruction manual to be available in English in the colony, *A Treatise*, published in 1825.

1825 Van Diemen's Land (Tasmania) became a separate colony from New South Wales.

1829 British colonisation began in Western Australia.

1830s Vine plantings now reached Port Macquarie on the mid North Coast and Raymond Terrace (near Newcastle).

1836 British colonisation began in South Australia.

1838 First British government sponsored migration of non-British labourers to New South Wales: six vinedressers from pre-unification Germany, and their families, to work at James and William Macarthur's Camden Park vineyard.

1840s First vine plantings southward at Wagga Wagga, Gunning (Canberra), Shoalhaven Coast.

1842–43 Worst years of the economic depression of the early 1840s.

1842 First vineyard association in Australia: Western Australia Vineyard Society first met and established an experiment to test vine cultivars which members hoped would become a model.

1843 The first partially-elected Legislative Council enacted a series of laws to encourage wine production and consumption and the first official record keeping of grape plantings and wine making.

1844 First known retail sales of New South Wales colonial wine: 'Australian Wine' from James and William Macarthur's Camden Park.

1847 Inauguration of the Hunter River Vineyard Association.

1850s First (known) vine plantings at Mudgee, Yass, Inverell, Armidale and Tamworth.

1850 First meeting of the short-lived New South Wales Vineyard Association, centred around Sydney and westward on the coastal plain.

1851 The colony of Victoria became separate from New South Wales, so that its wine industry now developed with different policies including higher tariffs protecting against wine imports.

1851 London Exhibition at the Crystal Palace, the first of a long tradition of international and intercolonial exhibitions in the western world. A small quantity of New South Wales wine was exhibited to some notice.

1855 Paris Exhibition, at which New South Wales wines were judged to be better than expected by an expert panel. Plus Napoleon III introduced the Bordeaux Classifications of wine.

1859 Queensland became a self-governing colony so that that its grape growing was now a separate industry from that of New South Wales.

1860s Vine plantings extended to Albury, Young, Pokolbin (near Cessnock) in the Hunter Valley and Forbes.

1861 New South Wales vineyard plantings represented 25 per cent of the Australian total.

1861 First *Land Act* in New South Wales, aimed at encouraging small hold agricultural land use, to dilute the dominance of large scale pastoral land use (sheep and cattle grazing).

1863 Holroyd's *Sale of Colonial Wines Act* which introduced a lower licence fee for wine shops in an effort to encourage moderate temperance.

1867–69 The vine disease powdery mildew (oidium) had spread to New South Wales after being detected in Queensland. Disagreement raged about whether to force all grape growers to use sulphur, which proved to be the best remedy to control the disease.

Late 1860s William Keene from the Hunter Valley created a new design for a saccharometer, for measuring the sugar content in ripening grapes to determine when harvest should take place.

1870s Vines planted in the Southern Highlands.

1871 New South Wales vineyard plantings represented 26 per cent of the Australian total.

1877 Australia's first official outbreak of the vine pest grape phylloxera was first detected at Geelong, Victoria.

1880s First vine plantings at Cowra (though it was possibly earlier); 360 wine presses in operation in New South Wales.

1881 New South Wales vineyard plantings represented 31 per cent of the Australian total.

1884 *Land Act* amendment; a new attempt to encourage closer settlement and wider crop farming and small hold mixed farming

1885 Grape phylloxera first officially detected in New South Wales at Macarthurs' Camden Park vineyard.

1885 Per capita annual consumption of beer in New South Wales was 13.19 gallons compared with 1.3 gallons of spirits and 0.64 gallons of wine.

1888 The total number of wine presses operating in New South Wales was 360 (see Appendix 2).

1890s First wine grape plantings at Junee (near Gundagai).

1890 New South Wales Department of Agriculture created; appointment of an expert viticulturalist (who had studied in Britain and at Pasteur's laboratory in France); first publication of the *New South Wales Agricultural Gazette*. One of the earliest initiatives of the new department was to encourage the production of grafted rootstock as a preventative measure against phylloxera.

1891–92 New South Wales vineyard plantings represented 19 per cent of the Australian total. There were more than 2100 growers of grapes for wine and table in the colony (see Appendix 2).

1893 Worst year of the international economic depression of the early 1890s.

1894 *Land Act* amendments which marked a renewed attempt to encourage agriculture closer to settled areas.

1901 New South Wales vineyard plantings had dropped to 13 per cent of the Australian total.

1905 Rise in economic prosperity and end of crippling drought

1913 First wine grapes planted at Griffith/Leeton (Murrumbidgee Irrigation Area).

1920s Drought reduces much of western New South Wales to a dustbowl; soldier settlement schemes post–World War I are declared a failure; formal end of hopes for an agrarian Australia.

1930s Depression and **1940s** World War II: Two decades of decline in wine growing except for Griffith and the Hunter Valley; one winery remained at Mudgee.

1950s New plantings begin to emerge in old wine districts in New South Wales.

1959 Australian Bureau of Statistics figures show wine consumption was 12 per cent of the total pure alcohol consumed nationally, compared with 76 per cent for beer and 12 per cent for spirits (see graph, p. 4).

1960s and 1970s The pace of vine plantings and wine production began to accelerate, along with increased economic prosperity and social changes, such as greater British Australian tolerance of the wine drinking (and other cultural practices) of non-British Australians and new drinking habits for all Australian women.

1980s New wine regions emerged, while other districts which had hosted vineyards in the colonial era were being replanted with vines. The new regions were Tumbarumba and Orange (plantings in 1850s at Orange may have been table grapes).

1990s The newest New South Wales wine region of Perricoota was created in the decade in which Australian white wine conquered the British and United States markets.

2011 Australian Bureau of Statistics figures showed the quantity of wine being drunk in Australia had reached 37 per cent of apparent pure alcohol consumed; beer was at 42 per cent, spirits at 20 per cent (see graph, p. 4).

Vineyards are captivating places, especially at harvest.
Photograph by Sam Hood, c1930.

MITCHELL LIBRARY, STATE LIBRARY OF NSW, DG ON4/7052 HOME AND AWAY - 7063

Introduction

I remember being tiny enough to duck underneath the trellising wires in my grandparents' vineyard in Mudgee, New South Wales. It was the early 1970s and I must have been about three or four years old. A drought had made the bravura Australian landscape colours seem paler than usual next to the lavishness of grape vines in full green leaf.

And there I was, just before harvest or vintage – we called it picking – at eye level with a tangle of spindly wooden canes amid a chaos of leaves; bunches of grapes clouded with bloom, sticky and sweet with juice and laced with spider webs. The webs made the grapes seem historic, even ancient, although they had matured in just a few months from buds to berries.

Like many Australians I have spent most of my life on the coast but this is the original sedimentary layer of my memory: vines, orchard, chooks, Grandma's vegie patch; the big stone house built by my great-great grandfather who migrated as a child in the 1850s when his father came to work as a vinedresser on an estate near Sydney. These members of my family, along with hundreds of others from pre-unification Germany, contributed to the earliest glimmers of a wine industry in New South Wales, an industry which was small compared with contemporary wine growing but beginning to thrive before the 1890s. That decade's Depression, followed by social factors and the economic crash of the 1930s meant that by the early 1950s wine vineyards all but vanished from the physical and cultural landscape of New South Wales and therefore – in most regions – from memory as well.

Some wine making continued in this lean mid-century. At Mudgee, for example, a single vineyard and winery remained where in the 1880s there had been fifty-five landowners growing grapes for wine and table. This surviving site had been one of many holdings of the remarkable Roth family, who arrived in the same wave of assisted German migrants as my family. The Roths' Craigmoor survived by producing fortified wines such as port and sherry, which had a small Australian market. Port and other heavy sweet wines such as Madeira were quite posh in Britain's Georgian-era drinking culture, but by the twentieth century were branded with ignominy as *plonk*. Really, fortifieds were the fashion victims of the Frenchification of wine. Frenchification is the colonisation of the very idea of wine by Frenchness: the correlation of a small number of French chateau-produced, long-aged wines with quality and authenticity. This influential notion that fine French wines carry the highest status and economic value may seem to have existed since time immemorial but is actually younger than the invention of the telephone.[1]

My grandfather worked Craigmoor's vines in the 1950s to supplement earnings from 26 acres left to him when half of the original family selection had been resumed to build Mudgee airport. Known as Rosebud Farm, this property had produced wine in the early part of the century.

> "
> *Shearing, cattle stations, gold and beer drinking are iconic parts of British Australia. Wine however, is not.*

Grandad used Craigmoor cuttings to begin to replant it with vines so that by the early 1970s, after harvest, in the new winery next to the old house, waxed concrete vats frothed with crushed grapes fermenting into wine. The mysterious alchemy of it, the seductive perfume in that high-roofed corrugated iron shed delighted me long before I was old enough to drink wine. At bottling time there were pallets of unlabelled bottles at one end of a simple assembly line. I puddled with the gum used to adhere wine labels to bottles and sorted the plastic capsules which were slipped cleverly over the corks. I admired the smart bottles ready for sale, the neat rows of tasting glasses and Grandma's wonderful way with people who drove in to purchase wine by the carton from the small cellar door at the side of the winery.

In this time too, my other grandparents, my parents and many others in the region were mixed farmers. They raised sheep, cattle, and grain and fodder crops near the old gold mining town of Gulgong. These pursuits, like the vineyard, are joyful sources of nostalgia for me. For all of the hours I spent sitting high on our stockyard fence, swinging my legs and watching cattle and sheep subjected to necessary indignities, I feel a jolt of pleasure at the sight of such yards on country roads. The aroma of shearing shed – an astringent cocktail of lanolin and urea – reminds me of them. And I am disproportionately proud of my one season as a shearer's cook for my father in the late 1980s. For four frenzied days I was perfectly happy to be known only as Cook, to butter oven loads of my grandmother's scones and to roast vast quantities of meat and vegetables. Needless to say I witnessed the consumption of a good deal of beer at the end of those intense four days; at cut-out, as it is called. I mention this because shearing, cattle stations, Central Western gold – and, for that matter, beer drinking – are well told, iconic parts of the story of British Australia. Wine, however, is not, as I discovered when I set out ten years ago to use papers left by my grandfather to piece together the origins of his enterprise.

Very little academic scholarship has been undertaken on the history of Australian wine, either as an agricultural commodity, an object of trade or a drink in everyday life.[2] This is not surprising since the entire edifice of Australian history for so long echoed the European style of historical narrative as celebration of the triumph and distinctiveness of nations. Unlike rural life in Europe and the United States, farming has had a relatively small social impact on the Australian nation. This, combined with the emergence of environmental history as a critical field of study for Australian land use, and no traditional Australian wine culture, means that you will not find wine in the indexes of general Australian history books. But if we look at the extent to which wine production has boomed in the past twenty years, how it has come to represent an appreciable part of national export income; how wine is, in fact, gradually replacing beer as the drink of the nation, then it is time to take a much closer look at early Australian wine history.[3] The story of wine in colonial New South Wales complicates our understanding of the multifarious contrivance that was the making of Australia.

Fortunately, the wine industry itself has for many years gathered together the scattered fragments of its record. Without these efforts I could not tell the story in this book.[4] Among these industry histories, I first encountered the idea that the elite of the colony of New South Wales – that is, its educated middle and upper class; officials and wealthy settlers

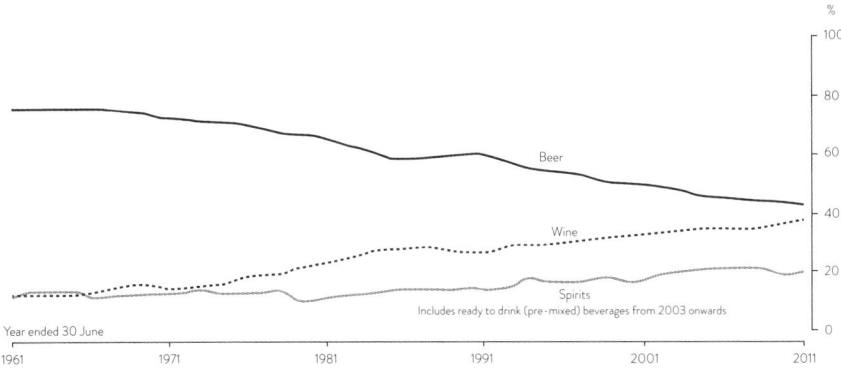

Australian Bureau of Statistics 2012, Apparent Consumption of alcohol, Australia 2010–2011, Cat. no. 4307.0.55.001, <www.abs@nsf/97>, viewed 9 July 2012

Comparative consumption of alcohol by volume in Australia shows a decline in Australian beer drinking, a rise in wine drinking and steady spirits consumption for the past half century.

– envisaged the complex and diverse colonial project as a future 'vineyard of Great Britain'.[5]

Not possible, I thought. What is more, if I had not been taught in school or university that this 'vineyard of Britain' plan existed from the beginnings of the colony of New South Wales – if no reference to it existed in general Australian histories – then it must be a rogue idea; a notion to be rejected out of hand.

But it *is* true. The *First Fleet* carried wine grape vines, barrels and bottles of wine and, crucially, British ideas about the cultural status and material profitability of wine growing.

The vision for colonial Australia from the first comprised a very determined intention to create a wine industry to supply a local market and ships' officers in maritime trade, and eventually for export. Rich and aspirational colonists were closely engaged in this vision for the production of barrels of colonial wine; some even tried to encourage a taste for colonial wine in preference to rum among their labourers.

In the minds and on the maps of colonists, New South Wales at first constituted the entire east coast of the continent, until Victoria and Queensland became separate colonies in the mid-nineteenth century. Within New South Wales, and later its neighbouring colonies, the vision for wine growing and a wine drinking culture were not ideas that simply sparked and flickered in the early promise of colonial expansion and then died back until the second half of the twentieth century. The vision was expressed in private correspondence as well as public debate, in thousands of column inches of the colonial press and in many books. Elite men and women were talking to each other about wine growing; they were exchanging vines, drinking each other's wine, and sharing resources such as skilled labourers, wine presses, bottling equipment and mail order sales processes. Supporters of the vision for wine spoke of how to grow grapes and how to create a market. They imagined Australia as a highly civilised part of the New World.[6] Wine was to be a part of achieving this.

Detractors of colonial wine – and there came to be several in the New South Wales legislature in the second half of the nineteenth century; mainly mates of pub owners – exercised themselves about a perceived failure of wine growing compared with other commodities and how, basically, beer was better. Temperance activists argued that the better option for health and wellbeing would be no alcohol at all but this did not significantly impede wine growing in New South Wales in the colonial period.

Grand seigneur of Australian wine writing, James Halliday, quite rightly considered it inevitable that 'right from the outset attention would be paid to vine propagation and winemaking'.[7] But why did some colonists experiment with growing grapes and fermenting them into wine when others did not? Those engaged in early experiments enjoyed wine socially and were fascinated by its manufacture, from vine to fermenting vat. This formed part of their motivation. But there were broader forces at work. Individuals were influenced by ideologies of progress and improvement, grand ideas about what it meant to be civilised; conceptions which seemed to be confirmed as the empire swelled towards greatness. To understand these broader forces, I have followed threads of inquiry within historical landscapes in much the same way as do food historians. These fields of study include the history of ideas and of the rise in imperialism, colonisation and migration throughout the Age of Empires; that enthralling and tragic transmission of people, plants, animals and ideas from the fifteenth century to the mid-twentieth century. Across these great panoramic expanses of the past we can more clearly see the coalescence of the ambition to introduce wine grapes in New South Wales into an industry. The furthermost starting point of the historical threads I am tracing begin earlier in time than you might expect. And, as we follow them through to the colonial era, they wind in unanticipated twists and turns so that you will find some chapters in this book go over the same periods of the past to explore each of the different themes which make the story of wine in New South Wales.

Although the natural order of this story might seem to be to first consider colonial grape vines before moving on to look at grapes grown, wine made and so on, this would actually be a back-to-front and upside-down approach. To understand why there were European grape vines and wine on the First Fleet in the first place, let alone what happened after that, it is necessary to contemplate the long inheritance of ideas about wine and

NATIONAL LIBRARY OF AUSTRALIA, CALL NO. PIC/8729/8 LOC ALBUM 757

One of the most successful vineyards of the lean mid-twentieth century in New South Wales wine growing: McWilliam's Mount Pleasant in the Hunter Valley. Photographer Max Dupain took this shot during the 1950 vintage as part of a series which depicts an Australian Arcadian ideal at Mount Pleasant. It shows, too, how women and children were a crucial part of seasonal vineyard labour.

wine growing that contributed to British culture in the 1780s. The culture that shaped the forceful imaginings of the colonial vision for wine growing contained the confluence of various threads, including classical revivalism and Christian thought evolving into Enlightenment philosophies about human progress and the creation of wealth and power.

In the 1780s, Georgian Britain could boast of a strong wine trade which meant that British merchants, or vintners, influenced the manufacture of some European wine and knew how to sell it. The British middle and upper classes very much liked to drink wine. It had a vaunted position in their image of themselves compared with cultural conceptions of ale, beer, cider and spirits. Wine had come to be associated with elite British ideas of what it meant to be civilised. What Georgian Britain did not have, however, due to climate and trade history, was a home soil wine industry. This meant that while Britain and continental Europe shared elements of a wine drinking culture as part of the history of western civilisation, the British experience of wine diverged dramatically from the wine countries of Europe in daily life. In wine countries, grape wine was consumed by peasants as much as by aristocrats. Wine prices ranged from cheap and cheerful to incomprehensively expensive, not just medium to high end as in Britain. In Britain, elites traded and drank wine though no British resident lived near a winery; however, many Spanish, Portuguese, Germans, Italians, Austro-Hungarians, French, even some Dutch did live in vine growing regions. The folklore of a culture of contented and industrious peasants in the wine lands of Mediterranean Europe came to be perceived by British elites as the ideal model for sober and civilised colonial working classes. Colonial authorities in New South Wales preferred model workers since theirs was a post-Abolition colonial project with convict and free labourers who were not as readily controlled as slaves.

British imperialists saw that established Old World powers, Spain, Portugal and the Netherlands, had wine industries which extended into

> " *When British officials planned the First Fleet, they could see the potential for a wine industry at Botany Bay.*

their colonial territories, and in some cases had done so for hundreds of years. At established maritime outposts, vineyards supplied wine to visiting trade and military ships. The British had tried to create wine industries in the eastern colonies of North America which possessed suitable climate and soils but once the thirteen colonies rebelled against British rule, the temperate zones of the new United States of America could no longer be vineyards of Britain. When British officials planned the First Fleet, they could see the potential for a wine industry at Botany Bay, along with other survival foods and luxury crops.[8] The broad colonial project required the exploitation of natural resources which the British mistakenly considered to be under-used by Indigenous Australians.[9] Architects of the colonial project of New South Wales drew on a vast store knowledge of prior British and European imperial experience and they intended the enterprise to succeed. Marines and convicts sent to New South Wales were not selected at random but for their potential to contribute to the colony's development. To provide familiar food crops and other potential cash crops, the fleet transported what was probably the most comprehensive list of plants sent to establish a European outpost to that point.[10] Among these plants were European wine grape plants (*vitis vinifera*).

When my grandfather Alf Kurtz made his first vintage in the early 1960s, his humble undertaking was one of many in an awakening of wine growing across the state, the nation and indeed other parts of the western world; the bubbling up of a renaissance, a renewal. What was being revived had begun more than 170 years earlier with the arrival of *vitis vinifera* on the First Fleet. What of the first vintage in New South Wales? We will get to that. First, however, let us consider the culture of wine that accompanied the first vines.

1

Ideas of wine on the First Fleet

A preference to not to have to live without wine arrived in Australia with the First Fleet in the habits of a handful of elite British colonists. It was a desire which came from more than the pleasure of drinking; it came from a history of grape wine as part of the traditions of European everyday life – sacred, refined and ordinary culture – which extended back into the mists of time. It has been recently shown how influential food has been in human development; how access to food, and food production, has effectively *made history*.[1] Compared with the inarguably central role of such an essential requirement for survival, wine cannot be said to have made history. Yet it is a distinctive commodity with roots in western ideas of civilisation almost as deep as the growing, processing, trade and eating of food. Wine ranked as a first food in ancient European culture. In its unpreserved pre-modern form, wine constituted an inexpensive foodstuff in vine growing regions in times of food shortages. When available cheaply, it could be used as an alternative to unsafe drinking water. It was thought to prevent disease on long sea voyages. It featured as a vital substance in religious worship, becoming the blood of Christ in the Catholic communion through the process of transubstantiation. Wine, if manufactured in specific ways from certain grapes, can also be stored for very long periods of time, during which it may improve, become more subtle and complex; a singularly miraculous quality in a comestible product. All of these characteristics have imparted wine with sophisticated social and cultural meanings compared with other forms of alcohol, and indeed some foods. We do not need wine to survive yet many, over thousands of years, have gone to great lengths to obtain it, including colonists in eastern Australia from 1788.

But what is wine?

Grape wine is a form of European and (prior to the rise of Islam) Middle Eastern fermented liquor as old as the domestication of plants and animals. The European wine grape (*vitis vinifera*) – generally distinguishable as smaller and more acidic than grapes used for eating fresh or drying – is believed to have originated in the Transcaucasian region of Georgia in Eastern Europe.[2] Grapes were among the earliest cultivated fruit crops in the Old World: temperate Europe, the Mediterranean and south-west Asia. Other fruits domesticated around the same time were olives, dates and figs. Archaeo-botanical evidence shows that wine production likely occurred from as early as three and a half thousand years before the Christian era, in the Early Bronze Age.[3] For millennia, grape wine belonged to the crucial Mediterranean exchange of 'sacramental foods': oil, bread and wine; and into the Middle Ages the most traded European foods were fish, grain and wine.[4] In the early modern era in Europe, wine production occurred throughout the southern regions below the forty-ninth parallel of latitude (from the west coast of France to Georgia) and wine consumption extended across all European trade routes, including into Britain.[5]

Domesticated grape vines developed deep root systems, making them seemingly ideal for poor soils. Once a suitable site has been selected for planting grapes the soil may be trenched, or dug to loosen the top soil, particularly if it has not previously been cultivated. This allows the young roots greater ease of growth so the plant establishes well.

Grapes must be propagated from vine cuttings to ensure new plantings have the characteristics of the parent vine. Plants grown from seed are likely to revert to their wild state, which would result in fewer and smaller berries than a cloned plant. In order to produce grapes with sufficient juice to make wine, vines are carefully pruned to control the number of grape bunches produced on each cane. The growth of the leaf canopy can also be controlled to either increase or decrease sunlight on developing grape bunches. For example, cooler climate ripening of grapes is achieved by removing leaves to create a lighter canopy and allow more light and warmth onto the grapes. Vine growing practices varied dramatically in wine countries even into the nineteenth century, from unsupported gooseberry bush vines to trellising on trees or arbours and espaliering, the method most used today, where rows of vines with a central stem have canes guided each way along a wire between posts.

Grapes do not bear fruit until the third or fourth year after planting so there is no quick return on an investment in wine growing. With careful pruning and adequate water wine grape vines will produce berries of suitable ripeness (or acid–sugar balance) to achieve fermentation from naturally-occurring yeasts in the cloudy bloom on the skin. The role of these yeasts became a part of oenological knowledge only during the nineteenth century. Today yeasts are added to aid grape fermentation but colonial wine production depended on these occurring naturally.

Colour in red wine comes from the natural dye in grape skins, so if the juice to be fermented is strained from the skins soon after crushing or pressing then the wine will be white. This is how red grapes can be used to make sparkling white wines. White wine is pale after first bottling and, if suitable for cellaring, can become deep golden with age. Tannins in the skins of red grapes is an important factor in giving red wines their potential to age – that is, to mellow over time and remain suitable for drinking, sometimes for several decades – more readily than white wine varieties. Some white grapes picked at a very ripe stage and those infected with botrytis, or noble rot, can be made into richly sweet dessert wines without the addition of brandy or sugar.

In the eighteenth century, grapes processed in many European wine countries were still pressed by foot because of the lower cost of this method. Wooden wine presses were also used. The length of time that the must – or grape solids – is left in the liquid determines the length of fermentation; too long and the wine may over-ferment and become vinegar. Before refrigeration could be used to cool the must and slow fermentation, the conversion of grape sugars to alcohol was stopped by rudimentary cooling methods such as sulphur fumes. Removal of solids from the liquid is called racking. Smaller particles of solids still remaining in the wine after this process are removed through fining, in which substances such as egg whites or milk are used to attract the sediment and produce clear wine.

Developments in technology have played an important role in the manufacture, trade and taste of wine. In recent centuries, wooden barrels were used for wine fermentation, storage and transport. For some wines the porousness of the barrels allowed a gentle exposure to oxygen over time which improved them by smoothing out rough tannic flavours. Other wines were over oxygenated or spoiled in other ways and became undrinkable inside of a year after manufacture. Spoilage led some vitners to adulterate wine with substances to mask the taste, with the result that wine merchants had a very poor reputation in British culture. An English statue of 1661 declared grape wine should not be mixed with wine from other countries, with cider, honey or sugar nor with brimstone, flesh or blood![6] These alarming practices dated from at least the mid-fourteenth century to the late nineteenth century when Louis Pasteur identified the souring effects of bacteria and measures such as sterilisation of equipment were introduced.[7] In the seventeenth century the invention of the corkscrew made it possible to more effectively seal glass bottles with cork stoppers which still allowed some oxygenation. But, because of the high cost of bottles, not all wine was sold this way and until the eighteenth century bottles were not the shape we know today. With the phasing in of cylindrical bottles, wines could be bottle-aged and wealthier consumers had the choice of wine in bottle or barrel. All wine still needed to be rested after it was transported, and then decanted to remove the sediment.

Wine, beer, cider, spirits and 'civilisation'[8]

Wine and beer have a similar antiquity in European history but have developed quite distinct cultural associations and symbolic meanings. Classical Greeks considered wine to be a 'civilised drink'.[9] Their vineyards were known to be a profitable way to exploit otherwise depleted soils; and they grew rich from trade in products such as wine. So it continued for the Romans, who borrowed heavily from Greek life and philosophies. In the second century BC, the Roman Marcus Cato the Elder said that the best farms consisted of 'every kind of cultivated field; and in the best situation; the vineyard is of the first importance'.[10] Many centuries later, in the 1600s, as classical thinking was joined with biblical wisdom to form the twin threads of emerging European philosophies, an Englishman said, 'For as Seneca, Cato, Varro, Columella, &c. do affirm, the planting of vineyards hath been more gainful than any other act of husbandry whatsoever'.[11]

An eminent United States brewing scientist has written a whole book which argues that beer (which he prefers to drink, as well as being a specialist in its production) is no less culturally sophisticated, technologically complex or nutritious than wine. He laments, for example, that wine is seen as being *nobler* than beer.[12] The perceived nobility of wine derives from its full range of representation as fundamental first food and artisanal peasant product through mystical religious qualities to the height of expressions of civility and status. Curiously, Charles Bamforth's contention only serves to emphasise the cultural significance of wine in the western world.

In contrast to wine and beer, cider consumption barely existed in Europe beyond Britain in the early modern era, and has very little complex cultural meaning. Spirits distilled from fruits and sugar cane were introduced in the sixteenth century. By the 1700s, a culture had emerged: the British poor drank gin, the middle classes preferred rum made from plantation sugar in the West Indies but only the very rich could afford

French cognac (brandy) made from wine grapes.[13] Spirits were more potent than other alcohols and by the early nineteenth century were blamed for an enormous rise in European alcohol consumption.[14] In the nineteenth century the ancient link between wine and civilisation gained ground among British elites who supported the reduction of high levels of alcohol consumption but were unwilling to stop drinking wine.[15]

The creation and maintenance of early modern European ideas of civilisation began with habits that distinguished the behaviour of those who were civilised from those who were not. 'Good behaviour' by 'fine people' came to mean things we now take for granted such as using handkerchiefs in preference to sleeves to wipe noses, hand washing before meals and the use of cutlery instead of hands when eating.[16] We see this in colonial New South Wales when the gentrified upper and middle classes who were predisposed to drinking wine in moderate quantities, expressed disgust at the 'savage' culture of bingeing on beer or spirits by squatters and labourers alike.[17]

Quite apart from other forms of alcohol, the line between being civilised and uncivilised in the consumption of wine is captured in the dichotomy that it is the 'food with two faces … praised when consumed in moderation, condemned when consumed in excess'.[18] Nowhere has this been clearer than in the Bible.

Wine in the Bible

There are more than a hundred direct references to wine in the Bible. Early New South Wales colonists of all classes – those accustomed to divine study and convicts forced to undertake it for moral rehabilitation – would have been familiar with at least some of these. To start at the beginning of the Old Testament: it is not stated whether there were wine grapes in the Garden of Eden but an eighteenth century commentary on the Bible assumed this to be the case.[19] The earliest biblical reference to wine rather than grapes is the disgrace of Noah who, after the flood subsided and he could leave his ark, planted a vineyard. He later harvested his grapes, made wine, and consumed enough of it to be found drunk and naked in his tent by a family member. There was such shame in this (though the reason is not precisely revealed in the abbreviated style of biblical narrative) that Noah banished the family member who found him.[20]

In the early books of the Old Testament, first fruits – corn or wheat, wine, oil, ox or sheep meat and honey – were expected to be sacrificed to the Hebrew god after harvest to ensure prosperity.[21] Wine 'maketh glad the heart of man'[22]; wisdom personified 'hath mingled her wine'.[23] A virtuous woman 'considereth a field, and buyeth it: with the fruit of her hands she planted a vineyard'.[24] The grape harvest was celebrated with singing.[25] On the other hand, priests in the Old Testament were forbidden to drink wine[26] (while in the New Testament bishops and deacons were urged to limit their intake).[27] For lay people 'wine is a mocker, strong drink is raging: and whosoever is deceived thereby is not wise'.[28] Wine featured metaphorically: 'in the Land of the Lord there is a cup and the wine is red; it is full of mixture; and he poureth out of the same: but the dregs thereof, all the wicked of the earth shall wring them out, and drink them'.[29] There was 'wine of astonishment';[30] 'wine of violence';[31] and of Babylon – the enemy of the Israelites – 'the wine of the wrath of her fornication'.[32]

> "
> *Virgil wrote of the desirable advancement in transforming landscapes with vines and olives.*

In the New Testament, Jesus taught humility with the parable of the landowner who underpaid his vineyard workers.[33] He turned water into wine to prevent the hosts' embarrassment at a Canaanite wedding feast.[34] Later, as he was paraded through the streets of Jerusalem on the way to his crucifixion, Jesus refused an offer of wine mixed with myrrh.[35] Wine has many faces in the single most influential text across gender and class divisions in late eighteenth century Britain and therefore nineteenth century New South Wales.

As alluded to above, educated colonists would also have been familiar with representations from classical literature which emphasised the link between wine growing, commercial-scale cultivation and civilisation. While this connection is implied in the Bible, it is explicit in classical writing. Like Cato the Elder, Virgil – the Roman poet who grew up on a farm – wrote of the desirable advancement in transforming even the most rugged of landscapes with vines and olives.[36] On a less sober note, an early modern English drinking song echoed the connection between the classical era and wine:

> Aristotle that Master of Arts/had been but a dunce without Wine/And what we ascribe to his Parts/is due to the Juice of the Vine/His Belly, most Writers agree/Was as big as a Watting-Trough/He therefore leapt into the Sea/Because he'd have Liquor enough/And liv'd by the Scent of the cask/and liv'd by the Scent of the cask.[37]

Here were the faces of wine parodied.

The paradox of wine in classical texts meant Hippocrates regarded it as a potent medicine as well as a dangerous intoxicant.[38] Plato's Law included an age limit for consumption which foreshadowed modern regulations: 'boys under eighteen shall not taste wine at all; for one should not conduct fire to fire'.[39] Pliny the Elder believed 'there are two liquids that are especially agreeable to the body, wine inside and oil outside' but for men only. Women, it seemed, should not drink wine.[40] Thankfully such restrictions did not apply in Georgian Britain or in New South Wales. Elite women do not have the same presence in the historical record as men but they too were part of the story of wine.

A brief history of wine in Britain, as distinct from Europe

Wine grapes may have arrived in England with the Romans or to make sacramental wine for Catholic priests who came after the fall of Rome. Even if the Romans did not grow wine in England, they certainly imported it.[41] After the Roman era, vines in England are known to have been maintained by the Catholic Church but at this time only priests took wine at Mass so the quantity used in worship is often overstated. A far greater volume was consumed by the clergy and the secular nobility as part of everyday life.[42] The Domesday Book recorded that there were thirty-eight vineyards in England at the time of the Norman Conquest but any English hopes which we might imagine existed to establish a wine export trade in the medieval period (as opposed to its later, successful wine *re-export* trade) were disappointed by the cold, damp climate and the influx of French wine from 1070.[43] Germanic wines were more popular than European until the development of trade relations with Bordeaux when, in 1154, Henry II of England took the throne with his wife, Eleanor of Aquitaine, whose inheritance included vast French wine lands.

Three hundred years later, the English in Bordeaux surrendered to French forces and from 1451 the famous region again became French. Exports of Bordeaux claret to England were allowed by the French king but taxed heavily.[44] By this time any remaining English grape wine production had stopped, as it could be readily purchased from Europe and European colonies; trade specialisations were beginning to take shape within the European world.[45]

Wine imported into England continued to be purchased by large royal and noble households, consumed by many within the household and distributed to armed forces maintained by the English monarch. It has been said that 'there was probably no import with which the medieval Englishman would have dispensed so unwillingly as wine'.[46] Indeed, it influenced more than the disposition of its consumers: ships were described according to the quantity of wine they could carry.[47]

Wine in England referred also to fermented liquor made at a cottage level from honey, berries, fruits and vegetables.[48] Malt liquor, called *vinum britannicum* by Thomas Short, commanded a certain loyalty due to its taste and affordability. In 1727 Dr Short claimed it was better for cool climates than grape wine, and sufficiently nutritious for people who ate food from fertile soil which, he argued in the spirit of age-old rivalries, European wine producing countries did not.[49] His efforts were in vain, however. Wine remained the more widely used medicine, especially as an antidote to scurvy; crucial in an age of frequent sea voyaging.

Wine relieved the hardship, not just the nutritional restrictions, of maritime travel. Sailors would rather have surrendered their dignity than their wine. On the *Endeavour* voyage, Joseph Banks wrote of the ducking of all on board (including pets!) passing the equator for the first time. Banks, ship's captain James Cook and the naturalist Daniel Solander were all due to be initiated by those who had previously undergone the ritual. Also on the 'black list' were Banks's servants and his dogs 'which I was obliged to compound for by giving the dunkers a certain quantity of brandy for which they willingly excused us'. Boys were always initiated this way but adult crew could stay dry only by forfeiting up to four days wine allowance, 'so that about twenty-one underwent the ceremony' and retained their rations of wine.[50]

Exactly which wines were the British drinking? Several sorts, depending on fashion and availability. In the seventeenth century, for example, it was imports from the Spanish colony of the Canary Islands: sack (or Sherry), also called Canary. A century later, King George III favoured hock (Riesling) from the Rhine region and claret. But the English generally drank more Portuguese wine than any other – luxury versions for conspicuous consumers among the upper classes, more common varieties for wine-drinking yeoman – most of which was 'port'. The British developed a taste for these strong, and later fortified, wines of the Portuguese Douro Valley as a result of the Methuen Treaty. Signed by Britain and Portugal in 1703, this trade agreement ensured Portuguese wine entry to the British Isles at two-thirds the rate of French wine. The British in turn secured a monopoly on the sale of woollen cloth to Portugal, which protected their sheep grazing and woollen cloth manufacture. In a broader sense, the Methuen agreement represented a master stroke which claimed cloth manufacture for Britain. The production of woollens and later cotton fabrics proved central in Britain's early industrialisation.[51] Of the more than 17 000 tons of wine imported into England by 1786, three-quarters were from Portugal.[52] Although 'perhaps only a couple of hundred thousand Britons consumed wine in the last years of the eighteenth century, they drank considerable amounts of it … excess was not considered disgraceful: on the contrary it was manly and convivial, an aid to wit, good humour and fellowship'.[53]

British men of the middle and upper classes used wine ritualistically. An ongoing round of toasts followed the evening meal; a practice which may have originated in the pledging of allegiances during the English Civil War. Once the toasting began, each round was responded to by all at the table. There was a sense of being contracted to fellow drinkers for the duration of the ritual. British taste for wine in the late eighteenth century even mirrored affairs of state. Overconsumption of wine allowed a sort of heroism denied to them in the perceived emasculation of the loss of the colonies of British North America. It was manly to drink at least three bottles in a sitting, to be a 'three bottle man' or to drink '*against* someone'.[54] Before the French Revolution British elites began to consider claret too feminine because of the elaborate grooming of noble Frenchmen, which led to a preference for port. Famed English wit Samuel Johnson exclaimed, 'claret is the liquor for boys; port for men; but he who aspires to be a hero … must drink brandy'. Since 'few men were heroic enough to drink brandy', port came to be 'a glass of manliness'.[55]

The Enlightenment and ideas about wine

Ideas about wine as the drink of rulers were newly inspired in the Georgian era by a new reverence for culture from ancient Greece and Rome, empires which provided blueprints for aspirations of British glory. A broad classical revivalism contributed to the formation and expression of Enlightenment philosophies (which are still with us) about ever progressive human mastery of the natural environment as a source of wealth and power.[56] Enlightenment thinking lay at the very core of the conception and of the colonial project of New South Wales and the manner in which the project proceeded.[57] One of the new ways of viewing the world which emerged during the Enlightenment established a deep faith in the power of *seeing* to determine what might be natural truths. For some natural philosophers (early scientists), the application of reason to the observation of material phenomena grew to replace biblical explanations for how the world had come into existence and continued to function. These nascent scientists drew what they saw, organised their observations into systems and described them in books. Such empiricism was epitomised by the Linnaean method of classifying plants for genus and species. *Seeing* contributed significantly to the vividly imagined possibilities for the creation of a wine industry in New South Wales, along with the British knowledge of the symbolism and value of wine growing, and the joy of drinking it.

Wine as art and science

Just as the Enlightenment shaped conceptions of wine so did Romanticism in poetry, literature and other art forms expressing passion for nature. In the late eighteenth century it became common among the leisured classes of Britain and Europe to observe natural landscapes as an antidote to the perceived squalor of urban life, as well as to improve the viewer's knowledge of the world. Grand tours of the cities and landscapes of Europe were intended to make young English gentlemen 'polished and accomplished'.[58] This same century saw a rise in Romantic landscape tourism which moved some to 'wonder'; to marvel at nature in a way previously associated with the experience of divine grace.[59] Romanticism held that the essence of being human requires artistic creation to understand the world, not scientific reason or rationalisations.[60]

In the age of industrialisation, from the late nineteenth century, wine as *art* came to be contrasted with wine as *science* and *business*. Romantics inferred that it was more authentic to consider wine as an art form, created in a way that exemplified the bounty of nature; passionate and red-blooded rather than profit-driven.[61] Wine writers James Halliday and Hugh Johnson have demonstrated that in the production of wine there is a meeting of art and science.[62]

The Frenchification of wine

There was one idea that it may naturally be assumed was carried to New South Wales on the First Fleet but which did not actually exist in the late

1780s: the notion of the absolute superiority of wine from France. As mentioned in the Introduction, this is quite new in historical terms. Early colonists were aware of French wines, claret of course and others, but not in the same terms as we are today. As it happens, the Frenchification of world wine did not precede but coincided with the rise of wine growing in New South Wales in the second half of the nineteenth century. For most of the colonial era it was not only claret (French Bordeaux made from Cabernet Sauvignon, Cabernet Franc and Merlot) and red Burgundy (French Pinot Noir) style wines that New South Wales growers aimed to imitate. Fine wines at the beginning of the nineteenth century included Madeira: sweet, heavy and dominated by Verdelho grapes; Hock from the Rhine, some port wines, Tokaji from Hungary; and Constantia from the Dutch colony of the Cape of Good Hope.

So how did French wine later come to be so influential? In 1855, the French held an international exhibition in Paris. This followed on from a very grand event in London in 1851, a show of shows which allowed Britain to display its wealth through its inventions and innovations and the diversity of produce and curiosities from its growing empire. For the 1855 exhibition in Paris, Napoleon III requested the creation of an official list of the best of France's wines from the Bordeaux region. Wine merchants obliged with the Bordeaux Classifications which listed *premiers crus* (first growths) as paramount wines, followed by second, third and through to fifth growths. Lower *crus* were produced in greater quantity but were lower in perceived quality, value and therefore price. The original red wine *premiers crus* were clarets: Châteaux Lafite, Latour, Margaux, Haut-Brion (which the British called O'Brion[63]) and the highest ranked white, Château d'Yquem.[64]

The next stage in the Frenchification of wine came in the early twentieth century as wine fraud threatened the reputation and profits of premium producers. The peddling of poor imitations of fine wine proved to be the final straw for struggling producers and they sought a strict system of regional delimitation to ensure reliability and authenticity in branding. By the 1930s, French laws controlled the labelling of fine wine for place of origin through the *appellation d'origine* (AOC), precursor of Australian regional Geographical Indications (GI). The AOC established a connection between the very finest French wine and the micro sites of distinctive soil types, grape-friendly climate and landscape aspects (directional slopes) known as *terroir*. A hierarchy of *terroir* provided the final feature of the powerful discursive framework which established the French industry as the reference point for fine wine. Owing to the subtlety and complexity of aged *premiers crus* it came to be held that because specific *terroir* produced them, the very land itself had inimitable qualities. This led in turn to the idea that French fine wines not only *tasted best* but were *in the best taste*.[65] The French make exemplary wines, there is no doubt, but it is entirely a matter of opinion that the most superior *terroir* micro sites in the world are in France and that the French make the only superb wines.[66]

And what is taste? Apart from physical sensory qualities such as smell, flavour and mouth feel, taste as an expression of a preference for wine quality depends on symbolic value. The Bordeaux Classifications and subsequent regulations on wine quality conferred this value on French fine wine through a process which has been called cultural consecration.[67] This cultural consecration is performed by rich consumers guided by opinion makers with particular expertise, such as trusted wine critics and wine show judges.[68] Cultural consecration is a way to explain the cultural processes that have made wine seem more refined and civilised than beer, spirits or cider. It is a complex but powerful means through which some wines are considered to be more desirable, have greater status and therefore attract higher prices than others. Superiority of fine wine can be understood within the concept of 'good taste' or *distinction*, symbolic value which in turn adds material value.[69] *Distinction* – founded as it often is on the idea of integrity earned over a long period of time – epitomises the authoritative but completely invented Frenchification of wine.[70]

Colonists experimenting with wine growing in early New South Wales were not influenced by notions of the superiority of Frenchness; in their era, other wines were also considered to be fine. They did, however, imagine that their colony could gain *distinction* through having a wine industry.

To make something new – such as colonial wine – requires factors that include individual initiative and action, knowledge and 'antecedent conditions'; that is, examples of the intended product against which a producer can benchmark their own.[71] But what if the intended products are utterly disconnected from their actual manufacture by a confounding tradition of names so that it is not possible to match one with the other? Next we join the First Fleet journey to see how the British named European wines. This brings into sharp relief the considerable degree to which making wine in New South Wales would require more than Enlightenment-derived ambition and Romantic desire.

2

British names for wine and why they mattered

After sailing from England, the First Fleet's first landfall occurred at one of the most famous sources of wine in British culture: the Canary Islands, a Spanish colony in the North Atlantic. Canary wine had long been sent to Britain; Shakespearean characters drank it and educated voyagers on the fleet were familiar with it. Canary comprehended a range of wine styles from several grape varieties. Consider this observation by First Fleet marines captain Watkin Tench at Tenerife, in the Canaries: 'dry wines, as the merchants term them, are sold from ten to fifteen pounds a pipe; for the latter price, the very best, called the London Particular, may be bought; sweet wines are considerably dearer'.[1] Semi-sweet, white London Particular from the Canaries should not be confused with London Particular from Madeira. Both wines were made from different varieties or a blend of them. Both wines had also been named by merchants for their status in the British market, not for their constituent grapes, a centuries-old practice

DE BORTOLI WINES

Claret, a popular French wine style imported into Britain for several centuries before the colonisation of Australia in 1788, gave its name to wines in New South Wales for much of the state's history. Here barrels of it are loaded at Griffith in the 1950s.

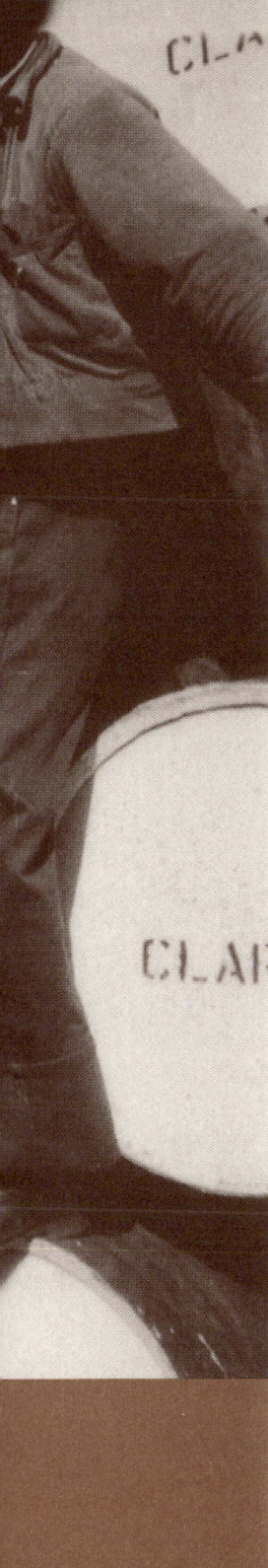

which did not take account of the need to one day divine the vine varieties that would be required to imitate European wines in a colonial setting.

It is possible to conjure some idea of how Canary London Particular tasted with the knowledge that it was made from the grape variety Vidonia. Its viscosity positioned it on a spectrum between Madeira and sherry, though it was reportedly better than each of these; 'being free from the occasional coarseness of the one, and the frequent acidity of the other'.[2] It did, however, need to be treated like Madeira wines. And, even after all of this, it should still have been bottle aged after purchase at the London docks, in quarter pipe barrels or large-sized bottles by the dozen.

A mid-eighteenth century encyclopedia shows the extent to which the British did not discuss wines using grape names. Instead, wines were:

> distinguished with regard to their colour into white wine, red wine, claret wine, pale wine, rose, or black wine; and with regard to their country, or the soil that produc[ed] them, into French wines, Spanish wines, Rhenish wines, Hungary wines, Greek wines, Canary wines, &... and more particularly into Port wine, Madeira wine, Burgundy wine, Champaign wine, Falurnian wine, Tockay [Tokay or Tokaji] wine, Schires [Shiraz] wine, &c.[3]

This naming tradition travelled with the British around the globe. Wine from the Canaries and the Portuguese North Atlantic colony of Madeira, for example, supplied British colonists in North America as well as the officers of ships heading westward to the Anglo Americas and those sailing southward along the African coast towards India and the Dutch East Indies (the Spice Islands; now Indonesia).

Madeira and the invention of a fine fortified wine

During the eighteenth century port wine styles changed because of demand and new technologies.[4] Madeira too was transformed from cheap to fine wine as a result of expanding maritime trade. In the early 1700s there were four grape varieties grown on Madeira: white, black, Malvasia and Vidonia; and its wines were made from blending white and black grapes. A hundred years later, twenty-three varieties were cultivated, including four of high quality, released as single varietal wines ranging from dry to sweet: Sercial, Verdelho, Boal and Malvasia Candida. British consumers preferred a sweeter, more full-bodied and golden wine than North American consumers, so exports were manufactured to suit each market. The need to prevent a second fermentation of the wine and other spoilage during long voyages led to the fortification of Madeira with grape spirit, before similar practices were employed in making port and sherry. It was also sold at greater age than had been common. But perhaps the most significant innovation was heating the wine – called Madeirising – to imitate the effect achieved by shipping it in barrels through warm Atlantic climates. Merchants consecrated Madeira into a luxury product by advertising it as:

> 'opulent', fit only for those in the metropolis with discerning palates, or for those on the periphery who aspired to live like them, or at least were familiar with their genteel ways … [these merchants] marketed wines of certain age as more suitable for intelligent drinkers; the older the wine, the more distinguished its drinker.[5]

Commensurate maturity in wine and its consumers remains persuasive in the twentieth century discourse of wine. With Madeirising of the *idea* of wine also came a curious foreshadowing of present-day celebrity endorsements of luxury goods. Testimonials from men of high status were used to reinforce the gendered, elite reputation of high grade Madeira and even its packaging reflected its invention as a status symbol. What of the actual wine transported to New South Wales on the First Fleet?

Wine on the First Fleet

When you think of alcohol on the First Fleet you probably think of rum but there was wine in the medicine chests of ships' surgeons and in the officers' mess. The quantity of medicinal wine on each of the eleven ships of the fleet can be calculated from the surgeon's list on the *Lady Penrhyn* which included 10 gallons of 'red port wine' (equivalent to five dozen bottles in our parlance).[6]

Although care was taken to provide for all on board the fleet, the British secretary of state in change of colonies drew up short at the idea of spending public funds to provide alcohol for the marines who would act as convict guards in early New South Wales. This alarmed fleet commander Arthur Phillip. When he heard of the decision he pressed for its reversal. He considered it non-negotiable to have wine and spirits for the military. The absence of these provisions could, at the very worst, result in mutiny.[7] Phillip's appeal led to the allocation of £200 to buy three years' supply of alcohol for the marines but the colonial secretary said this was to be the end of it.[8] Historian Alan Frost believes this refusal to guarantee supplies of alcohol for the military beyond the first three years of the colony very likely stimulated the notorious New South Wales rum trade of the 1790s.[9]

All First Fleet supplies were carefully rationed. The marines' daily fare during the Tenerife layover comprised one pound each of bread and beef and a pint of wine (while convicts received three-quarters of a pound each of bread and beef and no wine).[10] Dispatches and journal entries give the impression that there were three sorts of wine obtained in addition to medicine: wine for rations on the voyage and to be stored for use at Botany Bay, both bought on the public account; and wine purchased by officers and officials for their own enjoyment. Although Tench mentioned London Particular, as a fine wine it would not have been affordable as fleet provisions but might have been purchased for private use.

At the fleet's second layover: Rio in the Portuguese colony of Brazil, Phillip found that he could not purchase wine except from retailers, which made it more expensive. And the price of spirits increased by 25 per cent on his fleet's arrival in harbour! 'Thirty pipes of wine is the quantity that was ordered for the hospital', he explained in his reports, 'but for the above reasons only 15 pipes have been purchased'.[11] It is likely this wine was port since a company established by the Portuguese government in 1756 had a monopoly on wine trade with Brazil[12] and there is no evidence Rio had a wine industry of its own.

The final stopover for the First Fleet, at the Cape, presented another opportunity to stock wine, which Phillip procured despite an apparent shortage. The Cape colony at the southern tip of Africa had been established by the Dutch in the seventeenth century to provide a supply point for fresh water, food and wine en route to the Spice Islands, India and China. French exiles and Dutch elites established vineyards with slave labour to produce wines which ranged from fine to ordinary.[13]

Marines private John Easty recorded the pleasure of being in harbour at the Cape. 'Monday, October the 15th 1787 ... served out fresh beef and mutton and soft bread and fresh butter ... and wine hoisted out the long boat.'[14] Which wine? Most likely a common style; not Constantia (named for the property where it was produced), the most famous and finest of Cape wines.

Seeing colonial vineyards and wineries

As well as material supplies, the First Fleet voyage provided a store of impressions about other European maritime colonies: how these colonies looked, the relationship between indigenes and invaders; plantations of European crops for trade.[15] Prior to his First Fleet journey Phillip had ample opportunity to see vineyards and therefore imagine them in the Australian landscape. His extensive naval experience had taken him to the ports of France, Germany, Spain, Portugal and Italy and perhaps into their interiors. Plus he had spent time in the French countryside as a spy for the British Government in the early 1780s.[16] It would not be surprising to find several of Phillip's fellow officers had also travelled in wine countries or had otherwise learned of the value of vineyards. For those who had not seen them previously, vineyards at Tenerife may have been within viewing reach. As Frost has pointed out, while First Fleet voyagers did not see the Canaries in the best season, they could have gained an impression of a European maritime colony in action:

Vegetables were scarce, and few fruits were in season. Still, in the solidity of the town's buildings, the fertility of its environs, the production of wines, dye, cotton and silk, and the establishment of regular government over the mixed population, they saw enough to gain a sense of how a small-scale European colonisation might succeed. Tenerife was the first in a series of such experiences during the voyage to prepare them for the business they were about.[17]

At Rio too, the colonists gained a sense of the wider business they were about (though not vineyards). While Phillip met old friends and bought supplies, his men mixed with the locals. A fort captain entertained surgeon Arthur Bowes Smyth and others with punch and 'a bottle of excellent port wine'.[18] But the fleet's head surgeon John White noted that the Saint Sebastians at Rio 'do not accustom themselves to high living, nor indulge much in the juice of the grape'.[19]

At the Cape, the fleet's final stopover before Botany Bay, it was possible to not only see vineyards but to indulge in wine tourism. White and four companions climbed Table Mountain and could, from its heights, have seen vineyards among the patchwork of cultivated estates below.[20]

David Collins, on the fleet to take up the role of judge-advocate in New South Wales, noted that wine at the Cape could be bought only in bottles rather than more cheaply in barrels, which may have curtailed his expenditure. He rhapsodised that the wine of Constantia, 'so much famed, has a very fine, rich, and pleasant flavour, and is an excellent cordial, ... formed a considerable article of traffic [at the Cape] ...; and the neatness, regularity, and extent of their wine-vaults were pleasing to the eye; but a stranger should not visit more than one of them in a day; for almost every cask has some peculiarity to recommend it, and its contents must be tasted'.[21] For Collins, the Cape and Constantia represented a last taste of European civilisation before the final leg of his journey to Botany Bay.

It was at the Cape that Phillip bought the first grape vines planted in Australia but to best understand the nuances of this part of our narrative we have to shift our thinking to vines rather than wines. To do this, it is necessary to return again to the earlier past to follow a new thread of the story.

3

Grape vines on the First Fleet

While wine grapes planted these days are selected scientifically to match *terroir*, the vines transported on the First Fleet were chosen far more randomly. Exotic plants for New South Wales, including vines, were bought at ports of call on the voyage to Botany Bay with little knowledge of the soils and climate they were destined for. The colony's British founders did not have access to vines directly from Europe as later colonists would. There were no experienced wine growers on the fleet; no one to identify potentially useful vines or to make the connection between source varieties and the wine that might be produced from them in New South Wales. It is no wonder that the names of the precise grape varieties on the First Fleet remain a mystery. Less of a mystery is that there were vines on the fleet in the first place, since they, with wine, had long been a part of early steps in building empires.

When Governor Arthur Phillip purchased grape plants for New South

Wales, it represented a first for Australia but a broader view of history shows us something more. It made Phillip the latest in a long line of (often less likeable) captains of colonisation to take vines to new frontiers beyond Europe. The Greek and Roman empires of the classical era had each contributed to the spread of viticulture. Apart from the Islamic prohibition of wine from 570AD, the subsequent fall and rise of European and Mediterranian imperial powers brought waves of change but did not impede the planting of vineyards or continued wine trade. In the Age of European Empires, from the fifteenth century, vine cuttings were a customary addition to the cargo of European invaders and colonisers of the New World. When Christopher Columbus sailed to the Americas in 1492, he carried vine cuttings from the Canaries, though these few plants did not survive.[1] A few decades later, conquistador Hernan Cortes took the vine to Mexico. From there the Spanish rapidly established New World vine growing. By 1524 a regulation decreed that 1000 vines should be planted for land grants equivalent to a hundred Indians. Francisco Pizarro likely had vine cuttings with him when he sacked and enslaved the Incan Empire and there are reports of extensive Spanish missionary plantings in Peru and Chile by the 1550s.[2] At the end of the sixteenth century the Mexican wine industry was so successful that Philip II called a halt to further development of vineyards in Spanish America.[3]

I doubt there were grape plants on the first English voyage to the Americas in 1589 but there were vines on later English invasion missions to the New World. Aspirations to develop a wine industry in Britain's American colonies were fuelled by a desire to maintain access to and create profit from this necessary luxury. The gentry imported rare and expensive European wines to the colonies in Virginia and New Amsterdam but still a seventeenth century regulation ordered early Virginian households to plant ten vine cuttings and learn the art of vine cultivation.[4]

Late in the same century the English parliament urged investors to set up experimental agriculture in the American colonies to solve the problem of an influx of French refugees, including vinedressers, to England. The indigenous American grape was found to be unsuitable for wine production so hundreds of thousands of European vines were planted over the next hundred years, using French expertise.[5] Despite attacks on imported *vitis vinifera* from the as-yet-unidentified American pest, grape phylloxera, the industry was showing some signs of success in the late eighteenth century. A Frenchman won the Royal Society of the Arts gold medal for wine production in 1772.[6] In this same year Louis De Saint Pierre published *The Art of Planting and Cultivating the Vine, as also of making, fining, and preserving wines &. according to the most approved methods in the Most celebrated wine-countries in France* aimed at settlers destined for New Bordeaux, South Carolina. He believed wine growing created employment for vinedressers, coopers, smiths and even ship-builders because of the mercantile traffic projected to arise out of increased production.[7] But, once South Carolina and the other twelve revolutionary colonies declared their independence in 1776, a North American wine industry had no potential to directly benefit the British Empire.

Less than a decade after American Independence, when former British American colonist James Maria Matra submitted his proposal to British authorities to establish the colony of New South Wales as a replacement source of taxation revenue, he included grapes on the list of plants to be trialled as a cash crop.[8] And, just as Matra envisaged, wine grapes were on the list of exotic plants acquired for the new colony of New South Wales.

Although the vines imported on the First Fleet did not produce the first commercially viable wine made in the colony, they provided the grapes for the very first wine made in Australia, so it is intriguing to consider where they came from and what we know of them. Fragments of evidence about Governor Phillip's purchase of seeds and plants for New South Wales suggest he bought grape plants at both Rio and the Cape.[9] But I am not convinced Phillip was able to purchase wine grape vines at Rio. Botanist Joseph Banks made no mention of grape vines in his detailed description of the produce of Rio only ten years before the First Fleet called there.[10] Another reason I have my doubts about Rio is that Judge-Advocate Collins wrote that vines were purchased only at the Cape.[11] Perhaps any grape vines available at Rio were warm climate table grapes. More likely is that vine plants and/or a store of wine grape cuttings came only from the Cape since it had an established industry. Phillip certainly

MITCHELL LIBRARY, STATE LIBRARY OF NSW, CY 3005/66 BANKS PAPERS, SERIES 37.13

have never mentioned receiving the difficult plants of
Ipecacuanha which I sent from Rio de Janeiro, by the
Master of the Sirius who ret.d to England, his Name is
Morton. as you was desirous of having those plants I
should be sorry if they have not reached you.

The Vines you are kind enough to promise
me will be very acceptable, tho' the few I brought from
the Brazil & the Cape, have increased so as to have put
it in my power to send five hundred cuttings to Norfolk
Island, & I suppose we have two thousand in the ground
here & at Rose Hill; then a Vineyard of two Acres will
be planted next year. last summer produced two good
bunches of Grapes, which may be mentioned, as being the
first this Country has produced, tho' being neglected they
decayed on the Vine. A tollerable Gardener came out
with the last Ships, so that we shall do better in future,
& no opportunity of sending Seeds or Plants will be lost.

A clue to the earliest wine grape vines in Australia. Arthur Phillip to Joseph Banks, 22 August 1790.

could have purchased vines there along with other plants. His contact to do so was botanist Francis Masson, the first plant specialist from Kew Botanic Gardens to work outside of Britain at this time of the birth of the age of scientific discovery.[12]

Although Phillip left no specific notes of the types of vine plants and cuttings he bought at the Cape, there are clues elsewhere to the varieties they may have been. In his *Endeavour* journal, Banks mentioned Cape wines such as Madeira, Frontignac and Constantia.[13] A list of vines purchased at the Cape by Banks' protégée George Suttor in 1800 constituted 'Tokay, White Frontignac, White Muscardine, Black Frontignac, Constantia and Muscat of Alexandria'.[14] The British seized control of the Cape Colony from the Dutch from 1806 and an 1824 newspaper article tells us that about 800 vine cuttings were imported from the Botanic Gardens at the Cape to the Botanic Gardens in Sydney, to be distributed to settlers interested in wine growing. Although this transfer took place nearly forty years after the First Fleet voyage, it offers a guide to Phillip's vine purchases from the Cape. The 1824 imports were: 'pontac, red and white muscadel, steen, large and ordinary steen, water and red hoenpoten, Frontignac, chrystal, Persian, green grape, and ordinary hoenpoten'.[15] (Contemporary names for these are provided in Appendix 1.) These vines were definitely for wine, not for eating fresh or drying and wines made from them were familiar to the British by names other than vine varieties.

> " *Wine served as a tool of British diplomacy in the first cross-cultural contact at Botany Bay.*

The vines first imported to New South Wales were carried on a convict transport crammed with exotic flora and fauna. Shortly before landfall at Botany Bay in January 1788, surgeon Smyth on *Lady Penrhyn* reported that warm weather had invigorated the plants and they were bolting to flower. Four days later, in the strongest sea swell encountered during the voyage from the Cape, grape vines, bananas and other plants were tossed out of their storage tubs and 'much hurt'.[16] Fortunately, not hurt enough to prevent them being planted in the new colony.

Wine and 'natives' of New Worlds

While grape vines were not customary cargo of British voyages, wine invariably was and as a result had a role in the first cultural exchanges with Indigenous peoples during the Age of Empires. In the first English contact with Indigenous Americans in the sixteenth century, voyager Richard Hakluyt described attempts to communicate with the peoples he encountered. 'After two or three days the king's brother came aboard the ships', said Hakluyt, 'and drank wine, and eat of our meat and of our bread, and liked exceedingly thereof'.[17] Two centuries later, on 15 January 1769, Banks' *Endeavour* journal entry for Tierra de Fuego (southern South America) records Indigenous Americans being first given beads and ribbons then offered bread and beef, which they ate 'though not heartily but carried the largest part away with them, they would not drink either wine or spirits but returned the glass, though not before they had put it to their mouths and tasted a drop'.[18] Two decades on, wine served as a tool of British diplomacy in the first cross-cultural contact at Botany Bay.

How this came about was that, on 20 January 1788, the advance ships of the First Fleet had been anchored off Botany Bay for two days when Phillip took a small party from the *Sirius* ashore in two long boats to look for a place to camp and to find fresh water. While they were ashore the party encountered several men and boys who began to follow them.[19] As Lieutenant Philip Gidley King tells it, the British offered these men beads and mirrors, by leaving them on the ground. After this the Aboriginal men continued to walk behind the colonists as they explored the area. Some of the British were armed, though Phillip approached the Aboriginal men without weapons. The Aborigines, 'armed with lances and short bludgeons' seemed to want closer contact and the colonists' first impulse was to offer more presents but their supply of trinkets was running low. At this point, King offered wine to the Aboriginal men: 'I gave two of them a glass of wine', he wrote, 'which they had no sooner tasted than they spit it out'.[20]

It is not surprising the men spat out the wine due to the shock of the alcohol, the unfamiliar taste and the absence of any reason to want to try to like it. With what it is possible to piece together of the incident, it seems likely other Aboriginal men at the scene laughed at their companions' reaction to the wine. There is no suggestion in King's account, for instance, that the men given the wine became aggressive because they thought they were being poisoned. And given the precise moment at which the wine appears to have been offered – when relations between the British and the Aborigines were uncertain – I imagine relief on the part of King and his companions, though they were careful to leave out any hint of their fear in their published accounts. Any danger posed by the Aboriginal men seemed to have passed; a barrier in cultural contact breached. Both groups began comparing words in their respective languages. When the Aborigines indicated they were confused about the gender of their visitors a British crew member removed his pants to make it plain they were men. Again, there may have been amusement from the Aborigines. Whatever their response, it did not constitute a threat. Surgeon George Worgan described it as all a bit of a lark. He thought the Aboriginal men 'became very funny fellows. They suffered the sailors to dress them with different coloured papers, and fools-caps, which pleased them mightily, the strange contrast these decorations made with their black complexion brought strongly to my mind, the chimney-sweepers in London on a May-Day.'[21]

Phillip's orders were to use 'every possible means to open intercourse with the natives, and to conciliate their affections, enjoining all our subjects to live in amity and kindness with them' but also to count the number of Aborigines he met to calculate how they could be 'turned to the advantage of the colony'.[22] The Botany Bay encounter formed the first meeting in which Phillip and his officers believed they exhibited kindness but also speculatively judged the potential of the Aboriginal men to be co-opted to the colonial project. Wine proffered by King provided a test which we can only wonder the British expected the Aborigines to pass. Without a shared language or conception of each other's way of life, it is not possible that the Aborigines could have responded in a manner approved of by the colonists any more than the colonists could have conceived of what the Aborigines communicated except in a very superficial sense.[23]

Could King just as likely have offered spirits to the Aboriginal men?

The most plausible answer is no. On other colonial excursions, Phillip and his most senior men routinely carried wine as refreshment. Worgan described a Romantic short journey he, Hunter and Bradley later took in bushland up river from Port Jackson:

> Having extended our excursion as far as we wished, we returned to the place where we landed and after regaling ourselves with a cold Kangaroo Pie and a Plum Pudding, a Bottle of Wine &c, all which comforts we brought from the ship with us, we returned on board.[24]

What might the Aborigines have actually made of wine? Indigenous Australians possessed highly evolved cultural meanings for food and intoxicants derived from regional plants but had no fermented liquid such as wine or spirits.[25] Since the wine did not impress the men who tasted it, it must – along with the beads and mirrors – have seemed to be a curious, even pointless, but not hostile offering.

The offer of wine by King at Botany Bay was followed by other such incidents which, to adapt an observation by historian Henry Reynolds, showed the Aboriginal response to British culture to be varied and individual, inquisitive and creative.[26] When wine and artefacts of Britishness were again offered to Aborigines to measure their capacity to be Europeanised, there was little that was civilised about the means by which Phillip compelled this process. When Aboriginal men did not present themselves to him for scrutiny at Port Jackson, Phillip – frustrated – ordered a kidnapping. In December 1788, he sent a party of marines to capture Aboriginal men.

The first Indigenous Australian taken into the British settlement was Arabanoo. When Phillip first showed Arabanoo what he considered his best courtesy by including him among his dinner guests, Arabanoo refused to try wine or any other alcohol. Tench tells us the Aboriginal man 'dined at a side-table at the governor's and ate heartily of fish and ducks, which he first cooled. Bread and salt meat he smelled at but would not taste: all our liquors he treated in the same manner, and could drink nothing but water'.[27] Just over a month later, Arabanoo (still presumably at a side table) began to like eating bread, very much enjoyed drinking tea but would not drink alcohol, turning away 'with disgust and abhorrence'.[28] Although Tench's reports contain an air of benevolent curiosity, they imply Arabanoo had not demonstrated sufficient refinement. Arabanoo was not subjected to such observations for long. He died of smallpox in May 1789.

Phillip mounted further kidnapping missions. These at first failed until, six months after the death of Arabanoo, marines netted two men: Colbee and Bennelong. In much the same way as he had with Arabanoo, the governor offered these men wine as part of his side-table diplomacy. Colbee responded in the same way as Arabanoo. He showed little desire to help the colonists' rationalist observations of his people and soon after escaped. Bennelong, however, used a creative diplomacy of his own.[29] Tench noted that Bennelong, unlike Arabanoo and Colbee, 'was the only native we ever knew who immediately shewed a fondness for spirits' and could drink quantities equal to the Europeans without any greater effect than, 'upon one of us, although fermented liquor was new to him'.[30]

Bennelong played along very well with the white men. Historian Inga Clendinnen judged him to be 'wily' and there can be no doubt Bennelong put his relationship with the migrants to good use when it suited him.[31] Tench said Bennelong learned English faster than Arabanoo and that he had the added quality of being an entertaining story-teller (especially, I imagine, when he drank spirits or wine).[32]

King, with his great sensibilities for refinement, gave a similar assessment of the Wanghal man and wine but insisted that Bennelong preferred wine to spirits. He believed that when the whites attempted to trick Bennelong 'by mixing very weak rum or brandy and water, instead of wine and water ... he would instantly find out the deception, and on these occasions he was angry'.[33] If Bennelong did indeed drink only wine it appears to have indicated to King that he possessed a high state of readiness to be converted to British culture.

Despite Phillip's hopes of keeping Bennelong in captivity, with all of its perceived enticements, the Wanghal returned to his own people. The two men next met some months later, the day the governor was speared by another Aborigine at Manly Cove in September 1790. This incident has been skilfully interpreted by Clendinnen as planned and ritualised punishment of Phillip – for 'his and his people's many offences' – which led to a new détente, from the perspective of the Aborigines, between Indigenous inhabitants closest to settlement and the colonists.[34]

Prior to the spearing, Phillip sighted Bennelong among a group of Aborigines feasting on a whale carcass at the cove. When the governor's row boat reached the shore, Tench informs us:

> the natives were found still busily employed around the whale. As they expressed not any consternation on seeing us row to the beach, governor Phillip stepped out unarmed, and attended by one seaman only, and called for Baneelon, who appeared, but notwithstanding his former eagerness, would not suffer to approach him for several minutes. Gradually, however, he warmed into friendship and frankness, and presently after Colbee came up. They discoursed for some time, Baneelon expressing pleasure to see his old acquaintance, and inquiring by name for every person whom he could recollect at Sydney … Baneelon's love of wine has been mentioned; and the governor, to try whether it still subsisted, uncorked a bottle, and poured out a glass of it, which the other drank off with his former marks of relish and good humour, giving for a toast, as he had been taught, *'the King'*.[35]

Two others mention this incident. It is possible that similarities between accounts are the result of the editing of the journallers' original papers.[36] The story would also have been told and retold in the colony.[37]

After an exchange of gifts, Willemering stepped forward, aimed and threw a spear which struck Phillip; not to kill but to wound as payback, according to Clendinnen's interpretation.[38] The colonists quickly retreated from the beach. Phillip made a good recovery from his wound and the people of the region appeared to be more accepting of the colonists' presence. Wine gave Phillip a means to reconnect with Bennelong through a British expression of civility, but the more resonant aspect of the encounter is Bennelong and 'the King'.

Bennelong's habit of calling wine 'the King' has often been quoted in relation to Aboriginal alcoholism.[39] But there is also the bleak irony that when Bennelong joined the chorused cry of 'the King' with glass or bottle raised, he clearly perceived something related to power of meaning and certainty of purpose in the triumphal tone. He could not have known that when the colonists toasted the King, they also toasted the power of empire, which they imagined swelled over the Australian landscape and its ancient civilisation, ostensibly providing legitimacy and protection for the colonial project against resistance from Aboriginal occupants.

Wine and Dreaming

Craig San Roque, a psychologist working in contemporary Aboriginal communities, has found that while Europeans have an embedded sense of alcohol culture, 'where it comes from, what it's for', a recent rise in alcohol abuse in some Aboriginal communities has highlighted that there is no Dreaming for alcohol. There are no origin stories for it, no guide as to how to contain its use or what sort of punishment should result from offences committed under its influence. To address this, San Roque told Aboriginal elders a version of the classical Greek tale in Euripides' *Bacchae* in which a group of people under the influence of wine unknowingly slaughter a family member. Once the killers sober up they demonstrate horror and great sorrow at their crime; a cautionary tale from European culture.[40] Meanwhile, Australia's only Aboriginal-owned vineyard, planted near

Lake Cargelligo in 1999, by Murrin Bridge Land Council, remains a proudly operated community project. Murrin Bridge Connections is only the second Indigenous wine producer in the world.[41] Its wines are available through Westend Estate at Griffith.

Alcohol has been one of the most destructive legacies of British colonisation in Australia. So I cannot help but think it is a very powerful chapter in the story of wine that while some Indigenous Australians may use ancient European stories of wine consumption to make sense of the devastating effects of alcohol abuse others have embraced vine growing as a friendly face of wine.

With this in mind, let's see where those vines Phillip bought at the Cape were planted.

4

First vineyards, first vintages

Once the Port Jackson site had been chosen for the colony of New South Wales in the early summer of 1788, gardens were dug and filled with the plants transported from across the world. The first vines in Australia can be seen in a watercolour by William Bradley of Arthur Phillip's first house at Sydney Cove.[1] These vines flanked the path from close to Circular Quay, through the subsistence garden planted under the supervision of Henry Dodd, the colony's most experienced farmer and gardener, to Phillip's front gate.[2] The vines had been placed in the ground gooseberry bush style; that is, unsupported with trellising as espaliered vines are today. The 1791 painting gives a deceptive impression of the grandeur of the building and the neatness of the garden. It may also exaggerate the size of the vines, although they were three years old at the time of the painting, just coming into bearing their first grapes and perhaps as abundantly leafy as portrayed by Bradley. The apparent vigour of the vines belies the fact that the natural environment of early Sydney would prove to be far less welcoming than the confident colonists assumed. Along with uncertain access to vine stock and lack of viticultural experience, colonial growing conditions such as soil fertility obstructed the earliest attempts to create a wine industry in New South Wales.

An English friend of mine has commented how frequently Australians speak of soils. This fixation has a long history which, as you might expect, dates back to 1788. Historian Grace Karskens' profound skill in revealing significant insights in the colonial everyday led her to notice that wherever Phillip and his officers ventured beyond their settlement, 'they had eyes only for soils. They had an entire lexicon to describe soils. They carried little bags to take samples for testing and blending experiments.'[3] These early colonists were looking for places to plant particular crops as part of the desire to use all the land they occupied, as they perceived it, productively.

Wine growers and connoisseurs, farmers and gardeners will recognise this obsession with soil. In wine growing it is a main constituent of *terroir*. A difference in early New South Wales vine plantings from today's, however, was the belief that poor ground should by default host vineyards. This idea echoed classical Greek use of depleted land for vineyards combined with the British impression that French vineyards were acre for acre more profitable than food grain crops. But early colonists took classical Greek advice much too literally. A visiting Austrian diplomat noted in the early 1830s that British colonists had a 'mistaken notion' that vines would do best in 'very arid, cold sandy soil' and in an extensive vineyard the 'grape vine cuttings were stuck into the sand … without any soil or manure'.[4]

And the climate, which is another aspect of *terroir*? An account of New South Wales rushed off the presses in London the year after the First Fleet arrived, announced that the colony's typical weather resembled the 'finest in Europe'; fruits and vegetables brought from Rio and the Cape were thriving and wine growing offered considerable promise. 'In a climate so favourable', the publisher embellished on behalf of Governor Phillip, 'the cultivation of the vine may doubtless be carried to any degree of perfection; and should not other articles of commerce divert the attention of settlers from this point, the wines of New South Wales may, perhaps, be hereafter sought with avidity, and become an indispensable part of the luxury of European tables.'[5]

In 1790, the colony's first chaplain, Richard Johnson – who marines captain Watkin Tench described as the 'best farmer in the country' – reported in a letter to a friend on the colony's progress that the climate could be better but the soil seemed ideal so 'we are in hopes of seeing these turn to some account. I promise you if ever wine be made here and not prohibited from being exported, I will send you a specimen and perhaps may drink your health in a bumper of New Holland wine.'[6] Why Johnson thought the wines might be prohibited from being exported is not clear but the topic of vines was prominent in the minds of colonists. In a letter dated the day after Johnson's, Phillip thanked Banks for his promise of grape plants for the colony and allowed himself a degree of pleasure in reporting that 'last summer produced two good bunches of grapes, which may be mentioned as being the first this country has produced'. But as he went on to explain, 'though being neglected they decayed on the vine'.[7] Despite this frank description of the fate of the first grapes, Phillip's letter is not dispiriting. It tells us that 2000 vines had been planted at the new government farm at Rose Hill (now Parramatta) and the vineyard would be extended to two acres in the following year. Dodd supervised much of the government farm planting at Rose Hill before his death in 1791 and most likely can be credited too with the early vineyard there.[8]

Five hundred vine cuttings were sent to Norfolk Island and formed a crucial part of the early colonial project. Thanks to art historian Robert Hughes, the island settlement of the 1830s has a reputation as a brutal place of secondary punishment. Prior to its role as a prison for repeat offenders, the island offered the only known extractable natural resources in the colony: pine trees for ships' masts and flax for sailcloth. The plan was to use convict labour to harvest and process these.[9] The first lieutenant-governor at Norfolk Island, Philip Gidley King, predicted grape vines would flourish to 'a great quantity in a few years'.[10] A few weeks later, King's replacement, Robert Ross, told Phillip that the number of vines at the island 'amounts now to between seven and eight hundred, which are all in high perfection, and two or three of the oldest are now bearing'.[11]

That grapes were perceived as symbols of hope in the early years of the colony of New South Wales was communicated by Tench in his New Year entry for 1791, following an inauspicious previous twelve months:

> No circumstance, however apparently trivial, which can tend to throw light on a new country, either in respect of its present situation or its future promise, should pass unregarded. On the 24th January, two bunches of grapes were cut in the governor's garden, from cuttings of vines brought three years before from the Cape of Good Hope. The bunches were handsome, the fruit of a moderate size but well filled out and the flavour high and delicious.[12]

He reported that Elizabeth Macarthur considered the grapes to be 'as fine as I ever tasted'.[13]

Phillip wrote to Banks in December of that year, that 'we have now many thousand young vines, here and at Norfolk Island … at present the old vines in my garden are loaded with very fine fruit'.[14]

Philip Schaeffer

Late in 1791 too, Tench conducted a walking tour of government farming in the colony. At Parramatta, the Crescent – site of the main vineyard –'in beauty of form and situation [was] unrivalled in New South Wales'. Eight thousand vines had now been planted from cuttings of maturing vines. The older vines were expected to bear fruit in a year and 'although the soil of the Crescent be poor, its aspect and circular figure, so advantageous for receiving and retaining the ray of the sun, is eminently fit for a vineyard'. Tench next visited the farm of Philip Schaeffer, 'a man of industry and respectable character'; the colony's first free settler and the first hope for private investment in wine growing.[15]

How did Schaeffer come to be a free settler but neither ex-convict nor ex-marine so early in the life of the colony?[16] After serving with Hessian (German) forces used to bolster British troops in the American War of Independence, Schaeffer arrived in New South Wales in 1790. He was aged in his forties and destitute after the wreck of his original ship of carriage, the *Guardian*, which had been loaded with much anticipated supplies for the colony. Schaeffer originally migrated to the colony to work as a supervisor of convict farm labourers but his limited English made this impractical.

Schaeffer's conversations with Phillip revealed that his family's estate at Hesse-Hanau, on the Rhine River, included a vineyard. Although Schaeffer had spent most of his adult life as a soldier, the experience of farming he described led Phillip to allocate him 140 acres of land on the Parramatta riverfront in 1791. This was at a time when ex-convicts were receiving only 20 to 60 acres.[17] Schaeffer seemed to be an ideal candidate for settlement within the governor's vision for agriculture to not only sustain the colony but to begin to build surplus production for trade.[18] Schaeffer called his farm The Vineyard and quickly set about clearing land and planting corn and wheat, wine grapes and tobacco.[19] It was 'to these two last articles', wrote Tench, that Schaeffer 'mean[t] principally to direct his exertions' though he thought the soil very poor compared with the river flats of the Rhine.[20]

"

Grapes were perceived as symbols of hope in the early years of the colony of New South Wales.

Very poor? Phillip, also a man of the land, described Schaeffer's soil as 'of a middling quality, inclining to a loamy sand'.[21] I think Schaeffer likely made the more practical assessment.

The year of Schaeffer's first vine plantings, Joseph Banks received a letter that implies he canvassed for information on viticulture to send to Phillip. The letter recommended that when grapes were planted, cuttings should be laid in a trench than had been partly filled with compost made of rotten manure and bread. The compost should be laid fresh around the plants and watered in as they grew.[22] But, with neither manure nor bread in great supply in New South Wales this method could not have been very helpful.

In October 1792, Phillip reported Schaeffer 'doing well'.[23] The governor would depart from New South Wales only a few months later.

In 1795, Phillip's successor, Acting Governor William Paterson, advised Banks that Schaeffer had produced 'ninety gallons of wine in about two years now ... the vines I think produce better than at the Cape'.[24] He predicted that within two years New South Wales would be self-sufficient in wine and brandy.

Paterson's remark about Schaeffer's first wine raises a question. Had the Hessian settler made wine from the grapes at the government farm even earlier? If so, this would be the first vintage in New South Wales. A tiny shard of evidence suggests that he had.

First vintage

In 1794, Banks opened a letter from German scientist Johann Frederic Blumenbach, based at the Georg August University, Göttingen. Banks and Blumenbach (a student of Carl Linnaeus) shared a deep interest in natural philosophy and corresponded regularly as part of the robust intellectual conversation that took place across European borders during the Enlightenment.

The sliver of testimony about the first Australian wine in Banks' letter from Blumenbach is as follows.

> Yesterday I received from a friend of mine [a clergyman] ... a curious present of a small bottle of a strong red wine from Rosehill near Sydney Cove ... (as he says) he had received from a friend in London. He adds that the wine was brought over by Captain Phillips [in 1792]. Though I know that wines flourish now in New South Wales and also that my good clergyman himself will not play me a trick, I take however the liberty of requesting your kind information with a few words, if you know, that Captain Phillips really brought with him wine from there to England?[25]

How extraordinary! Is it possible Phillip took wine made at Rose Hill back to England when he sailed from Port Jackson in December 1792? Was this not only the first New Holland wine but the first colonial Australian wine sent to England? The possibility deserves careful consideration as it is widely held that colonial entrepreneur Gregory Blaxland was the first to send wine from New South Wales in 1822 to be judged by Britain's Society for the Encouragement of Arts, Manufactures and Commerce.

How could Blumenbach's bottle signal an earlier export of Australian wine? The vines shown in William Bradley's painting of first government house at Sydney Cove might have borne sufficient fruit by summer 1792 to be made into a very small quantity of wine. More likely, the first grape vines planted at the Crescent had produced a small crop. Without knowing how many bottles of wine Phillip allegedly carried to England the quantity of grapes we are dealing with is highly speculative. If wine had been made before Phillip left New South Wales, Schaeffer would have almost certainly been involved.

Of course, another potential scenario is that an unscrupulous British merchant counterfeited the Rose Hill wine. Wine fraud proliferated as much as wine adulteration and reports of agricultural activity in the colony would have fuelled great curiosity among British gentlemen, so colonial wine could have fetched a high price. But how marvellous if Blumenbach's bottle was genuine.

Vines and vignerons

The state of flourishing colonial vines described by Blumenbach (probably as a result of earlier correspondence with Banks) proved to be an exaggeration and, given the recurring problem of blighted (diseased or wind scorched) vines at the nearby government farm, it is likely Schaeffer's were also afflicted. No wonder he did not persist with wine growing, let alone his other intended Parramatta plantings.[26] In 1797, after being granted a lease of land elsewhere in the colony, Schaeffer sold The Vineyard to Captain Henry Waterhouse for £140.[27] The property retained its name but the vine plantings were not extended.

Paterson returned to the colony from England in 1799 and wrote to Banks the following year that:

> I am sorry to observe that the cultivation of the vine has been to-
> tally neglected since I left the country; there are not so many more
> as there was in the year 1796, other fruit trees are however doing
> very well, such as apples, pears, apricots, peaches and almonds, the
> peaches have borne fruit eighteen months after the [seed] was first in
> the ground.[28]

This unsatisfactory progress in the acreage of vine cultivation had absolutely no economic or cultural impact in the colony. So why did it matter? To the architects of the colony it mattered a good deal.

Neglect of vineyards disappointed elite visions for New South Wales. Without vineyards, the imagined picture of the colony remained incomplete. These notions were held by government officials making policy for the colony in England, other key members of the project such as Banks, gentlemen observers of imperialism (the audience for accounts of the colonial enterprise and British newspapers), European scholars such as Blumenbach and colonial governors and elites, including interested wives and daughters of colonial office holders.

A year earlier, Banks – now Director of Kew Botanic Gardens – had written to Governor Hunter with the reassurance that although the British government was distracted by Napoleon, the acting governor should know that, 'Your Colony is already a most valuable appendage to Great Britain' and within time the British government would see this. Banks' commitment to the future of the colony led to the dispatch of plant collector George Caley on the same ship as newly appointed governor Philip Gidley King (returning from London) along with plant nurseryman George Suttor and more plants for the colony. Prior to his departure, Suttor had discussed vine cultivation and its potential in New South Wales at a meeting of the Board of Trade in London.[29] Plants that Banks ordered for the colony included, he told Hunter, 'grapes of the sorts from whence the valuable wines of Europe are made' which 'I hope, will encourage you to plant vineyards, and some of them surely will produce marketable wine'.[30]

The vision could not be clearer.

Suttor received charge of the plants for the colony in a special purpose-built cabin on the *Porpoise* in 1799. In his regular correspondence with

Banks about the health of plants in the cabin, Suttor often mentioned the vines first.[31] Unfortunately, all of the plants in Suttor's special cabin rotted en route to the Cape so he had to purchase replacements there.[32] These appear as imports from the year 1800 in Appendix 1.

Philip Gidley King, Ante Landrien and Francois de Riveau

Healthy vine plant clones, from the Cape or elsewhere, were still of little use without skilled viticulturalists to tend them. The solution to this appeared to present itself with the singling out of two Frenchmen captured by the British early in the Napoleonic Wars. The prisoners claimed to have wine growing experience. The project with the Frenchmen did not only comprehend the idea of a marketable wine, however. A rapid rise in colonial consumption of spirits led to visions of a new role for wine. Governor King's orders included implementing measures to sober up the colony. To achieve this, King raised customs duties on spirits to limit their trade. He also tried to introduce an informal policy of substitution. That is, encourage production of beer and wine to reform colonial culture by substituting rum with an alternative cheap, light alcohol.

British Home Secretary, William Bentinck, Duke of Portland (at this time British government minister responsible for the colony), had high hopes that the French prisoners, Ante Landrien and Francois de Riveau, would soon fill the government stores with colonial wine and readily funded the tools they requested to do this. [33] But, at this time, only two acres of vines remained in the colony and the Frenchmen would have to start from scratch with their vineyard. King allocated six convicts to assist them with planting out the cuttings at Parramatta.[34] Norfolk Island vine plantings were also to be rejuvenated, the whole project being seen as 'an eventual means of discouraging the importation and use of spirits'; a substitution of colonial wine for rum.[35]

Which vines did Landrien and de Riveau plant? Probably those Suttor purchased at the Cape in 1800. Suttor too planted a vineyard in 1801 using the vines he had imported.[36] Plans continued to create another government vineyard at Castle Hill, with 10 000 vines and eventually 30 acres in extent.[37]

Along with the Frenchmen, Portland sent a document titled 'Method of Preparing a Piece of Land for the Purpose of Forming a Vineyard'. This described how to make red wine, white wine and brandy.[38] King at first had no means of distributing this document. Then, astonishingly, given the extent to which early wine growing later disappeared from historical consciousness, portions of JB Laideau's 'Method' were published in the first edition of Australia's first newspaper, the *Sydney Gazette and New South Wales Advertiser* in 1803, and two subsequent editions.[39] Unhelpfully, however, Laideau's instructions were not revised for southern hemisphere seasons. They advised vine growers to prune in January and February, which in Australia is the height of summer growth and the grape harvest. Pruning takes place in the cool months when vines are dormant after leaf fall.

King sent the same instructions to Lieutenant-Governor Joseph Foveaux on Norfolk Island with word that the Frenchmen had said red wine grapes would do better than white; Foveaux should have as many cuttings as possible planted and the Frenchmen would soon visit to supervise the vineyard (which does not appear to have eventuated).[40] New Secretary of State for the Colonies, Lord Hobart (replacing the Duke of Portland), reminded King in strong terms of the 'advantages that would result to the inhabitants of the colony if the vine could be brought into such a state of general cultivation as to supply even an ordinary wine'.[41] As such, the governor eagerly anticipated the wine from the first harvest of the new vines. About 40 gallons was made but when it proved too poor to send a sample to the colonial secretary, King blamed the drought for the disappointing results and guaranteed efforts would continue, although the Frenchmen's contracts had been completed.

This episode in Australian wine history ended with one of the Frenchmen remaining in the colony. He reportedly made a reasonable peach cider. The other decided to return home.

> "
> *The governor eagerly anticipated the wine from the first harvest of the new vines.*

When Suttor's vines also failed, he put it down to being 'too much occupied with the raising of the necessities of life'.[42] Since the colony began to be self-sufficient in grain production during King's tenure, surplus grain could be legitimately directed towards brewing and malting to satisfy the need for colonial alcohol with less strength than spirits, and the governor called for hop plants to be sent from Britain to encourage local beer manufacture.

Vines as symbols of colonial wealth and respectability

While King despaired over the failure of the Frenchmen to deliver a wine industry at short order, a few entrepreneurial settlers maintained the vision for wine growing. Evidence for their faith in the power of vines to make them civilised and rich is reflected in objects of the time. It was not unusual for vines to represent wealth and civility in British World expressions of classical revivalism. For example, a Scottish trader incorporated repeated motifs of grape vines and olives into his renovated estate house in Scotland as symbols of his wealth and respectability. In New South Wales, a decorative Chinese-manufactured porcelain plate, ordered as early as the 1810s by entrepreneurs Elizabeth and John Macarthur, has a grapes and vines pattern. Among the colonial treasures of the State Library of New South Wales is a punchbowl depicting early Sydney in great detail, including a group of Aborigines. At one side is a grape vine motif.

The motif of vines and olives features on the crest of the Australian Agricultural Company, the first significant investment of private British capital into New South Wales farming and grazing. Created in 1824, the AA Company's inaugural colonial committee included prominent members of the Macarthur family and the company aimed to produce fine wool, beef cattle and luxuries: 'wine, olive-oil, hemp, flax, silk, opium, etc as articles of export to Great Britain'.[43] The design of the AA Company crest incorporates a length of grape vine joined to an olive branch stretching upward around a royal crown and holding aloft a beribboned sheep: symbols of wealth and respectability.

Two other private investment ventures established to exploit the land resources of New South Wales – the Scottish Australian Company and the North British Australasian Company – were also early colonial wine growers.

Unlike icy cold Scotland, where the trader mentioned above could possess only images of vines, in the temperate climate of New South Wales, British migrants could create vineyards as expressions of wealth and civility. The first private garden vines known to have been planted in the colony were on the property of the Macarthurs at Elizabeth Farm, Parramatta in 1794.[44] As they exploited opportunities such as land grants and trade, men and women such as the Macarthurs could afford to fashion their surroundings to suit conceptions of a privileged life, decorated with real and representative classical revivalism. Robert Townson named his colonial estate (at Minto near Sydney) after the Roman agriculturalist Marcus Venetius Varro. In the 1820s, 'Varro Ville became a show place for its beauty, abundance and variety in orchard and garden' and the colony's second most extensive vineyard.[45] Curiously, Townson had been based at the university of Göttingen when Blumenbach received his bottle of Rose Hill wine. Townson also completed a study tour of Hungary – perhaps the first British scholar to do so – where his exploration included close observation of 'Tokay' wine, the prized Aufbruche, made partially from highly-ripened, possibly botrytised grapes called Troken-beers.[46] Townson also grazed cattle inland at a property he named Murrumbateman, which today is within the Canberra wine region.

Obstacles such as blight of young vines and poor knowledge of where to most suitably locate vineyards meant that the symbolism of vines contained a promise not yet realised.

5

Intelligent industry

The earliest experiments in vine growing in New South Wales made it clear that if ambitious British colonists hoped to ever share toasts of drinkable colonial wine, they needed to know much more about how to start vineyards. Grain crops and orchard fruits were well established by the early 1820s, since plant stock and skilled labour for these could be readily imported. Why then did wine grapes not show their anticipated promise? Enlightenment confidence in the power of humankind over nature, combined with potential wealth and status to be gained from colonial wine growing, meant that the desire to create a wine industry was not simply abandoned at the first signs of obstacles. When French vinedressers Landrien and De Riveau did not produce rapid results, a British bureaucrat from the office that dispatched convicts – and who had a hand in employing the Frenchmen – remarked that 'without intelligent industry nothing can be expected'.[1] Intelligent industry in wine growing required specialist knowledge from outside the British World, but the Napoleonic Wars restricted British travel to European wine countries. Then, in 1815, almost as soon as these restrictions were lifted, John Macarthur and his sons James and William became the first established New South Wales colonists to set about gaining first-hand experience of wine growing in France and Switzerland.

Let us briefly consider the notion of intelligent industry. The observation about this requirement in colonial wine growing came in a private letter to Samuel Marsden, the clergyman better known for his contribution to early initiatives in wool growing. It is not widely reported in Australian history that Marsden first imported the grape variety Miller's Burgundy (Meunier) to New South Wales before 1817.[2] He also had the distinction of introducing the first European vine cuttings to New Zealand in 1819.[3] What, however, did his correspondent, Ambrose Serle, mean by intelligent industry? A search for similar uses of the phrase turned up a reference from Henry Swinburne's travels in Spain and France in the 1770s. 'The road hither is excellent', he wrote of a district in south-western France, 'and passes through a rapid succession of grand, romantic and pleasing prospects, where the uncommon richness of the soil is ably seconded by the intelligent industry of the cultivators'.[4] In these terms, intelligent industry could be defined as the clever use of resources to hand. For elite colonists, access to land was far greater in New South Wales than in Europe but as Serle intuited, the colonists needed to be much smarter about planting it with vineyards.

Macarthur and sons

By the time the Macarthurs set out on their wine study tour in 1815, John Macarthur had been in exile in Britain since 1808 for masterminding the ousting of Governor William Bligh. The so-called Rum Rebellion against Bligh has been judged variously by historians but most recently and persuasively, as not at all about rum but motivated by British notions of property rights.[5] The Macarthurs' journey probably served partly as a grand tour of sorts for seventeen-year-old James and fifteen-year-old William. The trip also fitted into a tradition of exploratory travel. But Macarthur's intention was not to publish an account such as Townson's on Hungary or Arthur Young's well-known comparison of British and French farming. He wanted to *see* how to create a crop which had so far eluded him.

Macarthur and his sons travelled first to Paris. There they saw Napoleon and were unimpressed by him and his city. They then made their way, mainly on foot, through French wine regions to Switzerland where John Macarthur sought out a former migrant to the United States, Jean Jacques Dufour. Macarthur had read Dufour's 1802 publication on his efforts to establish a wine industry in New Switzerland, Kentucky. (We know this because Elizabeth Macarthur loaned a copy of Dufour's book to Gregory Blaxland from the library at Elizabeth Farm while her husband served out his exile.[6]) Dufour studied viticulture in Europe before migrating to Kentucky in 1796. By 1803 he had sent his brother to Washington with two five-gallon barrels of wine for President Thomas Jefferson, a great wine enthusiast. But Dufour's enterprise had been set up with investment subscriptions and when investors stopped paying because of disappointing returns, the business had to be wound up. In 1806 Dufour returned to Europe to raise the money to settle his family's debts in the United States, and it was 1817 before he could return to Kentucky.[7]

When the Macarthurs arrived in Vevey in 1815, John Macarthur senior wrote to son John – the family's business agent in London – that Dufour and his family were soon to begin pruning so, fortunately, he could see the whole cycle of the vineyard where practices were similar to those in the highly-prized French region of Burgundy. He knew the wines were not as good as French ones due to inferior 'soil, aspect, climate and other unknown causes' but Dufour had valuable first-hand experience of New World vine experiments. The young Macarthurs attended school in Switzerland and their father spent time with Dufour. In this time he also recruited two Swiss vinedressers but these men, for reasons not explained, were turned back to Switzerland when the party reached Lyon on the return journey across France.[8]

While in France, John Macarthur bought vine cuttings, at Tain l'Hermitage, for instance.[9] William later wrote that about 'thirty of the best varieties of the vine (from six to twelve cuttings or plants of each) … were collected in the vineyards in which they grew, and taken from the vines, in most instances, literally under our eyes', including 'the best varieties' from the Languedoc, Cote Rotie and the Cote d'Or. But when the collection arrived in New South Wales it did not contain all of the varieties purchased, instead only 'Gouais (La Folle), Muscat Noir, Black Hamburgh, little Black Cluster, Miller's Burgundy and Sweet Water'.[10] Black Cluster may have been Pinot Noir so all may not have been lost, but it seemed to be so.

Vines were purchased too at Madeira on the homeward voyage to Sydney, likely at the recommendation of Dufour. This Madeira collection arrived at Port Jackson in 1818 and a vineyard was planted out with advice from Thomas Hobbes Scott, a visiting Englishman who had been a wine merchant in Bordeaux.[11] Scott became a friend of the Macarthurs when he travelled to the colony in 1819 as secretary to the judge John Thomas Bigge. (Bigge had been appointed by the Secretary of State for the Colonies, Earl Bathurst, to investigate the state of transportation of convicts and other matters such as farming and trade. He also became a friend of the Macarthurs.) Scott – a French wine snob – thought John Macarthur a little mad for gaining knowledge from a Swiss wine grower. He recommended French literature on wine growing and reminded his friend that English botanists and horticulturalists knew best only how to 'raise grapes in a hot house or on a wall'. He also warned against Italian instructions for wine growing as 'nothing can be worse than their method or their wine'.[12] Italian influence in New South Wales wine making in the Hawkesbury and around Griffith has since proved to be of great value.

It would be several years before the Macarthurs' commercial scale vineyard bore its first fruit and William Macarthur, the vineyard's custodian, realised that the vine plants purchased during their tour amounted to very little. From the French collection, only three varieties were new to the colony, the others already being under cultivation. William thought only the first two had been obtained in France and the whereabouts of the rest of the collection remained a tremendously frustrating mystery. When the first vineyard matured, it became clear that the Madeira collection comprised only one variety instead of the expected seven, which deeply dismayed William and his father. Their wine 'did not answer expectation. In short, although the vines flourished, the vineyard seemed to be a failure, and ignorant of the true cause, we were half inclined to give the matter up.'[13] But this half inclination did not win out. William designed plantings near the family's new estate house on the banks of the Nepean River at Camden which would prove to be more successful.[14]

The Macarthur brothers, James and William, offer us a glimpse of why some colonists engaged so keenly with wine growing while others were uninterested. During the wine study tour, James wrote in his diary that:

> the vintage, which I expected to find a very beautiful sight ... is however very much the reverse. The grapes, when gathered, are put into large tubs, where they are pounded until they have much the appearance of hogs wash. They are then carried away to the house and before they are pressed, undergo another pounding with men's feet. In short no process can be in appearance more dirty.[15]

None of the romance of the vintage for James! His indignation is a rare counter-point to the passion for vines and wine expressed elsewhere. When the Macarthurs left Switzerland with new knowledge gained from *seeing* the process of the grape harvest and wine making, it was always going to be William, not James, who breathed life into John Macarthur senior's vision for vineyards.

Gregory Blaxland

While the Macarthurs rambled through European wine regions, entrepreneur Gregory Blaxland had planted his first colonial vineyard, sent wine to the governor and began a campaign for reforms to facilitate wine growing. Blaxland and his brother John had migrated at the suggestion of Joseph Banks and were among the first 'respectable' (non-convict) settlers in New South Wales.[16] It was probably Banks who alerted him to the potential for wine growing, just one of the industries Blaxland expressed interest in. During layovers on his initial voyage to Sydney in 1806, Blaxland observed wine growing, and as he settled in he discussed his plans, at least with Elizabeth Macarthur, who loaned him the Dufour book. Blaxland's ambitions had progressed sufficiently by 1816 for him to send a sample of that year's vintage to Governor Lachlan Macquarie, who had relaced Governor Bligh. Blaxland's first experiments used vines from abandoned vineyards and produced poor results but, he stated, 'I have now collected three or four good bearing sorts, which appear to me fit to make wine, and have acquired some further knowledge of their culture which induces me to persevere in my attempt, which render me more sanguine in my hopes of ultimate success'.[17] There is no surprise in Blaxland's lack of expertise in viticulture but it is intriguing to consider how he might have extended his knowledge. Only by reading the Dufour publication? Instructions from the *Sydney Gazette* in 1803? Blaxland's colonial ambition was demonstrated with the claim that he had led – not just participated in – the first successful crossing by British colonists of the Blue Mountains; a symbolic as well as tangible barrier to the westward progress of European civilisation.[18] (Blaxland, Wentworth and Lawson – the famous Blue Mountains expeditioners – would all, at some stage, have colonial vineyards.) Might he also have exaggerated vine expertise?

Blaxland's sample of colonial wine very nearly remained in bond on the London docks.

Blaxland, like other mid-century wine growers, made his income chiefly as a pastoralist but his contribution to wine growing included several innovations. By keeping convict labour in his employ for at least three years before they were granted tickets of leave, he believed he built a small semi-skilled viticultural workforce.[19] He requested that Macquarie support lifting restrictions on brandy production so grapes from vintages damaged by wet weather could be distilled, as occurred in France, ensuring some return on investment in the vineyard. Blaxland asked too that concessions be made on the export duty on brandy produced in the colony and refunds be made on duty paid for imported brandy to fortify wine, so wine growers were not hit twice by tariffs. Such requests might have seemed premature but, Blaxland argued, he wanted to begin the process of change since it would take some time.[20]

As a result of trials with different varieties of vines, Blaxland planted out two 200 young plants raised from seed. The best among his vines appeared to be 'the claret grape' (which James Busby later identified as Burgundy but could have been Cape Pontac).[21] Whatever the grape, Blaxland continued to show great initiative by transporting a pipe of this wine, fortified with 10 per cent brandy, to present to the Society for the Encouragement of Arts, Manufactures and Commerce (later the Royal Society). The Society promoted production in the British World, such as wool and colonial wine from the British North American colonies before Independence. In 1822, the Society had a section for wine growing in New South Wales under the category Colonies and Trade. Its members judged the climate of the colony to be 'healthful, and similar in temperature to that of Madeira' and the population 'well-disposed to exchange the new products of their laborious activity for the comforts, the conveniences, and even the elegancies and luxuries of civilised life'.[22]

Blaxland's sample of colonial wine very nearly remained in bond on the London docks. Faced with excise duties, he appealed for help to Bigge – now back in England – who knew of the great cost to which Blaxland had gone to experiment with wine growing. As Blaxland hoped, Bigge cleared the way for him to release his colonial wine from bond with little expense, on the grounds that wine growing 'if established will be of great importance to the colony of New South Wales'.[23] The Society went on to award Blaxland's colonial claret a silver medal, more I suspect in recognition of his enthusiasm than the quality of the wine. 'The general opinion', the Society reported, 'seemed to be, that although the present sample for the inexpertness of the manufacturer and the youth of the wine, is by no means of superior quality, yet it affords a reasonable ground of expectation that by care and time it may become a valuable article of export'.[24] Blaxland again sent wine to the Society six years later with better results. This time he received a Gold Ceres Medal and the judges decided the wine was 'sound and perfectly free from that flavour which characterises, not advantageously, the wine of another British colony'; meaning the Cape.[25] And although Blaxland might have taken heart from the comparison being so much in his favour it can also be read as a pejorative reference to Cape wine, which had replaced Portuguese products as the lowest-excised wine imported into Britain only fifteen years earlier.[26]

French ship captain Louis Isidore Duperrey visited the government farm at Emu Plains in February and March 1824 and observed that its vines were not pruned, as no one at the farm knew how to do so. Duperrey had heard of Blaxland's medal but could see no evidence of thriving viticulture, as opposed to garden-based vines. 'It is no secret', he reported:

> that the English are very anxious to possess vineyards and to rid them-
> selves as soon as possible of the necessity of paying a huge sum abroad.
> But I was able to convince myself here that all the boasted attempts,
> with the object of acclimatising the wine grape, amounted to very little.
> The table grape has succeeded very well in the gardens, where it has
> increased, and at the Governor's residence, and in one colonial garden
> I saw long espaliers yielding a very good fruit, where care is taken to
> cover it early in paper bags to protect it from birds, but especially from
> disease [blight].[27]

The British migrants did well what they knew: table grapes in gardens. Wine grapes, on a commercial scale, were another matter. Further knowledge had to be gained.

William Redfern

In the same year as Duperry toured Emu Plains, the former convict and respected colonial surgeon, William Redfern, visited Madeira on his return voyage from England to Sydney. Redfern had travelled to London to petition the king against recommendations from Bigge that emancipists have less right to property than non-convict settlers.[28] In Madeira, he took the opportunity, 'at considerable expense', to hire skilled vineyard workers and purchase vine cuttings.[29] The timing of Redfern's trip suggests he missed the drama of the Macarthurs' experience with vines from Madeira. Unfortunately, we do not know how well his vines grew or the fate of the Portuguese vinedressers his wife said he engaged in Madeira to travel to New South Wales.[30]

James Busby

While Redfern petitioned the King, young Scotsman James Busby – who had studied agriculture in Britain – was living in Cadillac on the banks of the Garonne, across the river from the more famous French wine districts of Sauternes, Barsac and Preignac. He observed vineyards and read several of the thirty or so French publications he knew to be available on vine growing and wine making. Busby's motivation to extend his informal studies to France included a British House of Lords report on trade which drew attention to the demand for wine in British India. The shipping route between New South Wales and India was shorter than New South Wales to Britain and trade between the two British colonial possessions had by this time become established. Supplies from India included tea, sugar and Bengal rum.[31] Busby calculated that the demand for wine in British India could be met from New South Wales and he prepared to migrate to the colony with his family by gathering intelligence on wine growing.[32]

On the voyage to Sydney, Busby visited Constantia and other vineyards at the Cape.[33] The long voyage also provided time for him to synthesise his knowledge into the work he published in the colony as *A Treatise* (1825). But he did not spend a whole year in France, so his seasonal observations were limited to bonfires used to keep the vines warm and thus prevent frost damage, and the grape crush.[34]

Busby's *Treatise* became the first English-language wine growing manual of the period and although he lacked knowledge of New South Wales conditions, he made a shrewd observation about the limitations of knowledge in the colonial environment. Busby found that French instruction manuals naturally assumed that aspiring vignerons could observe existing practices. French instructive literature said to French readers:

> You have, already, extensive and excellent vineyards, and in the lapse of ages, each variety has found out the soil and situation which fits it best, or has become naturalized to the climate and soil where it grows. Choose your plants from the best in your own neighbourhood, attend to their cultivation, and to the fermentation of your wine, and you will have the best your land is capable of producing.[35]

These knowledge pathways did not exist in New South Wales. This, said Busby, should not discourage colonial wine growing since although the French industry seemed to have been established since time out of mind, wine grapes were not indigenous to Western Europe and had first come from *other places*. While the French enjoyed the legacy of 2000 years of wine growing heritage, the best early nineteenth century wines came from vines imported from elsewhere only hundreds of years earlier. Cypriot wines, he said, were considered the best in the world in the fifteenth century and the prized Madeira, Malmsey and Malaga wines of the eighteenth and nineteenth centuries were from vines originally imported from Cyprus. French vines too came from Greece. And besides, Busby continued, due to the need to re-plant vines too mature to yield sufficient quantities of fruit, some French grape vines were only twenty-five to thirty years old.[36]

"

Wine grapes were not indigenous to Western Europe and had first come from other places.

Despite some colonial criticism of the pompous tone of the *Treatise*, its publication gained Busby the position of head of the colony's first Agricultural Institute at Liverpool; a project recommended by Bigge. Busby's instructions were to use a similar project in Switzerland as a model to educate orphan boys in viticulture and 'raising other products, which might be considered suitable to the climate, but which had hitherto been neglected by the Agriculturalists of the Colony'.[37] Strictly speaking, it was not just a viticultural school though it may have been the case that Busby concentrated largely on wine growing. He planted a vineyard with the help of the boys but did not get to make wine from it. A new management committee at the Male Orphan School decided his employment benefitted him too favourably and dismissed him. Private letters of Busby's suggest he had managed to make several enemies and he went on to spend several years protesting against his dismissal and seeking a new public position.[38]

Before leaving New South Wales for England, to challenge his dismissal, Busby wrote the *Manual of Plain Directions* (1830), with a great deal of help from Thomas Shepherd of Darling Nursery.[39] This book used less ornate language than the *Treatise*, advised on sources of vine stock and appealed to small scale settlers to plant vineyards as a means of transforming the culture of the colony from one of drunkenness to a colonial promised land. It set out estimated costs of establishing a vineyard to show how affordable and profitable it could be.[40]

Shepherd, a much-liked member of the early colonial community, migrated from Britain first to New Zealand in 1825 to supervise production for the New Zealand Company (established during the 'joint-stock mania' which also created the Australian Agricultural Company). On arriving there, he realised the company could not be profitable and recommended its dissolution. He and his family sailed to Sydney where Governor Ralph Darling granted him land at Black Wattle Swamp to establish the Darling Nursery.[41] As one of the colony's key plant nurseryman, Shepherd wrote to newspapers with advice for wine and table grape growers. He suggested how to select the best sites as well as details of treatment of disease, aspect and trellising. He referred to the practice of sheltering vines from harsh ocean winds on the island of Graciosa in the Canaries, which suggests he may have visited there.[42] In the early 1830s Shepherd completed the landscape design for Mount Adelaide estate at Mrs Darling's Point: an orchard, terraced vineyard, pleasure grounds, fish pond and wharf. Shepherd's sudden death in 1835, reportedly as a result of working too hard on a series of public lectures on plant cultivation, caused much sadness.[43] His name continued to be remembered for many years in the Hunter Valley name for the grape variety Semillon: Shepherd's Riesling.

We know from Busby's third book *Journal of a Tour* (1833) that the northern autumn of 1831 found the indefatigable wine advocate in Spain and France, collecting vine stock. He sought to gather as many varieties as possible of high and low quality wine and raisin grapes, to advance experimentation. 'It might at first appear superfluous to bestow attention on a collection which must include many of a very inferior description', he wrote to the British colonial office, seeking assistance with the cost of transporting the vines to Sydney. But, 'it is perhaps the most remarkable fact connected with the culture of the vine that even a slight change of climate or soil produces a most material change in the qualities of its produce'.[44] The best varieties in Europe might prove valueless in New South Wales, and vice versa. Busby felt too that since knowledge and vine stock had until then been sourced from colder climates than New South Wales, his tour of European wine regions should encompass climates similar to that of the colony.[45]

Busby's carefully assembled collection of vine stock constituted three portions: his private selection; vines purchased from Montpellier, the centre of viticultural training in France; and vines purchased from the Luxembourg Gardens in Paris. A whole collection of Spanish vines perished on the voyage to New South Wales, but an 1834 report on the vines by Shepherd, William Macarthur, John Jamison and others listed some hundreds of vines, only young and most not yet bearing, but offering great promise as a collection from which successive years' growth would provide further cuttings for distribution to colonists.[46] Vines from Busby's collection planted at the Botanic Gardens in Sydney were used to distribute cuttings, as were vines from the collection planted at Busby's sister Catherine Kelman's property Kirkton in the Hunter.

In the late 1830s Busby, by now in New Zealand, received a request to send vines to South Australia, where vine growing had not yet commenced. Busby organised for cuttings to be sent from his collection at Sydney Botanic Gardens. Busby's vine collection was not the first

MITCHELL LIBRARY STATE LIBRARY OF NSW, DG ON 4/7064 HOME AND AWAY – 7064

A tradition of children as vineyard labour dates back to the first agricultural school in New South Wales in the late 1820s where boys were taught viticulture and other farming methods. Two lads picking grapes into kerosene tins, c1930, photograph by Sam Hood.

MITCHELL LIBRARY, STATE LIBRARY OF NSW, PXD 390/70 [B]

The terraced slopes of Mount Adelaide vineyard, Sydney, landscaped by nurseryman Thomas Shepherd in the 1830s. Sketch by Georgiana Lowe.

substantial importation into the colony however (see Appendix 1). Before he left to return to England, Busby had brokered the distribution of as many as 20 000 cuttings from existing vines in the colony to fifty new growers, including George Wyndham. Much is made of the 1832 Busby collection which greatly increased the number of varieties available in the colony but the earlier distribution of vines had been very extensive and formative. William Macarthur would later comment that while Busby had performed a great service in creating the collection of vines, only a sixth of the many varieties were suitable as wine grape stock to prospective growers.[47]

Macarthur's experience of the vicissitudes of importing vine stock included the first Riesling vines in Australia. He paid 24 florins for 1000 rooted vines from the Rhine wine growing region and met the cost of their transportation to the colony via England with his second group of assisted migrant vinedressers in the 1830s. Of the 1000 plants, two survived the voyage but from these Macarthur created a supply of Riesling vine cuttings which were distributed widely in the Australian colonies.[48] Among other orders he made from Europe, was an 1840 consignment from a French wine grower later used by successful Albury wine grower and merchant James Fallon: Deinhart, Jordan & Co of Coblentz.[49] In 1850, more vines were imported to the Sydney Botanic Gardens by director Charles Moore. Moore did not demonstrate especial interest in wine growing and this appears to have been the last public importation of vines from abroad until, from the 1890s, the Department of Agriculture began to supply growers from its viticultural farms.

John Jamison

If Busby's first book had missed its mark due to the demographics of the colony, and his second so clearly targeted the more populous lower orders of New South Wales, then just how small was the number of grand estates for vineyards? In his inquiry Bigge calculated the population of the colony in 1820 to be approximately 24 000 people (not counting Aborigines). How many of these possessed properties which represented the ideal 'state of cultivation, and exhibit[ed] the greatest improvement'? According to Bigge, there were at that stage *six*. These were John Oxley, William Cox, Hannibal Macarthur, John Macarthur, 'Thoresby' (possibly Charles Throsby) and 'Howe' (likely William Howe).[50] Cox and John Macarthur were wine growers but another colonial who would prove to be a model improver, John Jamison, had grape vines just reaching maturity when Bigge inspected the colony.

Jamison inherited Regentville, at Penrith in western Sydney, after the death of his father Thomas, who had been a First Fleet surgeon. Construction began on the Regentville mansion in 1823 and two years later vines and other plants including olives were obtained from Sydney Botanic Gardens, presumably from stocks imported from the Cape in 1824. Jamison had an advantage in the employment of German vine expert F. Meyer, who had links with British garden specialist John Loudon. Impressively, Regentville had the first terraced vineyard in the colony. Some vines were trellised espalier-style, others on a single pole.[51]

In 1834, Jamison's new cellar contained 1400 gallons of wine in casks and another 400 gallons were anticipated from that year's vintage. Heat caused problems with the harvest, accelerating the fermentation, though the wine did not turn to vinegar as the coolness of the underground cellars was calculated to control fermentation and provide better storage for already manufactured wine. Busby described Jamison's wine, from Sweetwater mixed with Madeira grapes, as 'very tolerable'.[52] Jamison later sought approbation, as Blaxland had done, from the Society of Arts.

Governor Richard Bourke and a visiting judge – both of whom had travelled through Europe – declared Regentville's vineyards 'fully equalled if they did not surpass, anything of the kind they had ever witnessed in any of the wine countries they had visited'.[53] Visiting Austrian diplomat, Charles von Hügel remarked, 'the whole thing certainly looks like a vineyard, as these are painted in pictures' but he did not think the produce from Regentville could truthfully be called wine. Busby thought Jamison's vineyard looked impressive but the man himself insufferable.[54]

HISTORIC HOUSES TRUST, SYDNEY, RECORD NUMBER 30953

Regentville's terraced vineyard.
Sketch by Conrad Martens, 1838.

George Suttor

Knowledge of botany may seem to have been an advantage in unravelling the mysteries of wine growing but botanist George Suttor struggled just as much as other early colonists to produce wine grapes successfully in New South Wales. After a false start in his first years in the colony, Suttor achieved better results from the 1830s onward. In his quest for intelligent industry, he took an extended tour of European wine regions with his wife and daughter in 1840 which doubled as a pursuit of scenic wonder. His tour was chronicled as diary entries, interspersed with extracts of translations from contemporary works on wine, in *The Culture of the Grape-Vine, and the Orange, in Australia and New Zealand: Comprising historical notices; instructions for planting and cultivation; accounts, from personal observation, of the vineyards of France and the Rhine; and extracts concerning all the most celebrated wines from the work of M. Jullien* (1843). 'In our travels in France to see the vines, the vintage and the picturesque', Suttor observed that, 'the land is not so highly cultivated as in England, except where the vines are planted'.[55] He noticed soil types, vine height, trellising methods, the colour and size of grapes as well as the broader romantic beauty of French locales. 'I have seen the vine-covered hills and plains of Bourgogne', he wrote, 'and have thought that I would rejoice to see the hills and plains of Parramatta and Bathurst, to the same extent, covered with vines'. (Suttor's properties were at Parramatta and Bathurst.) In France, 'they venerate the vine' and the great age of the moss-covered vines in many of the stone-walled vineyards of the Bourgogne evoked a sense of historic gravitas.[56]

When Suttor visited vineyards on the left bank of the Rhine at Bonn he admired the neatness and cleanliness of the tubs used to carry harvested grapes. He saw that women were involved in picking the grapes, men in carrying and crushing them and the conviviality of the scene impressed

"
'I would rejoice to see the hills and plains of Parramatta and Bathurst ... covered with vines.'

him. In 1842, Suttor returned to France to visit Chateau Margaux to observe and record details of the vintage.[57]

Wine squires

We have considered some of the significant individuals engaged in early wine growing but there were even more ambitious colonists with vineyards, men I call wine squires, from a historian's remark that by the mid-nineteenth century, wine growing had become a 'distinguishing mark of the true-blue squire'.[58] When in 1843 the first partially elected Legislative Council took power (before this the Council members had all been appointed), eleven of its members made their principal income from other means but could also be counted as experimental wine growers or had connections to early wine production.[59] Among the wine squires were several times New South Wales chief secretary (premier) Charles Cowper, colonial powerbroker William Charles Wentworth, influential lawyer Richard Windeyer, emigration advocate Reverend John Dunmore Lang, surveyor Thomas Mitchell and, as we have already seen, second generation Macarthurs: James, William and Hannibal. Ten years on, New South Wales Vineyard Association president William Macarthur chaired a meeting and wine tasting which included the colonial secretary, the chief justice, the Legislative speaker, Wentworth and several other members of government.[60] At this point, wine growing reached its apogee as a pursuit of power elites. From the 1860s there were a greater number of wine growers in New South Wales but they were not from the ruling class.

Labour in colonial vineyards

The festive culture of the grape harvest witnessed by Suttor in Germany and France emphasised the far more limited degree to which such scenes yet occurred in New South Wales in the 1840s. Indeed, Suttor – when analysing the slow pace of wine industry development in New South Wales – complained that the Cape industry could use much cheaper slave labour when *all* labour in New South Wales was in short supply not just skilled vineyard workers.[61] In the long history of world wine growing, the Australian industry was the very first to be established without slave labour (though convict labour was used).[62] Who worked in colonial vineyards? In the 1830s Jamison had Meyer working for him at Regentville, while Ellen Ogilvie mentioned her family's Merton vineyard in the Upper Hunter was under the care of a German called Luther.[63] William Macarthur employed convicts Nicholas Papendross and Androni Tu Malonis at Elizabeth Farm.[64] Wurttemberger Georg Schmid had planted out Andrew Lang's eight acre Hunter Valley vineyard using the arbour-style *lusthaus* or trellised shade areas of his home region.[65]

But a few vinedressers here and there did not constitute sufficient labour to build an industry. In 1835, colonial clergyman and great improver, John Dunmore Lang, visited German provinces to recruit missionaries to work with Aborigines. Before his departure, his brother Andrew asked him to also hire vinedressers either from Germany or France. A dramatic series of events ensued. Lang found a group of willing workers but the Dutch Government refused them passage. Lang then managed to persuade 250 Germans stranded in France to follow him to New South Wales. He hired a French ship to transport them. Then, when the shipload of Germans arrived at Rio, the Brazilian Government reportedly poached them![66]

Serle, in his comments to Marsden on intelligent industry, had suggested Governor King could allocate convicts to wine growing.[67] While this did not exactly occur, a record of convicts with vineyard experience may have been kept in the 1830s. Convict superintendent Fred Hely made a list of the vineyards in the Hunter Valley, which provides a picture of the extent of early plantings but also implies a register of skilled workers.[68] At this time too, colonists were increasingly dissatisfied with the shortcomings and lack of respectability of convict labour. In response, Governor Richard Bourke announced a program of assisted migration where the government would pay part of the cost of settlers sponsoring British labourers to migrate.[69]

This had a two-way benefit: assisted migration also reduced the number of rural workers suffering social dislocation from enclosure of common lands in their British home counties. But there were no vinedressers to be had from Britain.

The Macarthurs quickly took up the offer of workers for their larger, non-wine enterprises. John Dunmore Lang and Edward Macarthur (second son of Elizabeth and John, and family company agent in London since the death of older brother John) also asked for vinedressers from Europe to be recruited under the assisted migration scheme. Bourke gave his assent but the plan encountered opposition from the colonial office in London. Edward countered by arguing that private investment in wine growing in New South Wales would be wasted if the investors could not secure skilled vineyard labour which was, through no fault of the colonists, not available in Britain. The vintage at William's 20 acre vineyard was less than a year away and by refusing to allow German migration, said Edward, the colonial office sentenced the Macarthur enterprise to failure. Plus, it limited prospects for the colony on which the potential to encourage future *British* migration depended. Government assistance in the 'introduction of a few families possessing the requisite experience and skill' would open new fields 'for the *employment of the surplus labor of the Parent Country*' (Macarthur's emphasis).[70]

Edward's appeal struck a chord. The colonial secretary very reluctantly agreed to his petition and Lang's, to allow the sponsored migration of workers from outside Britain. In making this exception, the secretary Lord Glenelg made it plain that favouring non-British migrants in any guise contravened the intention of migration as a means of easing social pressure. He could see the need for flexibility in policy but would not make any more concessions for 'foreign' immigrants.[71] Edward proceeded to search for a small group of families prepared to leave Germany for New South Wales when, amid the tumult of their own social dislocation, most were migrating to the United States not to British colonies.[72] Six married men were found: Johann Stein, Johann Wenz, Georg Gerhardt, Johann Justus, Casper Flick and Frederich Seckold. All but Stein had children and the twenty-eight German migrants sailed to Australia on the

Kinnear in 1837.[73] The men agreed to five-year work contracts with an undertaking to maintain standards of sobriety and civility. Employment at Camden ensured the workers free passage, an attractive enticement given the risks for Europeans migrating unsupported to the United States. The Macarthur vinedressers received £15 per year along with a cottage with a garden, a cow, access to grazing land and permission to raise pigs and poultry for their own use. The workers were prohibited from selling the livestock but each week received provisions of meat and flour. They could earn extra wages if they wanted, schooling for the children was free and there was no work on public holidays. After five years employment the workers could become tenants of Camden estate.[74] These conditions can be attributed to James Macarthur's critique of dramatic changes in English rural society resulting from the Enclosure Acts, which he observed between 1828 and 1830.[75]

"

The wave of German migration significantly benefited vineyard and wine making skill in the colony.

William Macarthur's first group of vinedressers worked well but he had trouble with later migrants and expressed concern that they would not adapt German vineyard practices to take account of the comparatively warm Camden climate.[76] Hunter identity William Keene would later argue that southern French viticulture better suited New South Wales than German methods.[77] But on balance the wave of German migration significantly benefited vineyard and wine making skill in the colony.

Vineyard owners soon received a more sympathetic response from the colonial office to requests for sponsorship of skilled vineyard workers from Germany. In 1847, more than a dozen wine squires received permission to import German workers: among them Henry Carmichael, Andrew Lang, Alfred Glennie, James Bettington, Charles Cowper, William Lawson and Henry Lindeman. Between them they applied for forty German workers: twenty-six vinedressers, five coopers and nine wine makers.[78] Between 1831 and 1860 more than 120 000 government-assisted British migrants arrived across all of the Australian colonies compared with 8309 Germans.[79]

Migrants from other wine countries were not encouraged to New South Wales through assisted relocation. One of only a handful of Frenchmen with wine growing experience in New South Wales throughout the century, Philobert Terrier, arrived to run the Scottish Australian Investment Company's property at Kaludah near Lochinvar in the Hunter Valley and later produced wines at his own nearby property, St Helena.[80] For a short while, Thomas Mitchell employed a French vinedresser.

Other colonial wine tours

Mitchell's gardener had purchased 7000 vine cuttings from William Macarthur in the mid-1840s and from the Hunter Valley's James King in the late 1840s, then hired a vinedresser through Macarthur to tend them for a year or two.[81] In 1847, Mitchell returned to England and took the opportunity to tour through the Spanish region of Andalusia, making practical observations. Two years later, on his return to the colony, he circulated his slim, illustrated and well-received report on vines and other Mediterranean fruits which the Botanical and Horticultural Society of Sydney published as *Notes on the Cultivation of the Vine &c., in Spain* (1849). Returning to Europe again in 1854, Mitchell and James Macleay, another prominent colonist, visited Cape wine farms and noted methods of vine cultivation and wine making. Mitchell recorded in his journal that Cape vines were not staked or trellised (as opposed to German and Greek practices) and leaves were removed at a certain time to promote ripening. After harvest, the berries were crushed by foot, no spirit was added to the must (as it was for port) and sulphur prevented a second fermentation of the wine.[82]

Forty years after his first journey through France as a young man, William Macarthur returned to Europe in 1855 as Commissioner of the New South Wales exhibit at the Paris Exhibition. During his stay, he toured vineyards in France, Switzerland and northern Italy: 'Clos Vaugeot,

Romanee Conti, Romanee St Vivant, Richebourg, La Tache St George, etc, producing the finest wines'.[83] In the late nineteenth century, further study tours were undertaken by James Fallon from Albury and Thomas Hardy from South Australia. Both contributed significantly to forging pathways for colonial wine exports to Britain. Fallon campaigned in England for more favourable terms for colonial wine and hired Frenchman Leonce Frere – who had experience in Bordeaux and Champagne – to work at his Murray Valley Vineyard in Albury.[84] Fallon's tours of European wine enterprises included the Rhine region, Chateaux Lafite and Margaux and various sites in Burgundy, and he attended the 1873 Vienna International Exhibition.[85] Hardy provided detailed intelligence on the Californian and Cape wine industries.[86]

By the end of the nineteenth century, colonial wine tours had become an established practice. George Graham, part-owner of Netherby Vineyard at Rutherglen, near the New South Wales–Victoria border, travelled through England and France and 'as usual with Australian vignerons when travelling, kept his eyes open for anything of interest to the industry'. He spent his time in France 'in the Southern and Medoc districts, chiefly at Montpellier', where several Australians had by this stage studied viticulture. Graham observed the vast extent of vineyards, the methods of vine cultivation and the successful recovery from the grape phylloxera plague. He had arrived after vintage and the 'new wine – not two months old – was being delivered for the purchasers, the roads being lined with long drays, holding five to seven barriques of 120gal each'. Graham noted that 'railway stations were blocked with wine as ours are with wheat'.[87]

Ultimately, experience from European wine countries comprised the intelligent industry required to advance early New South Wales wine growing. But British colonists were not alone in this. When a Southeast Asian–born Chinese entrepreneur with extensive capital resources established his wine grape business in China in 1892, he struggled to produce successful wine until joined by an *Austrian* diplomat who had genuine wine making experience.[88]

Remember the informal policy of substitution of wine for rum attempted by Governor King in the early 1800s? We next return to this and follow the thread of the ways in which New South Wales wine squires tried to encourage a taste for colonial wine among New South Wales working classes, as an antidote to drunkenness.

6

Colonial wine to create sobriety

The transfer of wine growing knowledge to New South Wales brought with it a new faith in ideas about wine culture. Of landscapes shaped by Europeans, vineyards had an ancient reputation as among the most civilised, not just for making poor soils profitable but for the improving effect of living among them. By the eighteenth century, of all Europeans, those living in the Mediterranean wine regions had a reputation as the most sober and industrious due to their proximity to vineyards and cheap wine. Of all alcohols, wine had a reputation for being not only the most civilised but for having the power to transform drunks from wilful bingers to contented workers. These ideas were very influential in early Australia and taken together formed a belief in the trans-formative powers of wine, the idea that uncivilised drinking could be cured by encouraging colonists to drink colonial wine instead of spirits or beer.

Early New South Wales is notorious for its high level of inebriety. Popular tales of the first years of the colony are rife with dramatic scenes of drunkenness and lawlessness. Yet the level of drinking did not actually exceed Britain's and the quantity of spirits being traded by the New South Wales Corps – known as the Rum Corps – has been exaggerated.[1] Why then did stories of drunken rioting among farmers on the Hawkesbury River, for example, gain such traction? Because the voices of the historical record were governors, judges, clergymen and settlers envisaging a civil society and morally stable environment ripe for creating prosperity.[2]

Despite the determination of administrators to influence the way of life in the very earliest years of New South Wales, lived culture – like the built environment – grew haphazardly and irreverently. As historian Grace Karskens portrays:

> Sydney quickly developed in precisely the opposite way to the original vision for the colony: instead of closely supervised, harsh, subsistence agricultural settlement, it was a distinctly urban place with considerable freedoms ... Much of the everyday urban landscape – buildings, paths, movements – was shaped by the tastes and habits of the convicts ... Governors wrote with some admiration of the domestic achievements of the convict townsfolk. But they were also spaces where people made their own lives, places where stolen goods could be stashed or sold, robberies planned and liquor illegally distilled, places for riot, revelry and conspiracy out of the eye of authority. As for labour, convicts did not even work to regular hours.[4]

Ordinary men and women of the colony preferred a self-regulatory culture in work and leisure, which did not sit well with official plans.

Hard drinking certainly caused misery among people of all classes however, as the unusual economy of the early colony meant that convicts, soldiers and free settlers could all buy imported spirits and wine, and the first peak in alcohol consumption occurred in the 1830s.[3] This coincided with James Busby's second book, described in Chapter 5, which recommended wine growing as a sober pursuit for the lower orders. Then, following the deprivations of the 1840s Depression, the gold rushes of the 1850s brought a new wave of drunkenness coupled with unreliability among colonial workers who deserted their bosses to seek their fortunes on the gold fields. Wine was seen as a solution to colonial intoxication owing to the national reputations of the people of the temperate southern European wine regions as more sober than those of northern European regions. Colonists in New South Wales tried to use policies of substitution to encourage the working classes to drink colonial wine; to promote a more general civility as well as commerce.

Wine in the colony

Botanist George Caley believed Governor King's 1802 imposition of a 5 per cent duty on the import of spirits had only driven colonists to measures such as making peach cider no better than 'hogwash' but eagerly sought after. 'I have witnessed it to produce a great scene of intoxication as I ever did from foreign spirits', Caley complained to Banks. 'What is to be done now? Will it be good policy to eradicate all the peach-trees?' Wine imported from the Cape, he said, at first quenched the high demand for liquor and 'a general intoxication prevailed for some time; but, from the people having spent their money, and being pretty well glutted, a deal of wine remains yet unsold'.[5] With no aristocracy and a ruling class commensurate with the British middle and mercantile class, there were less highly refined ideas of wine. A grand total of twenty people had official wine and spirits licences in the colony in 1810 (which does not factor in illegal trade) but most of their business appears to have been in spirits.[6] If we consider that price is often a measure of refinement, it is important to note that spirits fetched higher prices than wine.[7] In 1811, merchant Garnham Blaxcell sold Prime Tenerife for six shillings a quart bottle; half the price of gin.[8] Fine old port wine, when available, cost nine shillings a bottle, by the dozen. A new shipment of gin reduced the price, indicating the role of supply and demand.[9]

Merchant Hannibal Macarthur, nephew of Elizabeth and John Macarthur, had taken charge of the family's shipping business in this era. He assisted his aunt and kept his exiled uncle informed of business dealings, one of which demonstrated the fickle colonial market for wine and the risks of wine trade. In 1812, this younger Macarthur bought wine at Rio and Madeira, some of which came from France, but despite his best efforts, he had 'not had an application for a gallon of the French once yet!' A year later, the French and Madeira wine remained unsold. No one in the colony would buy it at its present age and the only other alternative would be to keep it in a rented warehouse in Parramatta until it improved or ship it to London so the voyage would improve it.[10] By 1814, the wine continued to be unsaleable and had proved by far 'the most unfortunate part of our adventure'.[11] The next year Hannibal proposed sending the wine to British India since it was not completely execrable and may have found a colonial buyer at a price which did not represent a loss of investment.[12]

VICTOR PAYNE COLLECTION

> " *Ideas of wine and luxury continued to arrive with free settlers and a wave of prosperity.*

Over subsequent decades, ideas of wine and luxury continued to arrive with free settlers and a wave of prosperity. In 1825 a report on wines stated that 'those of Champagne, though not the strongest, may be considered the best'.[13] In 1840 (before the Depression) an auctioneer advertised to 'the commercial, monied, speculative, operative and trading classes of the community, as well as to heads of families and captains of ships' that he had an attractive waterfront property for sale and that New Year would be celebrated with a 'capital Champagne Lunch' put on by the present owner of the house.[14] But getting drunk in New South Wales required little symbolic meaning of the alcohol. At an 'elegant home' in Sydney, a French visitor witnessed Aboriginal men being plied with wine and encouraged to fight each other. The men 'struck each other with repeated blows; two of them were stretched on the ground, dangerously wounded, and a third received a mortal blow … This scene took place in a civilised city; the spectators were respectable merchants, and elegant young ladies.'[15]

An informal movement to make wine the colonial alcohol of choice began to take shape.

Moderate temperance

As alcohol consumption rose across the English speaking world in the eighteenth century, so did resistance to it. In the first decades of the nineteenth century, organised temperance movements lobbying for law reform surged in Britain and the United States, ranking second only to the abolition of slavery in antebellum moral reformism in the United States. In New South Wales in the 1840s elite colonists supported temperance but, in contrast to the United States, the 'difference between the abstainers and the moderates centred on attitudes to non-spirituous liquors' (wine and beer) and they rejected the 'exclusion of wine-bibbing respectability'. New South Wales abstainers suspected the moderates of hypocrisy because they would 'deprive labourers of their grog, but not the rich man of his wine', while moderates recommended 'cheap wine' and 'wholesome sports and amusements' to protect labourers from the perceived evils of alcohol and debauchery.[16] Governor George Gipps actively supported the moderate temperance movement. 'Drunkenness, the fruitful parent of every species of crime, is', he lamented, 'still the prevailing vice of the Colony' *but* he refused to pledge abstinence.[17] The temperance movement's paper, *The Teetotaller*, with its sub-banner from Romans 14:12: 'It is good neither to eat flesh, nor to drink wine, nor any thing whereby thy brother stumbleth, or is offended, or is made weak' did not last long in the mid-century colony.[18]

Not surprisingly given the extent of wine growing advocacy in the Legislative Council in the early 1840s (see Chapter 5), Gipps presided over a flurry of legislation to encourage the production of light alcohol colonial wines as an alternative to stronger liquors. Part of this suite of laws formalised the collection of data to quantify vineyard acreage and wine production (see Table 1: First returns of vineyards in New South Wales 1844–50 in Appendix 2). One of the three new licensing regulations raised the fee for selling spirits, rather than wine or beer, to £30 a year. A second raised the quantity of colonial wine that could be sold without a licence from 2 to 10 gallons.[19] (As one Sydney newspaper reported, such legislation could not, however, control taste. Frankly, 'the appetite for strong liquor was as far beyond the power of legislation to control as was the appetite for sex'.[20]) The section of law preventing colonial magistrates who produced wine from granting liquor licences had to be abolished since both legal authority and wine growing were largely the preserve of the same elites.[21]

In a revealing amendment to earlier legislation, controls were tightened on the practice of adding spirits to colonial wine to make it more palatable. The same practice in Britain did not affect government revenue because the alcohol in wine was taxed at a higher rate than the alcohol in rum. In New South Wales, where Cape wine for instance could be imported at a very low duty compared with spirits, revenue collection would be affected if wine and spirits were mixed, so this was discouraged.[22]

A third law urged military officers to drink imported wine instead of spirits by allowing them to purchase it duty free, but the British colonial office pointed out very tartly to Gipps that *nowhere else in the empire* were military officers granted this indulgence.[23] The New South Wales legislative council also sought permission to import light alcohol French wine directly from France or French colonies in French ships, but such trade had been outlawed across all British possessions and the Committee of the Privy Council for Trade in London refused to allow an exception.[24]

Then came the gold rushes, which created enormous social and economic change. In 1857, Lower Hunter Valley wine grower and pottery manufacturer James King published a pamphlet to help him sell his wines in Britain. King argued in the pamphlet, entitled *Australia may be an Extensive Wine Growing Country*, that once the gold rushes had exhausted the resources of a new wave of immigrants and the gold reserves were all run out then the migrants could work most usefully in the emerging wine industry. King claimed that if British colonies had been producing good wines for longer, the British working classes would have been a wine drinking people instead of addicted to spirits and beer.[25]

But where did it come from, this notion that wine countries had a more sober peasantry? Historian Lynn Martin has explained that it had little basis in fact but held great sway as a folkloric national reputation.[26]

One of the most articulate expressions of this national reputation appeared in Adam Smith's highly influential *Wealth of Nations* (1776), as follows:

> If we consult experience, the cheapness of wine seems to be a cause, not of drunkenness, but of sobriety. The inhabitants of the wine countries are in general the soberest people in Europe: witness the Spaniards, the Italians, and the inhabitants of the southern provinces of France. People are seldom guilty of excess in what is their [cheap] daily fare.

Not only did wine countries have less habitual drunkenness but if drunken types moved into wine countries, where light alcohol common wines were cheap, they were transformed into more sober folk. Smith wrote:

> When a French regiment comes from some of the northern provinces of France where wine is somewhat dear, to be quartered in the southern, where it is very cheap, the soldiers, I have frequently heard it observed, are at first debauched by the cheapness and novelty of good wine; but after a few months residence, the greater part of them become as sober as the rest of the inhabitants.[27]

Smith claimed drunkenness resulted not from being able to afford liquor, otherwise the rich would be the most inebrious; it was that light alcohol should be what working people could more readily purchase so they were not so inclined to be intoxicated. For commoners, the cheaper the wine, the more sober the people.

Smith's point actually served as evidence for what he considered to be the absurdity of high tariffs on lower alcohol French wines compared with higher alcohol Portuguese wines (see details of the Methuen Treaty in Chapter 1). But his statement, although not the origin of the idea of wine and sobriety, carried a good deal of weight and would be used in a plan to turn New South Wales into a wine drinking country.[28]

New South Wales legislators responded to the wave of gold rush drunkenness of the 1850s with a parliamentary select committee, but no solutions were forthcoming. By 1859 the situation became acute.[29] In 1862, Arthur Todd Holroyd, a member of the New South Wales legislative assembly (as well as a foundation member of the now-defunct New South Wales Vineyard Association), agreed to pressure from wine growers to propose a new Sale of Colonial Wines, Cider and Perry Regulation Bill to try to change the tastes of the working classes in favour of colonial wine.[30] Holroyd proposed a £1 licence fee – when a public hotel licence cost £20 a year – so that a greater number of wine shops would be established. Publicans were the main legal source of alcohol in the colony but Holroyd observed that of 500 Sydney pubs 'not above ten or twelve sold colonial wines'.[31]

Holroyd's Bill was based on British Prime Minister William Gladstone's *Wine Act* in Britain which introduced off-licenses, allowing grocers to sell wine by the bottle for customers to take home, instead of drinking in pubs. This British Act followed an earlier one which lowered the import duty on light wines from France (less than 40 per cent alcohol), which led to a new wave of French wine consumption.[32] Holroyd believed off-licence sales of even lighter wines (less than 20 per cent proof) could encourage consumption of colonial wine within New South Wales by making it easier and cheaper to buy in quantities small enough for working people to afford.

Holroyd's supporters included Hunter wine grower Archibald Windeyer, who 'hoped the time would come when wine would be drunk daily in the field of every working man, as was now the case on the continent of Europe'.[33] Among the opponents, John Robertson – although a wine grower and member for what would be the emerging wine growing area of Mudgee – believed the Bill would not necessarily encourage a wholesome habit of alcohol consumption because of the unchecked addition of sugar to wine which increased its potency. He said Holroyd's Bill could turn every farm into a sly grog shop. 'It was no use to gloss the matter over', he said, 'they would see wine shanties starting up all over the country, and particularly in those places that were beyond the reach of the police and the protection they afforded'. Another member said he had no trouble buying colonial wine but denied that it could create sobriety in the colony; he was 'aware that there had been much intoxication at sheep-shearing in some parts of the interior where this colonial wine was solely used'. On one occasion another member had seen 'a number of men in groups fighting with each other, many of them going about all but naked, in a state of imbecility from drinking the trash that was sold under the name of colonial wine'. John Dunmore Lang responded that he had seen evidence of greater sobriety in wine countries of Europe with his own eyes and had every faith in a policy of substitution. He believed however that colonial wines had such a varying degree of alcohol that simply encouraging sales of wine would not necessarily be a measure of temperance.[34]

Holroyd responded with great passion that his Bill had not received a fair hearing and that 'the evils spoken of as being likely to arise under [it] … were mythical only, and not worthy of a moment's thought'.[35] His opponents tried to have the Bill thrown out. Another supporter again invoked national reputations: he 'had been for a considerable time in Spain, but he had never seen a Spaniard drunk … He regretted, however, that he had seen his own countrymen intoxicated whilst he was there'.[36] What if the problem lay not in the inferiority of colonial wine but in its price? 'The class of persons who went to public-houses did not care for colonial wines', said one member, but, if the permission proposed in this Bill were granted, we should find the reapers and other classes of labourers drinking colonial wine; and having acquired a taste for it, they would never want anything else'. Another speaker reminded the Legislative Assembly that imported wines such as port, Madeira and sherry were heavily fortified and colonial wines could be lighter by not requiring the addition of grape spirit as a preservative. Holroyd responded again by directly quoting Smith's observation that 'the inhabitants of wine-producing countries were in general the most sober people in Europe'.[37]

The outcome? A much watered-down law so that publicans were not threatened: a £10 wine shop licence fee.[38]

Ten years later Lindeman was still deploring the dilution of the law which he claimed occurred because 'King Rum was found all too powerful'.[39] The wines themselves were not attracting consumers either. On a journey from his Hunter winery to his Corowa vineyard, Lindeman chatted with his coach driver about colonial wine. 'Oh, dear no! I never think of drinking colonial wine', his coach driver told him. 'I once took a drop too much, and felt so ill after that I hate the sight of it ever since.'[40]

Henry Lindeman and the medical argument

Dr Lindeman's role in the promotion of colonial wines as 'another civilising industry' constituted a key part of the arguments about wine and sobriety.[41] His daughter remembered many years later that his philosophy had been: 'the national drink of a climate like Australia should be light wines, Hocks & Clarets'.[42] Lindeman's letter to the *New South Wales Medical Gazette* in the early 1870s: 'Pure Wine as a Therapeutic Agent, and Why it Should Become our National Beverage' stated that:

> More than thirty years ago, when I first arrived in the colony, I was induced to plant the vine, and to impress upon my fellow-colonists the desirability of doing so likewise, seeing the great necessity there existed for supplying a pure exhilarating wine to take the place of ardent spirits and of adulterated [fortified] wines and beers then and now the popular beverage of our community, the use of which frequently induces the diseases I have found mostly to be guarded against in our climate – namely, those arising from derangement of the liver; to suffer from which too often robs life of enjoyment by enveloping it in a perpetual fog of mental depression, and for which depression relief is generally sought in the deleterious stimulants above-named, which invariably add fuel to the fire, thereby crowding our community with the inebriate and in the insane.[43]

Such mores reflected 'a greater refinement in manners and behaviour in which drinking to excess was no longer acceptable in fashionable society'[44] and other doctors also embraced the health benefits and civility of wine. Champagne, with its reputation as the most refined imported wine, came to be in demand in Victoria and presumably the other Australian colonies during the prosperous 1870s.[45]

But the £1 license law was often flouted and popular taste remained unchanged.

Arakoon vineyard near South-west Rocks, north of Port Macquarie, in 1910. As Henry Lindeman hoped, New South Wales began to 'smile with the vine'.

MITCHELL LIBRARY, STATE LIBRARY OF NSW. CALL NO: AT WORK AND PLAY 044801

Vineyards as a civilising influence

Faith in the transformative powers of wine extended to the civilising effect of vineyards which, in colonial New South Wales, came to be combined with the classical conception that vines were a highly profitable and refined form of cultivation. During his voyage to the colony in the 1830s, surveyor and educational theorist Henry Carmichael had schooled 'working men ... almost through Smith's *Wealth of Nations*'.[46] From Smith he learned vineyards were a high form of the agricultural state in human development, a theory he applied as a wine grower in the Hunter Valley. At first he encouraged widespread vine cultivation over wool growing since in Europe, shepherding represented an earlier stage of human development. This was before Carmichael and others realised that the theory of these stages – from hunting and gathering through pastoralism, settled farms and then commerce – had been subverted in New South Wales where all of the stages occurred simultaneously and pastoralism proved most profitable.

In his second book on wine growing, James Busby encouraged settlers of all classes to plant vines but particularly smallholders who over-indulged in strong liquors. He thought it:

> extremely likely, that if each farm-house possessed its vineyard, and produced a sufficiency of wine to supply the wants of all labourers employed on the farm, as well as the farmer's own family, a deadly blow would be given to the ruinous habit of the farmer himself indulging daily in the excessive use of spirits ... At how very few farm-houses in this Colony will you find even a solitary vine climbing the walls, or spreading over an arbour, to cover the farmer and his family with its shade, and to refresh them with its fruit, after the toils of the day! And yet, the man who could sit under the shade of his own vine, with his wife and his children about him, and the ripe clusters hanging within their reach, in such a climate as this, and not feel the highest enjoyment, is incapable of happiness, and does not know what the word means.[47]

Suttor too argued for the morally and physically transformative qualities of vines. He echoed Busby's use of biblical imagery in the epigraph of his

1840s book encouraging British migration to New South Wales for the purpose of cultivating wine grapes and oranges: 'They shall sit every man under his vine'.[48]

In the same decade as Suttor's book, ideas of decency, civility and the Arcadian vision of the cultivation of vineyards were captured in a letter from young Kate Hassall to her brother Reverend James Hassall. She told him that she and their sister had just returned from a neighbour's property with 'three good looking melons, a basket of grapes and a little colonial wine'.[49] The whole family turned out for vintage each year, and Kate's letter, and another from her sister Eliza to James two years late, communicated an exquisite Romanticism.[50] Surveyor Thomas Mitchell took pleasure too, during a long journey through the 'savage' colonial interior, in the memory of the idyll of the grape harvest at Parkhall estate. One of his sons had reported that the most recent vintage produced a 'good strong wine'. This sustained him on his travels and he wrote to another son that 'I shall live in the hope to see you [both at Parkhall] and put it to the trial'.[51]

Confidence that extensive vineyards would transform the colony visually, morally and demographically was crystallised by Lindeman:

> How soon our refreshing, exhilarating and restorative wine will take the place of poisonous spirits. We shall then rapidly become a sober instead of a drunken community ... and when the law will allow wine to become our national beverage, thousands of acres now encumbered with the 'dreary eucalyptus', will smile with the vine, and another civilising industry will spring up in our midst to employ thousands of families in the light and pleasing labour it requires, and to attract a desirable class of immigrant to our shore.[52]

The idea that the *quantity* and *quality* of settlers could be influenced by wine and wine growing was not Lindeman's alone.[53] It lay at the heart of a powerful ideology which its historian, James Belich, has called settlerism. To see this, we now take a wider view of the geo-historical landscape through which we have been tracing threads of wine in early New South Wales, to encompass the entire Anglosphere.

7

A new generation of wine growers

Hopes for a wine industry in New South Wales took on a vigorous and compelling tone from the mid-nineteenth century, which seemed destined at the time to shape the future of the colony. Such thinking did not happen in a vacuum; excited conversations about grape growing could be heard in other Australian colonies, and in the United States, during migration from the Old World to the English-speaking New World. This migration to new homelands represented a Settler Revolution linking Britain, North America and Australasia in a mass transfer of people, plants, animals and ideas which went on to entrench the economic and cultural dominance of the Anglophone world.[1] Ever wondered why so many Australians have a combined heritage of English, Irish and German ancestors? These were the main ethnicities of the Settler Revolution. Before and after migration these settlers had access to a proliferation of prospectuses, books, pamphlets and newspaper articles encouraging them to undertake a variety of pursuits, with wine growing high on the list. This did, however, lead to a tremendous irony. While many hundreds of New South Wales settlers from Britain dutifully became grape growers, the tens of thousands of other migrants who arrived with them were also of the British working class and uninterested in drinking colonial wine.

While the vision for a New South Wales wine industry had its genesis in imperial design and its flowering in refined British colonial ambition for civility, prosperity and sobriety in the first half of the nineteenth century, it bore its first real fruit from the 1860s through the rise of small settler farming, fuelled by settlerist migration and land reforms. This is the point in New South Wales history when blocks of land available to new farmers were again small, as they had been in the early colonial period, in contrast with the vast and exclusive pastoral runs of the intervening years; small enough for men and families of modest means to become land owners. Reforms known as the *Selection Acts* changed land access to benefit some mixed farmers, instead of squatters who had locked up large tracts of land for grazing.

Alongside changes in land ownership, the Settler Revolution makes it possible to make sense of a perplexing trend in the second half of the colonial era. That is: a significant literature encouraging wine growing in New South Wales for new land holders, despite its limited profitability. Yes, there are books after Busby's, from the 1830s, which instruct wine growers; but within this instructive literature is a strong theme of prescription. Books, pamphlets and newspaper articles were not so much providing a service to existing wine growers, as specialist literature does today; they were encouraging new wine growers, talking up the prospects for wine growing when little consumer demand existed for colonial wine. This type of literature did not resemble any general publications we are familiar with now. So how to explain it?

A particular characteristic of the Settler Revolution was export rescue, where commodity production received greater incentives during economic downturns through literature encouraging migration and enterprises such as grape growing. Indeed, grapes proved to be a favoured crop in what James Belich, the historian who identified the Settler Revolution, called booster literature. This was particularly the case in the United States but also in Australia, including New South Wales.[2]

When did the Settler Revolution begin? Not until the nineteenth century. In the eighteenth century, leaving Britain or Europe to settle in the colonies did not have broad appeal and most people did not have the means to re-settle anyway. In fact, until the Settler Revolution, it was seen as punishment indeed for convicts to be exiled from their homeland to British North America and later British Australia.

How did the Settler Revolution begin? The end of several centuries of conflict between European powers that came with the end of the Napoleonic wars in 1815 ushered in the opportunity for imperialist nations such as Britain to expand their colonies. This, joined with Enlightenment philosophies about progress and prosperity, led to a rise in formal settlerism (where governments encouraged migration to colonies) and informal settlerism (individuals encouraging family and friends to join them in the colonies) along with a new desire by people of the middling and lower classes to transform these new countries into homelands. Imagine a slow movement of 'people, money, information, and ideas' picking up pace then accelerating before exploding into an enormous tide of migration from the Old World to the New. Settlerist migration was driven by a groundswell of economic cycles of boom, bust and export rescue. The message of settlerism resounded most volubly in booster literature which glossed the riches and the political freedom to be gained through migration, and provided blueprints for how to prosper through particular pursuits.[3] Boosterism explains why wine growing continued to be promoted as an ideal crop for settlers in New South Wales despite being only modestly profitable compared with wool and wheat. For example, American migrant H Mortimer Franklyn's *Glance at Australia in 1880: Or, food from the south: Showing the present condition and production of some of its leading industries, namely, wool, wine, grain, dressed meat, etc etc* (1881), described Australia as potentially 'The Vineyard of the World'. Franklyn went on to list wine immediately after wool in 'leading industries', when statistically it fell well behind grain and beef production.[4]

I found it puzzling that commentators such as Franklyn were talking up wine growing when I knew full well it barely figured on a list of export commodities leaving New South Wales in trading vessels. In 1861, the reported area under wheat in the colony was close to 123 500 acres. In 1901 the harvest had increased more than tenfold and wheat grossed more than £2 500 000 from export. New South Wales pastoralists earned £1.8 million from the wool clip in 1861. By 1901 the figure had risen to over £9 million. In 1900–01 (as Federation meant New South Wales production became part of a national rather than colonial industry), wine production in New South Wales reached 900 000 gallons. In 1901–02 the first national tally of wine production showed the former Australian colonies combined made 5.26 million gallons (most of it in South Australia), with wine exports in 1902 totalling £148 983.[5]

With these figures to hand, it seemed on first reading Franklyn and others who waxed lyrical about wine growing that they must have been wearing rose-coloured glasses, and that these rose-coloured glasses had been handed down for several generations, beginning in the 1830s. It is one thing to talk about the potential for an industry in confident but abstract terms at the very start of a colonial project; to imagine and plan the transformation of a landscape and the creation of domestic and export commodities. Watkin Tench, for instance, thought in the 1790s that 'an adventurer, if of a persevering character and competent knowledge' might meet with success in 'raising tobacco, rice, indigo, or vineyards (for which last I think the soil and climate admirably adapted)'.[6] It is another thing entirely to continue to talk a century later about a prospective industry which has not shown signs of success when other commodities proved so much more lucrative. The continued strand of published encouragement for wine growing – despite the absence of any demand for colonial wine from the drinking public – can be understood in terms of wine as a tool of sobriety, as discussed in Chapter 6. Indeed, booster literature on wine growing employed the rhetoric of moderate temperance. But policies to substitute wine for spirits, beer and binge drinking is only part of the explanation. From the 1860s the continued urgency for wine growing can also be attributed more broadly to settlerism; encouragement of vineyard plantings to expand land use and provide export income.

Boosterism as an explanation of great hopes for wine growing in the second half of the nineteenth century became all the more persuasive when I discovered that the same phenomenon existed at the same time but *to an even greater extent* in the United States. There, grape growing constituted a civilising and refining 'social and agricultural high art' and formed an important nexus in 'national identity for Americans in the decades of superheated manifest destiny'.[7] A closer look at Franklyn's *Glance at Australia* indicates too that he borrowed boosterish predictions of the same destiny for wine growing in California.[8]

Belich argues that the potency of settlerism came from its timing in economic cycles. Recessions excited a rise in boosterism for export rescue – greater production and stronger exports from Anglo settler societies – which led to booms. As the booms wavered, a new boosterism and subsequent rise in primary production and exports propelled progress towards the next wave of prosperity. As Belich shows, this pattern fits for the Anglosphere, including Australia in the nineteenth century. Comparison of Belich's figures on economic booms with peaks in prescriptive wine growing literature indicates that, as for wider patterns of settlerist encouragement, wine growing boosterism in Australia coincided with economic downturns.

The table below compares Australia-wide economic cycles, boom cycles in Australian wine production and booster literature about wine growing. Columns 1 and 2 show that wine production cycles of growth do not exactly match broad economic booms. After all, a vineyard planted

Comparison of Australian economic booms with peaks in wine growing booster literature

Australian economic booms	Boom cycles in Australian wine production	Rise in booster literature on wine production as economic growth stalled
1828–1842	1830s–early 1840s	Mid 1840s
1848–1867	1854–1871	1860s
1872–1891	1881–1896	1890s

Plate 61.

ILLUSTRATION FROM GEORGE BROOKSHAW 'POMONA BRITANNICA...' LONDON, 1812, PLATE LVIII, MITCHELL LIBRARY, STATE LIBRARY OF NSW, RB/DS634/19

Pub.d by Sherwood, Neely & Jones, May 1.st 1822.

Black Frontignac, a common wine grape in colonial New South Wales, may have been among the varieties imported on the First Fleet, possibly from the governor's garden at the Cape of Good Hope.

The Vineyard, site of the first free settler vineyard in Australia. This painting was made a year after Philip Schaeffer sold the land in 1797. Artist unknown.

MITCHELL LIBRARY, STATE LIBRARY OF NSW, ML SAFE 1/14 OPP. P. 224

MITCHELL LIBRARY, STATE LIBRARY OF NSW, ML SAFE 1/14 OPP. P. 224

> James Busby aged about thirty. A miniature portrait made in 1832, when Busby returned to New South Wales from a journey to Britain to protest his dismissal from the colony's agricultural school for male orphans, at which he had planted a vineyard.

Under a tangle of wild olive, in a horse paddock within view of the Nepean River at Camden Park lie these wine fermenting vats and the remains of what is thought to be the room where William Macarthur and his German wine makers processed and stored wine from at least 150 years ago.

ALEXANDER TURNBULL LIBRARY, NEW ZEALAND. REFERENCE NO. NON-ATL-P-0065

ROSIE MARSON

MITCHELL LIBRARY, STATE LIBRARY OF NSW, CALL NO. R266

MITCHELL LIBRARY, STATE LIBRARY OF NSW, CALL NO. R265

Silver medal awarded to Gregory Blaxland by the Society for the Encouragement of the Arts, Manufactures and Commerce, London, in 1823

Gold Ceres Medal awarded to Blaxland in 1828 by the Society for the Encouragement of the Arts, Manufactures and Commerce, London

MITCHELL LIBRARY, STATE LIBRARY OF NSW, CALL NO. XR10

A great rarity in the State Library of New South Wales' collection, this Chinese manufactured, enamelled porcelain punchbowl depicting early Sydney before 1820 includes a grape vine motif.

WYNDHAM ESTATE

Dalwood House built, and possibly designed, by George Wyndham is the oldest surviving Greek revival building in Australia and an enduring symbol of Wyndham's embrace of neo-classical culture. These Doric columns on the east wing of the house led to his bedroom.

Australian Agricultural Company crest with the classical revivalist symbols of vine leaves and olive branches c1820s

NOEL BUTLIN ARCHIVES CENTRE (NBAC), CANBERRA

ILLUSTRATION FROM GEORGE BROOKSHAW, THE HORTICULTURAL REPOSITORY, CONTAINING DELINEATIONS OF THE BEST VARIETIES OF THE DIFFERENT SPECIES OF ENGLISH FRUITS, LONDON, SHERWOOD, JONES & CO, 1823, PLATE XXX, MITCHELL LIBRARY, STATE LIBRARY OF NSW, DSM/Q634/B

Known as Sweetwater but later identified as the sherry grape,
Palomino, this variety was common in early colonial vineyards.

MITCHELL LIBRARY, STATE LIBRARY OF NSW, DSM/Q634/ B

Black Hamburgh, a common colonial wine grape

Vinedressers at work in South Australia, demonstrating staking and leaf removal practices known to have been used by German migrants to New South Wales from 1838. Painting by Samuel Gill, painted between 1841 and 1843.

NATIONAL LIBRARY OF AUSTRALIA, CALL NO. PIC R3294 LOC BOX A49

MITCHELL LIBRARY, STATE LIBRARY OF NSW, CALL NUMBER: ML 88

An American ship tied up in front of James Grocott's Wholesale Wine and Spirit warehouse at Circular Quay, Sydney. Wine has been imported to Australia since 1788. Watercolour by Frederick Garling, 1854.

The Vineyard. One of Ten Australian Views, London, c187-?. The Arcadian vision of wine growing, unknown location and artist.

NATIONAL LIBRARY OF AUSTRALIA, CALL NO. PIC H531 N:6316 PLATE 5 LOC NK SHELVES 7

MITCHELL LIBRARY, STATE LIBRARY OF NEW SOUTH WALES, CALL NO. PXD 740 P15

PLATE 17ᴾ

WYNDHAM'S
CELEBRATED AUSTRALIAN WINES.

WINE AWARDS

DALWOOD VINEYARDS, BRANXTON, N.S. WALES.

PRINCIPAL ESTABLISHMENT

JOHN WYNDHAM,
PROPRIETOR.

MESSᴿˢ WOOD BROˢ & Cº NEWCASTLE.

— AND —

MESSʳˢ DAVID COHEN & Cº MAITLAND.

NOTE.

The Wine from Dalwood Vineyards was awarded a Silver Medal at Paris International
Exhibition 1867. The highest award obtained by any of the Australian Colonies.
A Bronze Medal was also awarded at Paris Exhibition 1867, to the Manager (JOHN WYNDHAM)
as a wine maker.

Part of an album of photos taken at John Wyndham's Dalwood Estate in 1886 showing barrels in the cellar and showcasing prizes for Dalwood wines at international and colonial exhibitions. Dalwood was one of the colony's most awarded wine businesses between the 1860s and 1880s, which was used as a selling point.

MITCHELL LIBRARY, STATE LIBRARY OF NSW, DL PD 265

McWILLIAM'S WINES

DE BORTOLI WINES

Who said Australia was not a wine drinking country? c1920s

> *Early 1930s: winery workers at a traditional lunch on the veranda at the De Bortolis' Bilbul home near Griffith.*

< A view of George Suttor's vineyard and orangery at Baulkham Hills in Sydney. Watercolour by William Simpson, 1855.

> One of the earliest New South Wales wine artefacts, an Irrawang vineyard and pottery bill head stamp from 1838.

MITCHELL LIBRARY, STATE LIBRARY OF NSW, CALL NO: SSV1B / RAY 7 / 1

MITCHELL LIBRARY, STATE LIBRARY OF NSW, SSV/229

First cellar and wine press at the Wilkinson's Oakdale at Pokolbin in the Hunter. Built in the 1860s and shown here just before they were replaced c1908. A note on the back says this shows how grapes were crushed with heavy logs. Sketch by Florence Mary Hindmarsh Wilkinson.

> *Red wine from the 1880 vintage at George Francis' Douglas Vale, Port Macquarie received a bronze medal from the wine jury at the 1882 Bordeaux Exhibition. Isabella is from the North American* vitis labrusca *family of grapes, rather than* vitis vinifera, *most commonly used for European wine. Douglas Vale is now a living museum with some Isabellas still planted.*

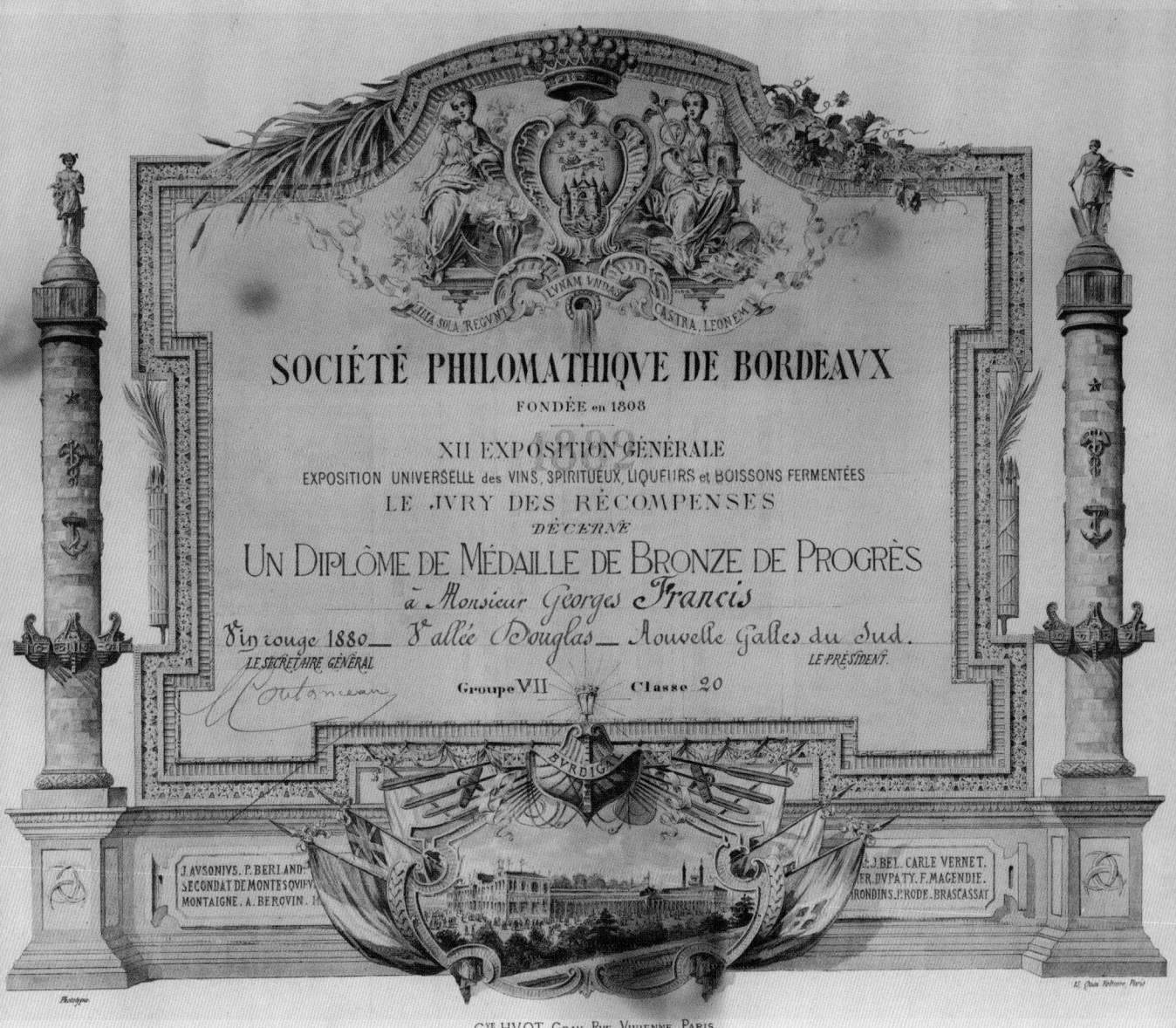

Notification of a Colonial and Indian Exhibition 1886 commemorative medal presented to Port Macquarie wine grower George Francis for his contribution to the event. The classical revivalist artwork captures conceptions of the grandeur of empire. Each colony is listed on the certificate; New South Wales at the top left-hand corner.

during years of economic prosperity will not produce its first crop for at least three years and yields then increase to a certain level of maturity. The important comparison as a means of understanding the proliferation of prescriptive literature is columns 1 and 3 together, which show that as economic boom cycles lost energy, literature recommending wine growing production rose.

Comparison of columns 2 and 3 show wine growing boosterishness seems to have had less effect on increasing wine production than a boom across all sectors. Ultimately too, investment in table grape growing exceeded investment in wine grapes in the late nineteenth century. Table 2 in Appendix 2 shows how few wine presses there were compared with vignerons in fruit growing areas in Sydney and its hinterland (Cumberland), for example.

How extensive was booster literature on wine growing as distinct from private correspondence discussing its potential? In the United States it constituted thirty-seven publications by the 1860s.[10] The figure is not as high in the comparatively lower population of the Australian colonies but here printed material did appear in concentrated periods, beginning with James Busby's three books. His *Manual* (1830) is credited with sparking an upsurge in requests for vine cuttings and advice on wine growing.[11] This was helped along by the increased migration of settlers with capital. Busby's third book, *Journal of a Tour* (1833), had elements of early boosterishness but throughout the 1840s more material on colonial wine appeared across Australia. Historian W. P. Driscoll attributed this to book publishers and the colonial press responding to interest in the industry but it was part of a wider picture: colonial ambition, the drive for economic prosperity and the perceived role of wine growing in this.[12] George Suttor's *Culture of the Grape-Vine* appeared in London in 1843 to encourage settlers to grow vines (and oranges) in the Australian colonies. In the same year, South Australian gardener George McEwin's *Vigneron and Gardeners' Manual Containing Plain Practical Directions for the Cultivation of the Vine* was published to assist new settlers in their land improvements.[13] William Macarthur contributed vine stock to the vineyard McEwin managed, as well as other early South Australian ventures. Macarthur's *Letters on the*

Culture of the Vine followed McEwin's, in 1844. The *Letters* were the collected practical contributions which appeared under the pen name Maro in *The Australian* in 1842, with additional autobiographical comments by the author.[14] Macarthur's work had a more instructive than prescriptive tone but contained a good deal of personal experience which encouraged perseverance in wine growing. Also in 1844, a translation from German of J.S. Kercht's *Improved Practical Culture of the Vine* and Henderson's *History* could be purchased in New South Wales.[15] In 1845, Richard West Nash authored *A Manual for the Cultivation of the Vine and Olive in Western Australia*. Dublin-born Nash acted as honorary secretary of the western colony's Agricultural Society from 1842 to 1845 and played a key part in early farming experiments.[16] In 1850, Thomas Mitchell's *Notes on the Cultivation of the Vine* provided instructive details, and another surge in prescriptive material – which often included instructions – occurred from 1859.[17] In this, newspapers – as the mass media of the era – played a central role.

When British migrants established the Port Phillip settlement (now Melbourne), as historian Alan Atkinson detected, 'newspapers, like fairy godmothers, had told the community about itself and, as with fairy godmothers, their prophesises were self-fulfilling'. By the 1840s, the Port Phillip press clearly had a 'social vision'.[18] In New South Wales, the *Sydney Gazette* reported the first wine made west of the Blue Mountains in the tones of a supportive aunt:

> Considering that it is a first attempt, and that that species of grape is the least suited of any of the varieties for the making of wine, we think the experiment a very encouraging one. It is the character of the light French wines. We shall place the bottle in our Advertisement Office, where the curious will be welcome to taste for themselves. Thus we are gradually creeping towards those halcyon days when Australian hearts will be 'cheered' with the sparkling produce of their own vintage.[19]

The wine had been made from sweetwater grapes grown in the garden of Fitzherbert Hawkins, a navy captain and former public servant who had moved into Wiradjuri country before 1820 and was one of several Bathurst landholders to trial wine grapes.[20]

Twenty years later, a newspaper report boosterishly predicted that colonial wine could do more than cheer hearts; it could create conditions for the 'the advancement of the peculiar interests of the British population … the direct employment and maintenance in comfort of a dense and industrious tenancy … a boundless sphere [for the] employment of the teeming multitudes of the mother country'.[21] That is, fulfil the settlerist vision of migration to the colonies.

Migration, wine growing and export

Migration into New South Wales had begun to rise after 1815 and gradually increased following the end of convict transportation in the 1840s, due to an increase in supported migration of labourers and then the impulsive migration of the gold rush era. Between 1861 and 1871 the population of New South Wales increased by about a third. From 1871 to 1891 it doubled to 1.12 million; almost level with Victoria's gold-fever figures.[22] Settlerism in Australia resulted in greater migration to coastal cities than into an agricultural heartland exemplified by the American west. Even so, thousands of smallholders invested in viticulture – a good deal of them in wine grapes – until the 1890s Depression led to widespread financial losses. In 1866, Joseph Reymond and Auguste Nicolas, for example, took up a selection of 320 acres on the Lachlan River at what is now Forbes and created Champsaur which included wine production; reportedly 80 000 gallons a year by the late nineteenth century.[23] The extent and location of vineyards is given in Table 2 of Appendix 2.

Wine economists Kym Anderson and Robert Osmond have argued that a ten-fold rise in wine production across the Australian colonies from mid-century to the 1870s created a surplus which drove the need to export wine to ensure the survival of the emerging industry in the absence of a domestic market.[24] I think the desire to export existed well before this and the surplus simply made it more viable, along with increasingly sophisticated wine business structures such as interest from British importers. Settlerist principles meant the Australian colonies believed Britain had an obligation to buy colonial wine. If Britain did not do so, it neglected its role in the economic cycles of empire from a colonial perspective: migration from the imperial metropole; production in the colonies; export to the metropole. What aspiring New South Wales wine exporters came up against was a decline in British wine consumption, changing tastes, and policies encouraging wine imports of lighter level alcohol. A British refusal to embrace Australian colonial wine at the rate hoped for by producers led to some bitterness. As early as 1861, South Australian wine grower Alex Kelly decided that the British were not civilised enough to recognise the merits of colonial wine:

> In the extensive dominions of Great Britain, embracing every variety of soil and climate in Europe, Asia, Africa, and America, nearly every product that can minister to the wants of civilised man is produced, with the exception of wine, and for this she had to depend on foreign countries. The poor coarse wine hitherto supplied by the Cape of Good Hope need hardly be taken into account … with singular perversity John Bull [the Englishman] refuses to deal at the nearest shop where he can get the article he wants … This perverse conduct on the part of that very obstinate individual would be laughable were it not for the lamentable results of his absurdity in the vitiated tastes and degraded habits engendered by the habitual use of coarse and heavily intoxicating drinks.[25]

Victorian wine grower Hubert de Castella, a Swiss migrant, made a similar argument in *John Bull's Vineyard* in 1886.[26]

The first Australian firm to be established in London to market colonial wines was Patrick Auld (the Australian Wine Company, later Emu Wines) in 1862, followed by Peter Burgoyne in 1872.[27] In the ten years to 1872, Britain imported 245 000 gallons of Australian wine. London merchants Elders and D. Cohen & Co listed several Australian wines for sale in the late 1860s, including from Wyndham's Bukkulla at Inverell. But wines from the warm Murray District, such as James Fallon's, with its high naturally-occurring alcohol, were discriminated against under new British licensing laws introduced by Prime Minister William Gladstone in 1872.[28]

Fallon used settlerist rhetoric to campaign in Britain for lower duties for Australian wines with higher than 26 per cent naturally occurring alcohol. No doubt the Irish-Catholic Fallon had sharpened his skills of persuasion in the failed case against Victorian customs duties on New South Wales wine. Fallon's wines were produced near the Victorian border; closer to Melbourne than Sydney.[29] His argument that British customs duties for colonial wine were discriminatory centred on the logic that stimulating greater income from production in the colonies increased colonists' power to buy English products. 'Thereby', said Fallon, using the language of export rescue, 'assisting in providing for the employment

What remains of the Pokolbin home of
Edward Tyrrell who crushed his first vintage
in the Hunter Valley in 1864

TYRRELL'S WINES

of English artisans, and preventing the reoccurrence of such seasons of industrial depression as the present ... The interests of England and Australia are identical'. Colonial wine, said Fallon:

> is doubtless destined to be one of the leading staple articles of produce in Australia, and one which will not only give healthful employment to a number of Australian vignerons, but also open up a large field for the occupation of the surplus labour of Great Britain ... [B]y honest exertion in a few years a man could purchase his homestead and be his own master.[30]

Migration and drinking culture

Although there were ethnicities other than the British involved in wine growing in New South Wales, by the end of the century working class Britons represented nine out of every ten migrants to the Australian colonies. This overwhelmingly British flavour to New South Wales culture meant that although vine cultivation rose steadily, calls for greater consumption of colonial wine fell on deaf ears. A Carlton Brewing ad of 1870 summed it up by saying a 'standard feature in the composition of the Briton is his partiality for malt liquor, in preference to fiery spirits or washy wine.'[31] The principal alcoholic beverage consumed in New South Wales was no longer spirits as it had been in the early years of the colony, and certainly not wine, but beer. As historian Richard Waterhouse noted, in pubs 'customers were by then less likely to drink rum scooped in mugs from a bucket than to sip on cold beer drawn by tap from a keg', while the culture of the 'shout' or sharing rounds of beer became common, like extensive rounds of toasting in the earlier era.[32] By 1885, per capita annual consumption of beer in New South Wales was 13.19 gallons compared with 1.3 gallons of spirits and 0.64 gallons of wine.[33] The bush shanties of the first half of the century and the sly grog shops of the goldfields gave way to pubs in great numbers. In New South Wales, for example, Armidale (a town of 1300 people in the New England district) hosted ten pubs by

ILLUSTRATED SYDNEY NEWS, 12/6/1880, PAGE 16, MITCHELL LIBRARY, STATE LIBRARY OF NSW, TN115

Etching, 'The Vintage at James Fallon's Murray Valley Vineyard'

Wine shops were far fewer than pubs despite reforms from the 1860s to encourage their establishment. Colonial wine & dining rooms, Hill End, c1870–1875.

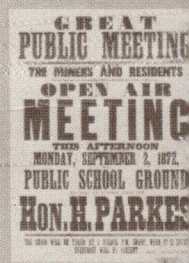

GREAT
PUBLIC MEETING
THE MINERS AND RESIDENTS
OPEN AIR
MEETING
THIS AFTERNOON
MONDAY, SEPTEMBER 2, 1872,
PUBLIC SCHOOL GROUND
HON. H. PARKES

MITCHELL LIBRARY, STATE LIBRARY OF NSW, GMS BOX, NO 18630 HOME AND AWAY - 5791

1870; Lismore in the Northern Rivers, population 1000, had eight pubs by 1879; Narrandera in the Riverina in the same period boasted seventeen pubs but only one church.[34]

By 1887 there were over 400 colonial wine shops in New South Wales, including 126 in Sydney.[35] But in the same year the number of pubs in New South Wales totalled 3270; 846 of them in the capital.[36] In 1889, the *New York Times* published a report by a British visitor to Australia who commented that at first, 'I had the impression that, as beer is the national drink of England, whisky of Scotland, and wine of France, tea was the national drink of Australia'. There were in Australia more teetotallers than in England but on closer observation it became obvious that 'the labourers living in towns are in the habit of drinking freely … a large number of men drinking up country usually drink tea, but … when they come into the towns, many of them drink very heavily'.[37] These seasonal workers, such as shearers and cane cutters, blowing their pay after cut-out, were not likely to be drinking wine.

Proximity to wine production did result in the town of Seaham in the Hunter boasting 'several wine saloons' even before the 1860s but they were by far fewer than local pubs.[38] Colonial wine shops opened in the goldfields as a result of lower licence fees. In the early 1880s when the New South Wales government tried again to discourage working class consumption of stronger liquors in favour of wine, a new law lowered the annual licence fee for colonial wine shops to £3 and allowed sales of wine by the glass or up to 2 gallons. But publicans were still opposed to lower fees for wine shops and they had greater support than the wine lobby among colonial authorities. At Wagga Wagga in 1892, vineyard owner James Beattie applied for a colonial wine license only to be told by a police officer that since colonial wine could be purchased cheaply enough at local pubs there could be no need for him to sell wine. Beattie replied that pub owners refused to sell his wine and the one who did charged four times as much as they should have and he wanted to be able to provide fair prices to buyers at his own premises. In eventually approving Beattie's application for a wine license, one of the magistrates reminded the police officer that the law had intended to 'encourage the cultivation of the [vine], and help

BRITANNIA HOUSE, WILLIAM-STREET, BATHURST.

CHRISTMAS DISPLAY!
SEE OUR WINDOWS
THE ATTRACTION AT ALL TIMES,
—— BUT ESPECIALLY AT ——
THIS FESTIVE SEASON
—— BEAUTIFUL GOODS FOR ——
CHRISTMAS-BOXES & NEW YEARS' GIFTS.

OUR CHRISTMAS TREES, LOADED WITH CHOICE AND INEXPENSIVE ITEMS, should be seen by Everybody Disposed to Purchase Useful & Seasonable Presents.

N.B.—Dainty real Lace Handkfs., Scarfs, and Collars and Cuffs, to be only at Britannia House, specially purchased for the Christmas Trade.

Dress Lengths in Prints and Stuffs, Very Cheap for Christmas.

JOHN MEAGHER & CO.'S
SPECIAL LIST
FOR CHRISTMAS WEEK

CHRISTMAS. CHRISTMAS. CHRISTMAS.

EVERY person, no matter how poor or humble, looks forward to having a GOOD TIME AT CHRISTMAS. In order, therefore, to enable all to enjoy themselves during the Christmas Holidays we have made

SPECIAL REDUCTIONS
—— IN OUR ——
Grocery, Wine, & Spirit Departments,
For the WEEK ONLY, from
MONDAY, 19th, to SATURDAY, 24th.

At the Prices we quote we will not Book the Articles for an instant; the Goods have to be paid for at the time of purchase.

We are prepared to lose £500 During the Week by the Reductions, Which we consider as trifling to the pleasure and happiness we will confer on thousands.

Colonial Wine by the Single Bottle!
Reduced Prices!

Reduced Prices.

Case Spirits, Porter, and Ales.

GROCERIES. GROCERIES.

We would recommend customers, when they make their purchases to ask for a price-list from the young man that will wait on them, and then order your supplies from it, as it may be possible for the young man to make a mistake, as he may not remember the reductions.

Our reductions already advertised in our Drapery, Ironmongery, and Furniture are too well known and appreciated to need any comment from us. We will say, however, that there is not a house in New South Wales selling goods all round as cheap as we are.

Wishing everybody the Compliments of the Season, and hoping our efforts to enable the public to enjoy themselves through the holidays will be appreciated—

JOHN MEAGHER & CO.

IMPORTANT!
XMAS NOVELTIES
CONSISTING OF THE LATEST DESIGNS OF
Diamond & Gold Jewellery,
Sterling Silver & Electro-plated Ware (BY THE BEST ENGLISH MAKERS),
Watches, Clocks, etc.

ESPECIALLY SELECTED FOR US FOR THIS YEAR'S CHRISTMAS SEASON

E. CURTIS & CO. (E. ROOS),
JEWELLERS, WATCHMAKERS, &c.
HOWICK-STREET, BATHURST.

WEBB'S SALE!
ENORMOUS SUCCESS
GOODS FLYING LIKE FUN!
WEBB'S CHRISTMAS BOOM.

Boys and Girls, and everybody pleased at WEBB'S Sensational Prices!

TOYS—1d, 2d, & 3d; Reduced from 6d, 9d, 1s, & 1s 6d.

Webb's Xmas Bargains
Regardless of Cost.

Wonderful Bargains in every Department!

DRAPERY,   Clothing.   TOYS.
GROCERY,   Hats.   MILLINERY.
BOOTS & SHOES.   Crockery.   IRONMONGERY

WEBB'S EXTRAORDINARY CHRISTMAS LIST for Cash Down at Time of Ordering.

THE SUPERIOR QUALITY of WEBB'S GOODS Need no Comment.

Department of Public Works.
Government Architect's Branch.

TENDERS.

12 Prime Fat Vealers!
AT THE CORPORATION YARDS, BATHURST.
ON THURSDAY NEXT
E. S. TAYLOR & CO.

A LA VILLE DE BORDEAUX,
JEAN JOSEPH RALPH, Importer and French Agent of Wines, Spirits, &c.
LIST OF PRICES FOR CHRISTMAS ONLY.

BRANDY.
RUM.
HOLLAND GIN.
WINES.
CHAMPAGNE.
CLARET AND BURGUNDY.
ENGLISH BOTTLED ALE AND PORTER.
SYRUPS AND CORDIALS.
SPIRITS OF WINE.

J. J. RALPH,
Importer in Sydney, New South Wales.

DEAN'S FURNITURE WAREHOUSE
NEW GOODS BEING OPENED,
WILLIAM DEAN,
CABINETMAKER and UPHOLSTERER,
Late of City Theatre, Market-street.

LATE FIRE IN PITT-STREET.—J. KEARNY begs to call the attention of his customers and the public in general that he still continues to carry on the business of Furnishing and General Ironmonger, down the gateway, and has now on hand—

BARGAINS IN IRONMONGERY.
Important Notice.

The largest colonial wine producers succeeded in selling their products alongside imported wines.

VICTOR PAYNE COLLECTION

Grape harvest at Douglas Vale, Port Macquarie; one of more than fifty vintages at the Francis-Wilson property, beginning in 1867. Vineyard owner Margaret Wilson is on the left, surrounded by her family at work.

the producers of colonial wine, and to offer them every facility to dispose of their produce'.[39] To do so wine producers had a few bars in Sydney, Newcastle and Albury.

The lack of a wine drinking culture translated into the absence of wine in Australian colonial popular culture. Working men and women with British ancestry did not sing songs of wine. Characters in Banjo Paterson's *Waltzing Matilda* were not likely partial to a glass of colonial claret. The last three verses of *Click Go the Shears* (a revelation to me since they were not taught with the rest of the song in primary school in the 1970s) celebrate over-consumption of beer. One verse, for instance, enjoins, 'Down by the Bar the old shearer stands/Grasping his glass in his thin bony hands, Fixed is his gaze on a green-painted keg/Glory, he'll get down on it, ere he stirs a peg'.[40] Mateship and drinking were inextricably linked. Henry Lawson wrote that, 'in spite of all the right-thinking person may think, say or write, there was between us that sympathy which in our times and conditions is the strongest and perhaps the truest of all human qualities, the sympathy of drink … We were drinking mates together'.[41] How often did mates drink colonial wine? Statistically we would have to conclude that it was very rarely but when Victor J Daley followed a mate from Victoria to the New South Wales goldfields in the 1880s he penned *In a Wine Cellar*, an uncommon ode to Australian colonial wine. In it he claims that, for all the romance of European wines, colonial poets found true inspiration in colonial wine, for it alone contained the stories and culture of Australia. In this excerpt 'it' is colonial wine:

> But he may wholly/Become a seer/
> Who quaffs it slowly/For he shall hear,
> Though faintly, lowly,/Yet sweet and clear,
> The axes ringing/On mountain sides/
> The wool-boats swinging/Down Darling tides,
> The drovers singing/Where Clancy rides,
> The miners driving,/The stockman's strife/
> All sounds conniving/To tell the rife,
> Rich, rude, strong-striving/Australian life.
> Once more your hand in/This hand of mine!/

And while we stand in/The brave sunshine,
Pledge deep our land in/Our land's own wine![42]

From the first vine plantings to 'our lands' own wine' remained a far from complete process at the end of the nineteenth century. In Phillip Muskett's *The Art of Living in Australia* (1893 and reprinted several times), the chapter on wine opened with the boosterish epitaph that, 'with time and care Australia ought to be the vineyard of the world', a quote from a publication called *Greater Britain*. Muskett shared the vision of campaigners for wine as a tool of sobriety. He urged Australian colonists to take advantage of their climate to embrace a more healthful Mediterranean lifestyle – including wine culture – instead of an unchanged British lifestyle transplanted to a warmer part of the world. Muskett discussed the art and pleasure of fine wine and the refreshment to be had from good common wines. He advised how to grow grapes and make wine. He recommended that the colonies introduce a viticultural college to improve training in this area of cultivation and manufacture. Wine tastings were common among wine producers but Muskett provided a guide for others to taste wine as a means of educating themselves to gain a greater appreciation of it. 'In all

Trade mark, registered 1888. It refers to honours at the 1862 London Exhibition plus the French Premier cru classifications: 'first growth'.

LINDEMAN (HOLDINGS) LTD PAPERS, 24-8 BOX 148. NOEL BUTLIN ARCHIVE CENTRE

Harvest required additional hands and adaptation of resources. Here workers are emptying grapes into a woolpack or bale bag for transport to a winery. Photograph by Sam Hood, c1930.

MITCHELL LIBRARY, STATE LIBRARY OF NSW, CALL NUMBER: HOME AND AWAY - 7052

these many ways public interest in the Australian wine industry would be continually sustained; and, he concluded, 'rising from its unfairly neglected position, it would speedily attain to that pride of place which is manifestly its destiny', which sounds very much like manifest destiny, the ultra-boosterish phrase used in the United States.[43]

While wine consumption had little impact on the idea of Australianness in the first half of the twentieth century, wine production came to occupy a pride of place in some regions until the Great Depression. In the 1930s, in the spirit of the triumphal stocktaking of centenaries, the author of a souvenir booklet on a hundred years of Hunter wine wrote that: 'Old as is the history of wine-making in the European World, so in this land of ours the wine industry ranks next to wool and wheat as the third oldest of the agricultural industries'.[44]

When had wine growing become an industry? Economist Kenneth Boyer recognised in the 1980s the lack of a specific definition of 'industry'. He set about defining it in such a way that a business belongs to an industry of 'that group of sellers with which a firm would find it most profitable to collude'.[45] In the 1850s there was barely a group of sellers of colonial wine in New South Wales. A British newspaper correspondent described it as 'more a fancy than an industry.'[46] During the 1860s, the era of wine squires who drove experimentation gave way to the era of second generation wine family businesses, and more sophisticated distribution and retail. Layers of the new industry comprehended grape growers selling to wineries and wine businesses of the scale of Douglas Vale at Port Macquarie through to larger enterprises. Wyndham's, Lindeman's, Fallon's and Wilkinson's created brands which by the 1870s competed with each other and against imported wines from overseas, though colonial customs duties prevented a significant trade with South Australia and Victoria. Wyndham's and Lindeman's had vineyards in different regions, as would the McWilliam family and Penfold's in the early twentieth century. This coalescence of experimental wine growing into an industry occurred as new wine science knowledge boosted production potential and new transport technologies facilitated long distance export. Just in time to face the challenge of modern vine pests and diseases, to which we now turn.

8

Wine, science and industrialisation

As the Settler Revolution brought a new generation of colonial wine growers, the emerging New South Wales wine industry began to be transformed too by the Scientific Revolution and the Industrial Revolution. Just as the mass transfers of settlerism accelerated throughout the nineteenth century, so did advances in scientific knowledge and the development of new technologies. Plant transfer took North American vine diseases and pests to European vineyards and then to New World wine regions such as New South Wales. In the chaotic interconnectivity of cause and effect in innovation, these threats to large-scale wine grape production were first caused and then solved by explosions of curiosity and ambition. New forms of energy and new means of production resulted in dramatic changes to the quality and quantity of wine that could be made, no matter how ancient or new the wine region. From the mid-nineteenth century, wine growers world wide were witnessing, and contributing to, the earliest impact of machines in vineyard and winery, bacteria-free wine making, refrigeration and mass production.

We take it for granted that we are able to buy wine by the single bottle, at a bottle shop, almost any time of the day and certainly any time of the year. Prestige wines can be ordered online as their release is announced. The process of obtaining wine was far more ponderous and uncertain 200 years ago. British merchants of the Georgian era purchased European and European colonial wine as soon as it could be transported after fermentation. They sold it in wooden casks or, more rarely, caseloads of bottles, mainly to wealthy private buyers. Very cheap table wines could be purchased in wine regions but British drinkers experienced this only when they travelled. Most wine had to be consumed before it spoiled, within a year or two. Fine wines, manufactured to be aged were stowed at wineries and in the warehouses of merchants for more than a year, or, like Madeira, underwent long sea voyages to achieve their particular quality. It is thanks to scientific viticulture, wine making (oenology) and new technologies that seasonality and geographical distance no longer determine our choice of wine, any more than they do food.[1]

As New South Wales growers planted vineyards in parts of the world which had never before hosted *vitis vinifera*, they were swept with equal force into the whirlwind of industrialisation which – for better or worse – transformed European vine cultivation and wine making from ancient, artisanal practices into a modern industry. Despite its youth, farming in New South Wales and the other Australian colonies did not have to go through the same time frame of knowledge development as in Britain and Europe; it developed alongside new innovations and specialisations. Colonial agriculture was 'linked into the expanding and deepening international networks of technical information'.[2] With vines and wine the trajectory from first plantings to modernisation in New South Wales happened in less than two lifetimes, in contrast with the *longue durée* of Europe which had experienced thousands of years of wine growing experimentation.

In the nineteenth century, New World and Old World wine industries battled simultaneously against diseases and pests which threatened their vineyards. The imperative to find solutions to threats to vines was far greater in Europe because of the enormous importance of the industry but New South Wales newspapers reported on the progress of the development of these solutions, colonial experimental farms tested them, and the burgeoning colonial wine industry was progressively fortified against future natural challenges as was Europe's. Knowledge and infrastructure at first flowed *to* the Australian colonies but investment in scientific viticultural and oenological training led later to the flow of knowledge and technology *from* Australia to join a global exchange.

Wine growing in Australia is a product of modernity as much as it is a product of colonial ambition for civility and prosperity.

Dealing with pests and diseases

For the first few decades of vine growing experiments in New South Wales, the main threat to healthy grape production was blight. This condition afflicted several different plant crops and a French sea captain visiting Port Jackson in 1803 noted that the 'vine, which during the first years, yielded great hopes, has much degenerated, that it is matter of doubt whether it will be able to live there. The cause of this unexpected decay is not ascertained, it is commonly attributed, however, to the burning of the northeast wind.'[3] Gregory Blaxland claimed to have found the colony's most blight resistant grape variety, from which he made the wine he submitted to the Society for the Arts in 1822.[4] A decade later, debate on the causes and cures of blight continued for some months in the colonial press.[5] In the mid-1840s, William Macarthur believed it to be a parasitical fungus rather than some of the more far-fetched suggestions of the time.[6] Twentieth century diagnoses of the colonial problem have included fungus and drought.[7]

Macarthur listed other threats to vines: a borer grub that migrated from certain wood stakes used as trellises into the vine wood, a leaf-eating caterpillar, and birds and mammals that fed on the grapes. Possums and other nocturnal fruit-eating native animals were hunted by Aborigines who continued to live at Camden Park. Colonists who helped themselves to the crop were another matter. 'I presume', wrote Macarthur, 'that no one possessing a vineyard will omit the protection of a formidable hedge fence, as well as a watchman with a gun, assisted by faithful dogs, when the grapes are ripe' to keep out trespassers who thieved the fruit.[8] Drought reduced the 1851 grape harvest at Murrurundi in the Upper Hunter and grasshoppers attacked a vineyard at nearby Scone so that 'a few bunches of grapes, and a few bottles of wine, were the only proceeds of the vintage'.[9]

The progress of European farming in the nineteenth century realised Enlightenment ambitions but had unanticipated deleterious side-effects. As vine growing increased (for table and wine) so did vulnerability to diseases and pests. American agricultural historians have commented that, 'the rise of specialized and intensive agriculture, due in large measure to commercialization, mechanization and territorial expansion, resulted in rapidly increasing agricultural production but provided an ideal scenario for major plant disease outbreaks'.[10] The impact of the disease powdery mildew and the pest grape phylloxera on the European wine industry were among the highest (and largely forgotten) prices paid for agricultural expansion in the nineteenth century and a poignant irony of the Age of Empires. European viruses and infections travelled east-to-west with adventurers and traders and decimated American Indigenous peoples. In the west-to-east exchange, food plants such as maize and potatoes from the Americas led to cultivation of crops which underpinned unprecedented population growth in Eurasia.[11] For centuries this biological transfer benefited Europeans but the destruction of the European wine grape industry by powdery mildew and grape phylloxera represented unexpected revenge from colonised countries against European conquest.[12] For the European wine industry, powdery mildew and phylloxera were plagues of biblical proportions. For scientists working with the industry the defeats of these threats were remarkable victories; new chapters in the mastery of the natural world.

> " As vine growing increased so did vulnerability to diseases and pests.

Powdery mildew (*oidium tuckerii*)

Oidium is the French name for powdery mildew (and the name most used among early New South Wales grape growers), a fungus which attacks leaves and berries, reduces grape crop yield and produces foul tasting wine. First described in America, where it originated, in 1834, oidium arrived in England on American vine stock (not *vitis vinifera*) then spread to Europe in the mid-1840s.[13] In France alone, it devastated vine crops so that production plummeted from 880 million gallons in 1840 to 220 million gallons in 1854.[14] Oidium appeared in the table grape vineyards of Queensland before it was detected in New South Wales, prompting action from New South Wales growers aware, from overseas newspaper reports, of its destructive power. In late 1867, the Member for Patrick's Plains (present-day Singleton in the Hunter Valley) proposed to stop the importation of grapes, vines and vine cuttings into the colony from Queensland as well as from Europe and America.[15] The income of at least 200 New South Wales families was at risk from the vine disease. Opponents of this proposal believed that prohibiting grape imports from Queensland grape growers would harm those dependent on the larger New South Wales market. Supporters of the bill countered that few grapes were purchased from Queensland anyway.[16]

In 1868, Member for Queanbeyan, Leopold De Salis, thought oidium should be taken as seriously as threats to more lucrative industries: 'If this disease was likely to be destructive of property as the scab in sheep or a fire in George-street, surely it behoved the honourable members to take all necessary precautions to prevent it'[17] Such precautionary measures to protect the existing industry were favoured at this time but legislation can be flimsy protection against destructive natural forces and a year later the disease had travelled south to the Hunter Valley and the Cumberland Plain.

How to defeat this disease? Grape growers were urged to use the most recommended remedy from Europe and the Cape: thoroughly dousing whole vineyards in sulphur. Sydney vineyard owners, particularly table grape growers around Ryde, were in favour of forced sulphuring but Albury wine grape growers resisted. The southerners believed they were protected by distance from the march of oidium and should not have to wear the cost of a problem many hundreds of miles away. Petitions against forced sulphuring were received from Albury and nearby Corowa (on the New South Wales–Victorian border), Patrick's Plains in the Hunter and from the chairman of the Hunter River Vineyard Association.[18] One opponent asked why the parliament bothered to legislate against oidium when it appeared to be an act of God. Another called attention to the problem of grape vines growing as weeds. Who would treat them against oidium?[19] The matter was referred to a select committee of parliament.

Petitions for and against the Diseases in Grape Vines Prevention Bill indicate a broad spread of the industry by the late 1860s. Opposition came from the Hunter, Merriwa, Illawarra, Sydney, Yass, Dubbo, Carcoar, Bathurst and the Clarence River.[20] Petitioners in favour of forced sulphuring were sent from Boorowa, Central Cumberland, Appin, Port Macquarie and Clarence Town (in the Hunter Valley, as distinct from Clarence River), Camden, Narellan and Eden.[21]

Albury mayor George Day sent his protest by telegraph but it could not be formally received by the Legislative Assembly because the law did not yet recognise this new form of technology as a valid way to send a petition. Day had to use the post instead.[22] One MP told parliament the issue had been blown out of all proportion. 'Was it the intention of the government', asked Richard Driver, 'to introduce a bill to prevent the spread of aphis in cabbages? (Laughter)'[23]

The 1869 parliamentary select committee heard evidence from Charles Moore, director of the Botanic Gardens in Sydney, on the lack of a comprehensive understanding of the disease in any part of the wine growing world. Moore thought forced sulphuring would have little impact unless neighbouring colonies enacted similar measures and, he said (incorrectly), the disease would 'run itself out in a few years'.[24] Philip Adams, a grower and wine judge from Albury advocated leaving the remedies to growers; the prevailing view in his district. P.L. Cloete from the Cape of Good Hope explained that there was no comparative legislation in his part of the world but he implied that if there had been, it might have prevented a serious outbreak of the disease. Jules Joubert, secretary of the

Agricultural Society of New South Wales, supported legislation to ensure small growers acted against oidium. William Macarthur, now knighted and a long-time though reluctant member of the colony's Legislative Council, also strongly advocated legislation – by all colonies – to ensure all growers took action, particularly smallholders who might be tempted to ignore the problem because of the cost of treatment. One of Macarthur's own vineyards had recently been affected by the mildew and he advised that 'after being several times cleaned with sulphur, the disease was always noticed to begin again on the side next to a neglected vineyard in the neighbourhood'. He suggested vine inspectors be appointed to prevent local prejudice in identifying outbreaks of the disease. In the end, forced sulphuring did not become law and growers were left to self-regulate their treatment of oidium.[25]

In France, 'crackpot remedies abounded' for oidium, such as 'herbal bonfire smokes, douching the roots in brine, washing foliage with soapy water, distempering with bizarre chemical cocktails, planting potatoes among the vines to somehow draw away the poison'.[26] (George Wyndham had planted potatoes between his vines in the 1830s, perhaps as a result of practices he observed in France or Italy in the 1820s well before the outbreak of oidium.[27]) The most effective treatment, confirmed in the late 1860s, involved treating vines with a water-based spray of copper sulphate and lime known as Bordeaux mix, which is still used today.[28]

In 1871, the Albury growers who had so strenuously opposed measures to prevent oidium had to admit it had reached their district, though the editor of the *Albury Banner* still predicted an excellent year for wine production, saying that 'the disease seems to have appeared too late in the season to do much harm'.[29] In 1873, Henry Lindeman told a Corowa audience at one of his lectures on wine growing that Hunter growers had the best success with 'repeated sulphurings' of vines but only with the 'best of sublimed sulphur … not ground sulphur'.[30]

In the early 1870s too, news of phylloxera – the next challenge to the nascent colonial wine industry – began to filter through from Europe, especially of the speed with which it spread from region to region. There was great confidence that scientists could find a solution but unless the pest could be eradicated from French vineyards, it was feared the famous Hermitage vines could be destroyed within a few years.[31] In 1874 a South Australian grower, David Randall, hastily penned a letter to Henry Parkes, Chief Secretary of New South Wales, which portrayed a European industry in crisis. Randall recommended the Australian wine colonies take every advantage of the slump in wine supply that would result. He called it a 'golden opportunity' but warned that the chance to benefit would be lost if Australian governments did not take serious measures to keep phylloxera from the colonies.[32] Randall's thinking reflected conversations taking place in urgent tones around the globe as Old and New World wine countries saw it as a 'splendid opportunity to develop their export trade' while French wine production floundered.[33] Randall's warning did not have the effect he hoped, however. Officials did not stir into legislative action until phylloxera arrived in the Australian colonies, and finding solutions proved to be just as vexed as for oidium.

Grape phylloxera

What is grape phylloxera? Known in the colonial era as *phylloxera vastatrix*, this strangely named insect is a tiny yellow or orange aphid that feeds on the sap of grape vines. This stops the vigour of the vine as it emerges from winter dormancy. Like powdery mildew, phylloxera was inadvertently transferred across the Atlantic from the United States, most likely in the roots of north-eastern American grape vine varieties (*vitis* cousins of the European wine grape *vitis vinifera*) which host phylloxera without harm. It first appeared in England before 1863 but that country's vines were table grapes grown in greenhouses so its effects were not felt as profoundly as in Europe where the massive extent of wine growing, close plantings and vines as weeds increased the spread of the pest. In wine countries, the socio-economic effects of phylloxera are thought to have been as devastating as the Irish potato blight.

The British had few vines to be concerned with but their wine supplies were reduced by the widening impact of phylloxera: first in France from 1863, then Portugal from 1871. (The Cape industry first detected phylloxera in 1885, several years after the end of favoured trade status with Britain.[34]) In 1871 phylloxera had arrived in Turkey.

And then a horrific domino effect ensued.

In 1872 it had spread to Austria-Hungary, in 1874 to Switzerland and a year later (officially) to Italy. Spain confirmed infection in 1878, Algeria in 1885; Greece in 1898. First identifications were just the beginning of the story in each country. Phylloxera still rampaged through the Douro ten years after the first cases in Portugal. By 1884, the phenomenal wave of the pest across the Old World wine industry left France with the ruins of a million hectares of vineyard (close to 2.5 million acres). More than half a million more were dying.[35] The European wine grape crop plummeted to as low as a fifth of what it had been prior to the infestation. By way of comparison, total plantings in New South Wales at this stage totalled 1857 hectares or 4584 acres.[36]

Californian growers of European grape vines began to be affected in 1873.[37] Six years later, the first official case of phylloxera was declared in the Australian colonies, at Geelong, Victoria. With the urging of the South Australian government and £10 000 in funding from there and New South Wales to compensate growers, Victorian authorities ordered the destruction of all Geelong grape vines in an attempt to eradicate the pest.[38]

In 1878, Queensland prohibited importation of grape vines and grape vine cuttings from Victoria.[39] (The north-eastern state would not have phylloxera in its southern wine grape vineyards until the 1910s.[40] South Australia remained phylloxera free.) New South Wales enacted similar legislation the same year, with some members of the lower house of parliament reiterating arguments from the oidium days that grape vines were one of the colony's most valuable fruit crops, for table and wine, and that these developing industries should be protected. Other members quibbled that the £20 fine for breaking the vine importation law was too high.[41]

More committed measures to deal with phylloxera were introduced in New South Wales in 1883 when Henry Bonnard – a wine broker – was appointed, largely as a result of his own initiative, to assist Moore at the Sydney Botanic Gardens to assess the threat of phylloxera and the best solutions. Two years later, phylloxera was officially detected in New South Wales, though Moore and others believed it had been present for longer.[42] The offending vineyard was the four acres remaining of William Macarthur's wine growing enterprise at Camden Park. Macarthur had died three years earlier, so he was spared this heartache. That the pest first officially appeared in the vineyard of this elder statesman of New South Wales wine tragically echoed the earlier detection of phylloxera in the western United States at Buena Vista, vineyard of Agoston Haraszthy, California's great old man of wine growing.[43]

In 1885 legislation in New South Wales instituted fines of up to £50 for importation of vines; diseased vines were to be uprooted and destroyed and vineyard owners compensated. Anyone caught leaving the colony with diseased vines would be fined £100. Landowners planting vineyards with diseased vines would be fined £50.[44] But New South Wales growers resisted the institution of a carbon copy of Victoria's vine pull scheme. John Wyndham announced his Dalwood vineyard in the Hunter contained phylloxera but he expected this since it had been so substantially established from the Macarthurs' Camden Park plant nursery. (Wyndham's friend Jules Joubert claimed to have seen phylloxera at Camden as early as 1862.) Wyndham felt too that if his vineyard continued to produce despite harbouring phylloxera then the colonial government should not have the power to order the destruction of infected vines.[45]

Bonnard and another employee inspected at least 225 vineyards of wine and table grapes, totalling about 450 acres, and found a further five infected properties on the Cumberland Plain. Bonnard estimated there were 'fully 500 families within the Cumberland County alone, having largely invested in vineyards' (many of which would have been table rather than wine grapes) and their livelihoods were imperilled by the potential spread of the pest. He advised against eradicationism.[46] An 1886 law strengthening orders for vine pulling in New South Wales further incensed Wyndham. Joubert agreed that legislative amendments to compel vine pulling were contemptible. 'I consider "mad legislation" a worse enemy than a legion of men armed with even the latest war implements', he said, and rejected in the strongest terms 'the total destruction of a vineyard by force of law unless indeed a whole vineyard be so thoroughly impregnated with the disease that not one single vine be free from it'. Joubert thought the establishment of a viticultural college in the Australian colonies would be a better use of public funds than compensation for uprooting vineyards.[47]

In 1887, the Vinegrowers' Union of New South Wales (which included Bonnard) petitioned then Colonial Secretary Parkes to repeal the 1886 laws in favour of self-regulation. Apart from the insult of government intervention, the Fruitgrowers' Union also abhorred the 'absolute power' of a Vine Diseases Board with Moore in the chair, no representation from growers themselves and no process of appeal. Both unions believed (quite rightly) that the Geelong experience and that of others in Europe proved that eradicating vines did not prevent the spread of phylloxera, though they failed to acknowledge that a cure had not yet been genuinely confirmed. The growers did not want compensation. They did not want to put a value on their vineyards in case they had to be destroyed. They preferred to keep their vineyards, and protect their industry and their land values against uncertainty. If the New South Wales government wanted to do something constructive, one grower suggested to Parkes, it could fund scientific studies of phylloxera in the Australian colonies.

Parkes replied to the delegation that the Board's powers were excessive but the Board, for its part, believed it could not act effectively with less authority. As a result of this stalemate, said Parkes, 'it seemed the Vine Diseases Act was practically a dead letter. It was not being carried out at all so the vinegrowers had not much to fear from it … it was pretty well inoperative.'[48] A problem solved? Growers may have been appeased but the 'let alone' response alarmed other wine colonies.[49]

In 1888, the Premier of Victoria wrote to Parkes on behalf of the Rutherglen and Murray River Vine Growers Association (just across the border from Albury, as distinct from the New South Wales Murray River growers) to ask what was going on.[50] The South Australian Vine Growers Association – determined to prevent phylloxera from the eastern colonies infecting their vines – also firmly urged action in New South Wales.[51] This pressure had its effect. By early September 1888, an amended Act in New South Wales empowered a larger Vine Diseases Board than before – five members this time (still with Moore as director), greater representation from growers and a quorum of three (which allowed the growers to ignore Moore) – to authorise the inspection of any vineyard regardless of whether the district had been declared under the original Act.[52] If it was determined a vineyard contained phylloxera the Board and the vine grower had fourteen days to establish an amount of compensation or destruction of vines would proceed anyway.[53] The first area declared a Vine Diseases District under the amended Act was Camden Park, the first inspector, A.T. Pringle.[54]

New drama followed as a result of 1888 amendments to the *Vine Diseases Act*. Moore thought £110 per acre excessive compensation for vine pulling and likely to be exploited by any vignerons who wanted an exit strategy from an unprofitable venture.[55] Growers on the board believed this compensation to be insufficient however and, moreover, two of the vineyards of condemned vines were healthy enough to warrant compensation for future crop losses, not just a year's income.[56] In an attempt to resolve this deadlock, Moore sought advice from Victoria on rates of compensation. He also opposed methods of destruction recommended by the rest of the Board – experiments with oil and other pesticides – and instead favoured digging up and burning the vine roots.[57]

Fevered experimentation in Europe had so far led to some very unusual treatments, especially before it had been determined that phylloxera was an insect nor a fungus.[58] An agriculturalist and military commander who had worked in India thought the phylloxera resembled pests which attacked the sap of plants in tea-gardens and cotton-fields and recommended vines be grubbed out, soil regenerated and vines replanted. Another proposal suggested wine growers surrender to phylloxera and find another plant source for wine, such as the fermented pulp of beetroot! This suggestion appeared on April Fool's Day in the same newspaper which three years later recommended fermented orange juice from Florida as a substitute for grape wine.[59] At Montpellier, centre of viticultural learning in France, phylloxera infected vines were treated with black soap and water, sea water and chalk, gas oil, sealing wax on pruning cuts, chloride of lime and flooding.[60]

New South Wales had its own share of attempts to kill the vine louse without the loss of established vineyards. All the while, declarations of infected districts were made but no action could be taken while Moore and the remainder of the Vine Diseases Board were in dispute. Once Moore received confirmation of reasonable compensation measures from Victoria, the other members of the Board finally agreed that the maximum cost of creating a vineyard and nurturing it to bearing for three years ranged between £112 and £71. Moore made it clear that, just the same, this represented much more than the New South Wales parliament would agree to as compensation for vine pulling so the membership of the Board remained at odds and infected vines remained in production.[61]

> *Fevered experimentation in Europe had led to some very unusual treatments.*

Then Moore resigned from the Board. But when the colonial secretary ignored his resignation he continued to attend meetings. Next, acting Chairman John Kidd quit the Board. In utter frustration at this point, Moore demanded a government inquiry. He called the situation a scandal 'unprecedented in any body connected with the Government'.[62]

Several months later, the Corowa Vine and Fruit Growers Association, among others, was siding with Kidd against Moore in the ongoing stand off.[63] The Albury Vine and Fruit Growers Association thought the Vine Diseases Board must be incompetent if reports were correct that vines condemned for destruction near Sydney continued to grow luxuriantly despite being allegedly riddled with phylloxera. Growers from the Murray region suspected the Board lacked sufficient knowledge of phylloxera to be able to deal with the outbreak, and that the seemingly arbitrary allocation of compensation led to injustice.[64] In an effort to clarify the situation, Moore explained that vines identified as infested could still produce fresh shoots which gave the appearance of vigour despite the presence of phylloxera. Really, he said, despite the deceptive health of condemned vines, the only sensible measure to prevent widespread devastation was eradicationism, to prevent further infestation since poisons had no effect whatsoever on the invading insect.[65]

In 1889, three vineyards were destroyed in the Parramatta district and members of the Vine Diseases Board travelled to Dubbo, in the Central West, to inspect suspected cases of phylloxera there.[66] The following year, responsibility for the administration of the *Vine Diseases Act* moved – with other matters relating to farming and grazing – from the colonial secretary to the secretary for mines and agriculture. The Vine Diseases Board animosity seemed to evaporate and the new focus on government support for primary industry led to the expansion of the anti-phylloxera bureaucracy in the principal grape growing districts: Cumberland, Hunter, and Murray River. Infected vineyards continued to be named and shamed.[67] Two years later, more than 1800 vineyards had been inspected and Pringle's sweep across the colony had reached the Hunter. Vines in the Paterson and Gresford districts were pronounced to be phylloxera-free.[68] Growers remained convinced that even if their vines did host phylloxera they could live with it rather than employing eradicationist policies.[69]

So what halted the invasion of the ruinous pest? Ultimately, the most effective solution emerged from studies in Europe, and involved grafting *vitis vinifera* – whose roots were vulnerable to attack from phylloxera – onto phylloxera-resistant American *vitis* root stock; a marriage of New and Old World grape vines.

In New South Wales, this process of grafting began to be used in the early 1890s. Staff at the Department of Agriculture requested via Saul Samuel, New South Wales agent-general in London, that Kew Gardens' director William Thiselton-Dyer recommend a French source of American vine cuttings to grow plants for grafting since none were available in Britain. Thiselton-Dyer had represented the Australian colonies at the 1882 conference on phylloxera in Bordeaux. He insisted there was too great a risk of importing phylloxera to New South Wales with American vine cuttings and that seeds were 'the only safe course' but the Department of Agriculture staff member would not accept more seeds. Samuel wrote with strong emphasis that the department wanted '*from France, at once, one hundred thousand cuttings* of phylloxera-proof vine stocks'. Thiselton-Dyer replied that he thought it folly but provided contact details in France just the same. Samuel agreed privately that importing vines could be a

MITCHELL LIBRARY, STATE LIBRARY OF NSW, GOVERNMENT PRINTING OFFICE 1 - 34570

A double cleft vine graft of vitis vinifera
onto phylloxera-resistant American vine stock,
performed at Howlong Viticultural Station and
showing the tools needed to complete the task.

risk to the wine industry in colonial Australia. Phylloxera had struck very
close to home for him; his own vineyard in the Central West of New South
Wales had recently been destroyed due to its level of infestation.[70]

From 1898, American vines obtained as a result of this correspondence
were planted at experimental farms managed by the Department of
Agriculture.[71] The Minister for Agriculture hoped this would 'guarantee
the permanency of the vine growing industry, even if the disease should
spread'.[72] Not since the distribution of vine cuttings by Charles Moore
from the Sydney Botanic Gardens in the 1850s had there been such public
investment in grape vine stock.

The New South Wales Department of Agriculture

Much of the credit for protecting vine growing in New South Wales was due to colonial government investment in agricultural support. This included specialist staff to oversee scientific developments and dissemination of knowledge for horticulture, with substantial attention to viticulture. The experts in this role were, first J. Adrien Despeissis until 1895 and Michele Blunno from 1896. Despeissis studied at England's Royal Agricultural College and Louis Pasteur's laboratory in France. Blunno trained in viticulture in France. Each travelled widely through the colony, published advice for growers in the new *Agricultural Gazette of New South Wales* and supervised work in vineyards at new experimental farms. Indeed, 'viticulture and the fruit industries attracted the earliest and greatest attention of the primary industries in existence in New South Wales when the Department was formed … and have the longest departmental history of any of the agricultural industries'.[73]

From its first issue in 1890 the *Gazette* recognised that the French Government's library on phylloxera, for instance, demonstrated the importance of storehouses of knowledge and pathways for its transmission from the wider world and within the colony for the benefit of all of the agricultural classes (smallholders to pastoralists with large sheep and cattle runs). The *Gazette*'s founding editor predicted the publication could also communicate colonial knowledge to the wider world. At 'the present time', he said, 'we have been the happy recipients of the experience of many civilised countries, but have not been able to sufficiently reciprocate these courtesies'.[74]

Wagga Wagga Experiment Farm, established in 1892, included a small vineyard to produce grafted plant stock. From 1900, Howlong Viticultural Station near Albury provided phylloxera-resistant rooted vines and training in vine growing. When phylloxera was detected at Howlong in the 1920s, the site was sold to the South Australian Phylloxera Board for experimentation.[75] The spread of the vine louse around Albury contributed to the end of vine growing there despite the survival of wine grapes just over the border at Rutherglen in Victoria.

Ampelographic confusion (difficulty in identifying vine varieties) which plagued early colonial wine growing began to ease under the expertise of Despeissis and Blunno. Despessis, for example, shared knowledge of Italian grape varieties. In New South Wales these were fostered mainly by Thomas Fiaschi at Tizzana on the Hawkesbury. Seven Italian varieties were doing well in the colony into the early 1890s: Barbarossa in a vineyard at Wellington and one at Wagga Wagga (which also grew Malvasia); Barbera Fina of Asti, which Fiaschi reported existed in small vineyards in the Cumberland district. At Fiaschi's Tizzana: San Gioveto, Canaiulo Nero, Mammolo, Malvasia and Aleatico. These varieties were described as all being suitable for wine, often in blends rather than a single varietal and Malvasia could also be sold as a table grape.[76]

In an act of settlerist ingenuity, British brothers John and Fred Wilkinson trained formally in Europe prior to migrating to New South Wales in the 1860s: John studied wine science with the German chemist Baron Justus Liebig and learned about German wine growing in Hochheim (home of Hock) while Fred trained in Burgundy.[77] The Wilkinsons' first vine plantings at Oakdale, in the Hunter Valley, in 1866 were followed by other family vineyards: Côte d'Or, Mangerton, Coolalta and Maluna. To finance family ventures, Fred managed Wyndham's Bukkulla at Inverell in an era which built its reputation. He also worked for Alexander Munro at Bebeah in the Hunter.[78]

While some training in vine growing had been established in New South Wales, there was not yet sufficient demand for a viticultural college and engagement with new wine science did not match that of grape growing. Not all grape growers could afford to own a winery. Colonists interested in wine science were those investing in vine cultivation through to manufacture. The capital investment required for wine presses, fermentation vats, barrels for storage and transport, horses or bullocks and drays to carry barrels, exceeded the income of many grape growers.

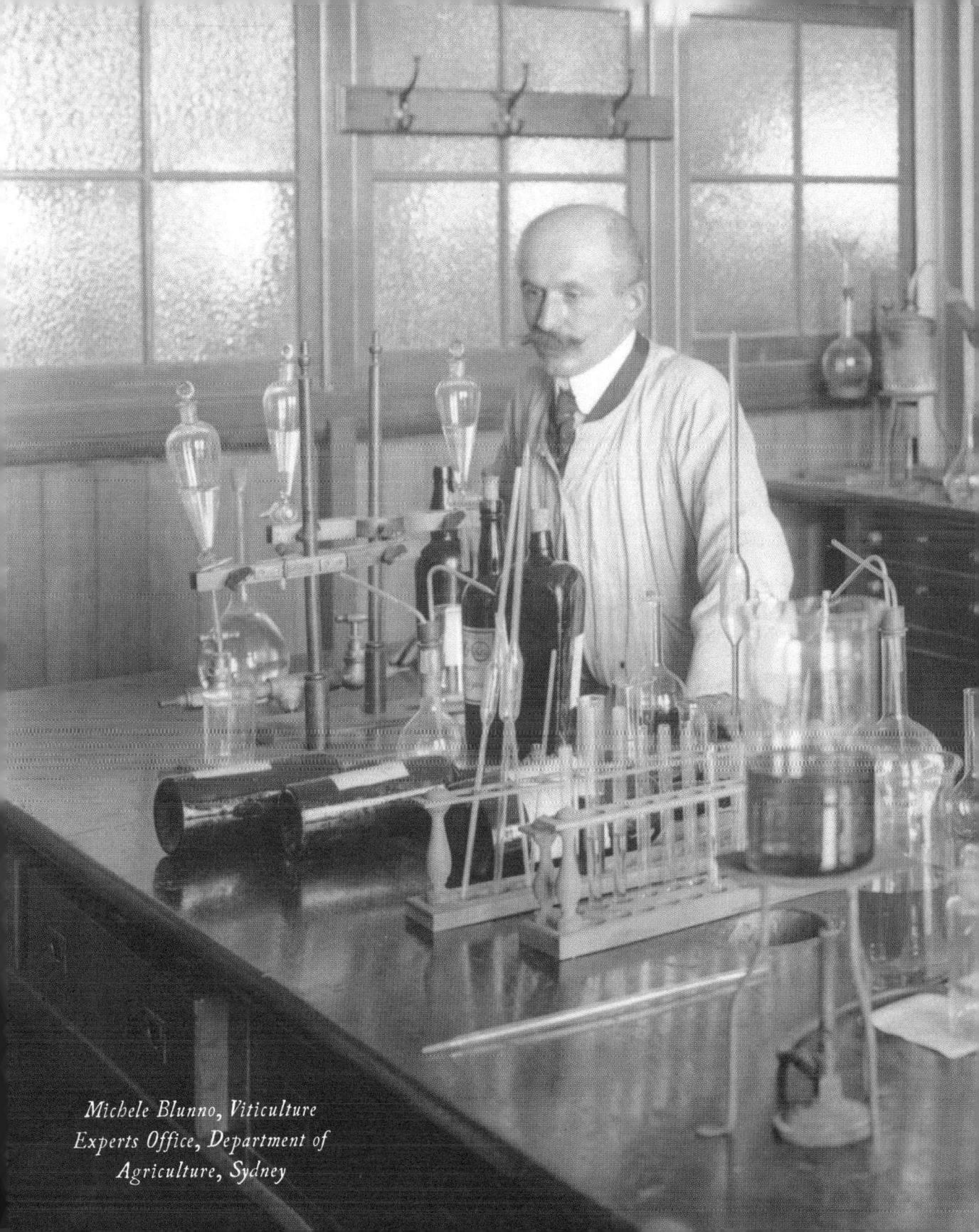

Michele Blunno, Viticulture
Experts Office, Department of
Agriculture, Sydney

MITCHELL LIBRARY, STATE LIBRARY OF NSW, GOVERNMENT PRINTING OFFICE 1 - 3267

Thomas Fiaschi, Hawkesbury wine grower, early importer of Italian grape varieties and president of the New South Wales branch of the Australian Medical Association from 1880–87

Thomas Fiaschi.
1889-90.

MITCHELL LIBRARY, STATE LIBRARY OF NSW, PXA 9-1 NO. 2

Wine science

William Macarthur, James King and James Fallon were early proponents of engagement with wine science. Macarthur and King corresponded with Liebig, whose 1840 report to the British Association – titled *Organic Chemistry in its Applications to Agriculture and Physiology* – marked the beginning of modern agricultural science.[79] Liebig conducted some of the first formal viticultural experiments with his work on manuring vineyards to increase grape yield and health. He also carried out revolutionary studies of the role of yeasts and sugars in wine fermentation and on oxidisation as a cause of wine spoilage. In 1849, the *Sydney Morning Herald* reprinted an article by Thomas Banfield, a specialist on the agriculture of Rhinegau in Germany. Banfield recognised – in the inverse style of one looking from the centre of empire to its periphery – that newer wine countries could just as readily apply new science as the ancient industries of Europe.

DRAYTON'S FAMILY WINES, MITCHELL LIBRARY, STATE LIBRARY OF NSW

Pokolbin winery and homestead of the Drayton family who arrived in the Hunter Valley in 1853. Photograph taken in 1900.

MITCHELL LIBRARY, STATE LIBRARY OF NSW, GOVERNMENT PRINTING OFFICE 1 - 34310

*Flourishing Chasselas Napoleon grapes at
Howlong Viticultural Station*

Workers cleaning the basket press at McWilliam's Mount Pleasant, Pokolbin. Photograph by Max Dupain c1950.

It will not appear singular [he wrote] that principles for wine-making should be wanted in distant colonies, when we consider that, with all the progress that has been made in chemical experiments, the true principle which ensures a constant quality of wine from the same grape, when ripened equally, has only within a few years been established satisfactorily in Europe.[80]

Banfield agreed with Liebig's findings on manuring but held that his recommendations for new methods of fermentation were harmful to wine flavour. Liebig's ideas may have come to colonial attention as a result of Banfield's critique as King and Macarthur sent wine samples to Liebig soon after.

Two years later King received a reply which he shared with the Hunter River Vineyard Association. King's red wine, according to Liebig, had 'many properties in common with Burgundy ... It might be possible to procure a sale for this wine in England and Russia, were you to succeed by carefully conducted fermentation, in producing a stronger bouquet'.[81] German wine expert F. Gerstaeker paid a visit to King's winery at Irrawang near Raymond Terrace, north of Newcastle in 1852. Gerstaeker believed King's white wine to be 'equal to our German hochheimer', a red 'equal' to Asmannhauser, and that Australia would 'some day become an extraordinary country for wine'.[82] In 1856 King met with Liebig in Munich, which he reported on with relish in his 1857 publication *Australia May Be an Extensive Wine-Growing Country*.

A decade later European scientists Ludwig Thudichum and August Dupre made enemies in colonial New South Wales when their *Treatise on the Origin, Nature, and Varieties of Wine; Being a complete manual of viticulture and oenology* (1872) declared the high level of alcohol in wine from the warmer regions of the colony resulted from fortification with grape spirit. Albury wine grower and merchant James Fallon knew this to be untrue and travelled to London to challenge the claim in an address to the (now Royal) Society for the Arts. With Thudichum in his audience, Fallon argued that not only were Australian wines unfortified but Thudichum and Dupre's misguided pronouncement created unnecessary obstacles to their competitiveness in the British market. (Wines of alcohol

NATIONAL LIBRARY OF AUSTRALIA, PIC/8729/15 LOC ALBUM 757

levels higher than 26 per cent were generally fortified and therefore, in this age of social reforms to reduce alcohol consumption, taxed at higher than the base rate of one shilling per gallon.) Thudichum protested loudly at Fallon's statement that Australian wines *naturally* exceeded 26 per cent; this, he declared, 'would simply upset the whole scientific facts hitherto established in the world'.[83] Fallon refused to be intimidated and demanded

"Oakdale" Vintage Staff 1919

AUDREY WILKINSON WINES

Monier concrete vats were installed at Audrey Wilkinson's Oakdale at the turn of the century.

the testing of colonial wines to show they were not fortified, as a way to settle the matter.[84]

In 1876 Fallon returned to London with the results of the tests of grape sugar which showed that out of twenty-three samples of unfortified wines, only one potentially fell below the level of 26 per cent naturally occurring alcohol. Questions were raised about the methods used to achieve these results. Thudichum said they were not valid since they were not conducted on grape must or at fine enough a level of weighing the density of the sugars. He demanded further studies. Fallon replied that all involved in the testing had been satisfied the results were reliable and saw no need to repeat them.

> " Fallon demanded the testing of colonial wines to show they were not fortified.

In a victory for Fallon's campaign for 'fair trade without favour', Britain's *Wine Trade Review* supported Fallon against Thudichum. According to its reporter, the chemist spoke 'in bad taste' against the colonial experiments. Several members of the Royal Society expressed support for 'pure natural' colonial wine and suggested improvements to the way in which it was transported to avoid spoiling.[85] Fallon's efforts paid off in the introduction of a sliding scale of duties on colonial wines.[86]

Technology

Apart from increasingly complex networks and energy technologies for transport on river, road and rail the principal technological changes for the wine industry in the nineteenth century occurred in manufacturing.

Presses to crush harvested grapes could be as simple or as sophisticated as a grower could afford. Very early in the century, Blaxland devised a wooden press with the help of a Sydney carpenter but reported a cheese press worked just as well.[87] By the 1870s, growers used log presses and designs were available for lever presses and screw jack presses. Basket

A Continuous Wine-press.

WHILE on a visit to the Goulburn Valley, Victoria, early in April last, I saw at the Chateau Dookie vineyards one of the above continuous wine-presses. Mr. François de Castella, the manager of this gigantic vineyard, informed me that it would be next to an impossibility to get through the vintage of this 600 acres of full-bearing vines in good time without the use of this great labour-saving appliance. The grapes are pressed in a perforated cylinder, as shown, and

every particle of juice extracted; the mark is ejected almost dry. By means of the press the first must from the grapes may be kept separate from the second pressing. The press when in full work is capable of putting through from 45 to 50 tons of grapes per day. The work is got through much more expeditiously and simply than with the best of the old wine-presses.

I am indebted to the proprietors of *The Australasian* for the excellent block to illustrate this press.—J. L. THOMPSON.

H

AGRICULTURAL GAZETTE OF NEW SOUTH WALES, VOL. 10, AUGUST 1899, F. 837, MITCHELL LIBRARY, STATE LIBRARY OF NSW, ML 630.5/6 VOL.10, P. 837

Victorian wine grower Francois de Castella's continuous wine press which could crush 45–50 tons of grapes a day presses also became commonly used. In the late nineteenth century the *Agricultural Gazette* published a line drawing of the elaborate machine used at the Victorian winery of Francois de Castella where 600 acres of bearing vines required a machine that could press 45–50 tons of grapes a day.[88]

Of 360 wine presses in operation in New South Wales in 1888, most were in the principal wine growing areas of the Hunter, the Riverina and Sydney districts. There were also clusters of presses in districts such as the Hastings, Manning, and Inverell, as well as a handful at smaller centres and sometimes a single press operating within an electorate.[89] Compared with the number of vignerons (see Appendix 2) we can see many growers did not own a press so must have sold their grapes to a winery.[90] When rain destroyed the fruit crop at Liverpool in outer Sydney, a local report predicted a co-operative wine pressing enterprise would do well in the district.[91]

In the 1850s, William Macarthur's German vinedressers built magnificent stone fermenting vats at Camden Estate, the ruins of which can be seen in a horse paddock close to a former vineyard site on the banks of the Nepean River. Other producers used old wine and spirits barrels or new wooden tubs until the innovation of cement vats such as those installed by the Wilkinsons at Oakdale in the early 1900s.

Wine barrels were often reused rather than imported new from oak plantations in the northern hemisphere. A French newspaper report in the 1880s blamed poor colonial wine production on the practice of storing wine in old European 'port, sherry, or brandy casks ... which tends to alter the character of the wines'.[92] Experiments with a range of Australian woods in New South Wales cooperage (barrel-making) met with mixed success.[93]

Saccharometers to measure grape sugars were in common use in New South Wales by the early 1850s.[94] In the late 1860s, the Hunter Valley's William Keene designed a saccharometer which came to be widely employed by colonial vignerons and James Fallon's saccharometer is still in use at Helm Wines, Murrumbateman.

Meanwhile, the wine industry benefited from advances in the bottling

NATIONAL LIBRARY OF AUSTRALIA. FLAGOV.AU.NLA.PIC.AN10691841

Horsley Park, western Sydney, wine grower working his screw jack press in 1900. Photograph by Henry King.

and storage technology used in brewing and soft drink manufacture. As with the labour-saving principles of wine presses, bottling machines created the potential for increased production. But, in the early twentieth century, bottled wine had not yet conquered the Australian market as it would a hundred years later.[95]

Modernity

As a product of modernity, Australian vine growing and wine making emerged alongside scientific viticulture and wine science. In Europe, by contrast, historically entrenched and widespread cultivation of wine grapes and making of wine underwent an astonishing arc of change as powdery mildew and phylloxera profoundly disrupted traditions of wine trade and consumption. Old World wine production is the product of modernity as much as New World wine, but European producers have resisted the growth of New World wine industries as competitors for the global wine glass by linking the very idea of wine authenticity and quality to their greater antiquity in wine production. In the 1880s, for example, a French writer marshalled his country's ancient links to wine growing as a sign of its greater skill and authenticity. The Australian colonies were, said the Frenchman, too young to make good wine.[96]

One of the most ambitious expressions of nationalist modernity in early twentieth century Australia created the Riverina farming district which now hosts the largest New South Wales wine producing region. From 1901, with the Federation of the colonies, the new Australian Government encouraged progress and improvement though projects such as the Murrumbidgee Irrigation Area. This scheme exploited emerging innovations in science and engineering to re-direct river flows to vast acreages of land lacking sufficient rainfall to produce water intensive food crops. New environmental knowledge has meant this scheme is no longer celebrated as a nationalist achievement and instead excites controversy but limits on water allocations from the irrigation scheme are of great concern

New technology: a 1930s corking machine. Photography by Sam Hood.

to Riverina wine growers who depend on them.[97] How to balance the environmental costs of wine modernity and wine success has become a twenty-first century challenge.

We have seen that New South Wales produced significant quantities of wine during the nineteenth century in the early phases of experimentation, long before Australia became a wine drinking country; but how did this wine actually taste?

DRAYTON'S FAMILY WINES

Old log press, on display at Drayton's Family Wines, Pokolbin

MCWILLIAM'S WINES

Wine production just over a decade after the launch of the Murrumbidgee Irrigation Scheme

Beelbangera Winery

Taste

Like wine from all wine countries, early New South Wales wines varied from undrinkable to highly-praised. At first New South Wales wines had the advantage of novelty value but this could only go so far in creating a market at home or overseas. Early Australian wines started well back in the hierarchy of prized imports to the large market in Britain compared with the familiar wines of Europe and European colonies against which they were constantly measured. Over many decades, however, colonists who were predisposed to New South Wales wines – usually producers themselves – provided a crucial testing ground for persistent efforts to create marketable styles. This occurred first in the grand homes of wine squires and other powerful families then, increasingly in the competitive and socially diverse environments of vineyard associations and regional shows, grand international and inter-colonial exhibitions. New South Wales producers worked hard to earn symbolic value: a taste *for* their wines as well as the taste *of* them but influencing wine culture would prove even more difficult than creating a vineyard culture. New South Wales wines were served to acclaim at royal tables in Britain but rarely warmed the bellies of the populous working classes of the colony. And whether to imitate familiar imported wines or to create new styles continually vexed colonial producers.

So how did the earliest New South Wales wines actually taste? If bottles of Rose Hill wine did indeed travel from Sydney to London with Arthur Phillip in 1792, as mentioned in Chapter 4, then we have a tiny precious detail from Blumenbach that the red wine was *strong*. Although it would be marvellous if this wine came from Sydney, this remains a mystery. In which case, let's fast forward thirty years for a glimpse of Blaxland's first contribution to the Society for the Arts in 1822, the first colonial wine officially tasted at the centre of empire where symbolic value or *distinction* was determined. The Society's committee judged Blaxland's wine to be light (not especially high in alcohol) but sound (not spoiled) 'with much of the odour and flavour of ordinary Claret, or rather, holding an intermediate place between that wine and the red wine of Nice'.[1] This implies a blend of Cabernet Sauvignon, Merlot, Cabernet Franc and a Grenache or Cinsault.[2] Blaxland had made it from a single variety. As discussed in Chapter 5, this may have been Cape Pontac. James Busby compared Blaxland's wine to Burgundy, and an 1830s writer in South Africa claimed Pontac produced wine similar to red Burgundy.[3] Essentially, however, the Society's judges tasted the wine with a view to what New South Wales could become and erred towards a favourable impression. They wanted evidence that hopes for the colony to produce wine had some foundation.

Contingencies of empire trade in the early part of the nineteenth century meant New South Wales wine producers were looking not just to the British home market but to British colonists in India. In 1822, John Macarthur junior, eldest son of Elizabeth and John senior and the family's first agent in London, urged his brother James to trumpet the acclimatisation of Mediterranean cultivars in the colony. 'I need hardly repeat', wrote John to his brother, 'that none of your pursuits are viewed with more interest than the cultivation of the olive and the vine ... [T]here is a prevailing horticultural mania here which makes it highly desirous that you should communicate your progress'. One powerful British gentleman, for instance, 'would be delighted to have a bottle of olives and I hardly know what he would not say in return for a bottle of wine'.[4] Two years later, John senior wrote to John junior that William had made a wine that resembled Hock which he hoped might find a market in India.[5]

In 1832, William Macarthur judged the year-old wines from his first vineyard to be sound but of common quality. The best he could say in a letter to his brother Edward was that they did 'not possess any particularly disagreeable flavour'. His brandy was promising, however, and he intended to send some of each to London. But 'if I do send them', said William, 'remember it is only to satisfy any curiosity upon the subject, and not because we think them worth sending halfway round the world, or indeed a twentieth part of the distance!' He knew Edward would want to promote the wines if they were fit for it, to create a taste *for* them. Plus I suspect William to have been not only a pragmatist but in possession of a very dry sense of humour. Despite his keen perception of the limitations of this wine, William intended to substantially extend his vineyard planting.[6]

> "
> The Bordeaux merchant thought it resembled 'port without brandy'.

When James Busby returned to England to argue against his sacking as head of the colony's agricultural school, he took wine made from vines he had planted at the school, though the wine had been made by his successor Richard Sadleir. Busby believed the quality of the wine to be 'very fair' despite the youth of the vines. What did it taste like? In the qualified opinions of Oporto and Bordeaux wine merchants: 'promising'. The Bordeaux merchant thought it resembled 'port without brandy' as it had not been fortified during fermentation. A bottle of the Sadleir wine, which Busby had with him when he returned to Sydney (so that it had travelled halfway around the world and *back again*), he pronounced to be sound, well-flavoured and strong-bodied.[7] Sadleir claimed many years later that he drank only colonial wine after making his first vintage in 1825.[8]

In 1839, Lady Jane Franklin, wealthy peregrinating wife of the governor of Van Diemen's Land, visited James King's Irrawang winery and pottery at the urging of her host in the Hunter Valley, Henry Carmichael. There she tasted 'white Rhenish sort of wine and red wine' and though they showed potential she liked to hear her colony's wines praised more highly than those of mainland Australia. She agreed with a travel escort who thought 'Tasmanian wine superior to Australian'.[9]

By 1844, William Macarthur began to sell bottled wine through Robert Porter's George Street, Sydney warehouse. Porter promoted it as Pure Camden Wine, a 'valuable produce of Australia', sure to become 'an important article of export from these shores' which could stave off 'misery and ruin' at a cost of 15 shillings per dozen bottles or 6 shillings a gallon.[10] The label designed for the Camden wine, with its fine detail of a grape vine in full fruit remained the same from its first use until as late as 1876.[11] Grape variety and vintage were written in to distinguish individual varieties. Sydney merchants Joubert & Murphy stocked Camden wine and it must have assisted these first experiments in colonial wine retail that Didier Joubert had been a Bordeaux wine merchant. 'We need not recommend you', Joubert wrote to William, 'to select the best you have now ready, as you are aware that we sell it as *Camden Wine* and endeavour to establish its character as a good and wholesome wine'.[12]

William sent eleven cases of Camden wine to India, but it did not travel well. The sediment had still not settled nearly two months after the wine arrived (a month was usually judged to be sufficient to allow sediment to clear after being shaken up during travel). The Calcutta agent advised the wine 'would make a pleasant drink in the hot weather' *but* 'people are so cautious of drinking wine which may disagree with them that it is very difficult to introduce any wine into this Country that is not commonly had, however good it may be'.[13] 1844 proved to be a crucial year in William's enterprise. He created a new vineyard, established an agent to sell plant stock, including vine cuttings in Melbourne, and also confirmed sales of altar wine to the Catholic Church in New South Wales.[14]

In 1849, Camden wine sales extended to Parramatta, where a shopkeeper stocked it at 10 shillings a gallon. The *Sydney Morning Herald* recommended the price be kept low 'in order to give the laboring classes the opportunity of using this beautiful beverage in preference to stupefying ale, or the grossly adulterated spirits, for which such an enormous sum is annually sent out of the colony'.[15] Was the beverage beautiful because it was a light form of alcohol in a small sea of spirits, or because it was of superior taste? Either way, Camden wine did develop ample reputation to attract the flattery and frustration of fraudulent imitations in the colonial market from 1850.[16]

Grape varieties or wine names could be written onto the Macarthurs' labels, which were in use from as early as 1844 up to the 1870s. This label is from the few still extant at Camden Estate.

ROSIE MARSON

Wine shows, associations and exhibitions

In 1847, when a wine from his Winbourne property won third place at the Richmond Show just outside Sydney, George Cox suspected the wine that took first prize was an *imported* sherry.[17] This inauspicious moment in the emerging practice of colonial wine judging belied the value of agricultural shows in fostering a culture of comparison and improvement.[18] With the first incarnation of the Agricultural Society of New South Wales formed in 1824, the first products attracting competition prizes were livestock, cheese and beer. The following year, the society added prizes for wine, sherry, peach cider and tobacco produced in the colony.[19] Shows and regular tastings among members of organisations such as the Hunter River Vineyard Association (HRVA) refined the quality of wine production.[20]

Organised societies and associations served a vital role in increasing knowledge of wine growing from vine to glass. The Western Australia Vineyard Society, the first to meet in the Australian colonies, in 1842, established an experiment to test vine cultivars which members hoped would become a model.[21] In New South Wales, the geographic and social fragmentation of settlement coupled with the 1840s Depression and the 1850s gold rushes left the colony without even an umbrella agricultural and horticultural society in the two decades from 1836. The *Sydney Gazette* lobbied vigorously for the revival of a colony-wide society from 1841 but, as historian Brian Fletcher has shown, circumstances were hardly favourable: 'few of the larger settlers could have been in any position to contemplate forming agricultural societies at a time when they were struggling to remain solvent'.[22] Separate societies were formed in the early settled districts from 1827, when the Hunter River Farmers' Club promoted agriculture, including viticulture. Its inaugural president, James Webber, was a known vine grower at Tocal in the Hunter region. The colony's first specialist society, the HRVA, formed ten years before the revival of the New South Wales Agricultural and Horticultural Society in 1857.

The Kelman family vineyard at Kirkton remained in production throughout the nineteenth century. This medal was awarded for best four bottles of wine at the Northern Agricultural Association Singleton Show in 1869.

MITCHELL LIBRARY, STATE LIBRARY OF NSW, CALL NO. R 499

The HRVA grew out of the Hunter River Agricultural Society (HRAS) when members divided over supporting viticulture. A chief dispute related to the payment of workers in wine at estates with vineyards, a practice which allegedly attracted labourers away from other properties during the depression of the forties. Hostility rose further at an HRAS dinner in 1846 when Henry Carmichael declared grape vines a more important crop than wheat. A year later, similar comments led to uproar among members not growing grapes. Carmichael claimed wine had no less importance than the 'now much vaunted main staple, wool' and declared an acre of vines could be as profitable as 100 sheep; ten acres of vines, 10 000 sheep, an opinion which he would later revise.[23]

Carmichael subsequently formed the HRVA and its first members were high profile growers from the district: King, Kelman, Lang, Archibald Windeyer and others. Membership excluded those not involved in winegrowing, a key difference from the New South Wales Vineyard Association (NSWVA) which was more of an organisation of privilege and power than practical wine growing. All members of the Hunter group were to contribute to the combined knowledge of the Association at least once a year and provide at least four bottles of wine annually to be tasted and discussed by the group. These wine growers aimed to turn vine growing to 'the most profitable account'.[24] In 1850, a Perth newspaper anointed the HRVA as the most successful institution established to develop and exploit colonial resources due to its narrow focus and business-like approach.[25] By 1855, the HVRA claimed, during a visit by Governor William Denison to the Hunter, that their collective efforts had been highly fruitful. The Association presented Denison with a copy of a tract by King summarising their achievements (though King wrote mainly about himself) and declared, further, that their success had come through faith in the suitability of the region for wine growing, 'the outlay of a large amount of capital' and ongoing experimentation so that some of their wines were now comparable with those of France.[26]

The NSWVA was formed in Sydney in 1850, chiefly under the influence of William Macarthur and Edwin Hickey, a steamship entrepreneur who had the distinction of being the only joint member of the NSWVA and

MITCHELL LIBRARY, STATE LIBRARY OF NSW. PXA 4358/VC. 7 NO. 124A

*Stereographic card of the young Elizabeth Macarthur-Onslow,
second from left; William Macarthur, third from left and James
Macarthur, far right. Although second-generation Macarthurs
shared the administration of the family business, William controlled
the wine growing branch of manifold enterprises.*

HRVA. The group's membership comprised colonial figures across a diverse range of occupations but few growers with the same determination to turn a profit from wine as those in the Hunter. Those who exhibited wines in the first two years comprised a relatively short list: Macarthur, Cowper, Cox and Macleay, among others.[27] The demise of the NSWVA came with the formation of the Cumberland Agricultural Society in 1857, a collective which evolved into the more enduring Agricultural Society of New South Wales (ASNSW) in 1859; a shift which reflected the broader agricultural interests of members of the NSWVA.[28]

In a social environment with a small ruling class, there were many intersections in interests with other booster organisations such as the Australian Society, which also supported the vision for colonial wine. Prominent colonist and Society member Thomas Mort captured the tenor of an emerging Australian bush culture when he remarked that, 'some of the finest colonial wine [he had] tasted' had been manufactured in a slab hut at Bathurst. Mort made much too of the news that Camden wine had captured the notice of a Russian visiting London, who subsequently ordered six hogsheads of it.[29] Across the Pacific, the first society exclusively for grape and wine growers began in the United States in 1849 and the American Wine Growers' Association was chartered in Cincinnati in 1851.[30]

Occasion to test colonial wines in international competition first occurred in London in 1851. The Great Exhibition of the Works of Industry of all Nations showcased the rise of western modernity and in particular the perceived burgeoning glory of the British Empire. To house the exhibition, Hyde Park's Rotten Row in London was transformed with the construction of a dazzling engineering marvel, the Crystal Palace. Manufactured products and processes from around the world were exhibited. Its 'nearly religious aura' in the Australian colonies was spoiled only by a disappointing lack of Australian colonial exhibits, reportedly due to apathy on the part of all of the colonial governments.[31] The Macarthurs sent several products to London for the Exhibition, including Camden wine, for which William drafted a catalogue titled *Some Account of the Vineyards at Camden on the Nepean River* which someone (most likely

Vineyard associations were crucial for knowledge sharing and testing wine quality. Pokolbin Grape Growers and Wine Makers Association dinner, 1900.

TYRRELL'S WINES

his brother Edward) revised to be more of a marketing document than a flat-out frank appraisal of the wine.[32] William had elsewhere expressed the opinion that he had long thought Verdelho (a Madeira grape) 'the most valuable grape for wine we have hitherto proved in the colony'.[33] His wines for London included a Verdelho, a blend of La Folle and Verdelho, a White Muscat of Lunelle fortified with brandy, a Red and Black Muscat of Frontignac, a Riesling, a blend of Muscat Noir de Frontignac and La Folle, a Syrah grown from cuttings from Hermitage in France and an unfortified variation of the Red and Black Muscat of Frontignac.[34] How did they taste? According to *Some Account*:

> These wines have a certain dryness and bitterness peculiar to the wines of New South Wales to which the palate becomes accustomed. but with age this bitterness passes off, as in the specimens now in England. The Wines at Camden are rarely fit for use until three years old, and greatly improve by the keeping. They are very wholesome, and are extensively used by persons who have acquired a taste for them.[35]

The bitterness cannot have been tannic if the whites were affected as much as the reds, so was more likely the result of the need for further wine making experimentation. William recognised how a predisposition to drink the wines, the acquisition of familiarity with them, played a role in their success in the colony.

James King had intended to send samples from Irrawang as well as neighbouring Porphyry (where he made the wine for Carmichael) to the Great Exhibition but due to a mix-up in colonial administration his wines missed out. He became so upset that he publically maligned the Macarthurs. He then sold the bottles of wine he had intended to send to London, had second thoughts, bought them back from the purchaser and dispatched them to London himself: directly to Prince Albert.

The Macarthurs ignored King's churlishness and when a royal response to the Hunter Valley wines arrived in the colony, William reported it to a meeting of the NSWVA. 'The white wine was considered neither good nor bad', began the letter to King, 'but the red, a sort of Burgundy or Hermitage, was considered excellent. It was tried at several parties at the palace, and deemed excellent at all of them, being allowed to take its chance at table, and being left to the opinion of the guests'.[36] King's antipathy seemed assuaged by the letter from the palace and William's public approbation for it. At a subsequent meeting of the HRVA, King said his earlier pejorative remarks about the Macarthurs were not intended 'in a spirit of silly cavil or childish antagonism'.[37] King knew royal assent went a long way to capturing elusive but much needed symbolic value for his wines and those of the colony more broadly.

A great clamour of excitement in New South Wales and the other Australian colonies followed the announcement of a Paris Exhibition in 1855 to rival the Crystal Palace event. William Macarthur served as a Colonial Commissioner for this exhibition and produce from Camden and Irrawang formed the principal part of the New South Wales display of wine, alongside other Hunter wines such as Maria Windeyer's from Tomago in the lower valley, Lindeman's Cawarra and wines made at Kaludah at Lochinvar by Philobert Terrier.

> It was tried at several parties at the palace, and deemed excellent at all of them.

The Macarthurs sent a range of their colonial primary produce to Paris but William's letters home to James were full of news of the wine.[38] Before the New South Wales wines were judged, he made sure to watch the Paris wine jurors. At first, the experience of witnessing the judges testing upwards of a 150 wines in a single sitting left William 'in a funk for our wine'; not at all sure that New South Wales would do well in such a competitive environment. But, when at 8 o'clock the next morning the tasting of the New South Wales wines began, according to his report, 'there was a long pause at the tasting of the first King's red of 1852, a look of surprise, and then of approval, "*jolie vin*" "tres bon"… and *ten* called out'.[39] (Scores were given out of twenty.) After the judging was over, William calculated 'the averages of the six samples from Irrawang, was 10-and-a-half to that of samples of Camden Wine [which] was 11-and-two-thirds'. Camden from King's Irrawang by a nose!

William later mustered the courage to speak to one of the Exhibition judges and was told the panel had been 'perfectly astonished at the quality of the Australian wines'; indeed, these experts had thought 'it [was] evident that in addition to soil and climate favourable to their growth, first care must have been taken in their manufacture ... They do your colony infinite credit', the judge said. William then asked him to which more established wines could the colonial wines be compared. The judge replied that he and his peers 'were unanimous in giving them a place in strength and flavour between the wines of *Madeira* and those of the *Cotes du Rhone* – they have some resemblance to both (William's emphasis)'. William went on to say to James, 'I cannot describe the number of applications as have since had to be showed to taste'.[40]

The *pièce de résistance* in hopes for a taste *for* colonial wines came the day after the judging when Queen Victoria and her entourage stopped at the New South Wales exhibit and she asked to try the wines. With this, New South Wales wine earned an enormous investment of symbolic capital in Paris and also in London, which was then communicated to the whole British World.[41] *The Times of London* reported that during the Queen and Prince Albert's visit to the Paris Exhibition, 'Mr Macarthur was too modest to tell the Prince a "fact" which is creating a great sensation here, viz. that Australia exhibits wine of extraordinary excellence, Tokay especially being fairer than the best produced in Hungary'.[42] Really it was outrageous to claim colonial Tokay was finer than genuine Tokaji at this stage but the favourable comparisons to Old World wine were no doubt welcome in New South Wales. King and Windeyer also received honours for their wines at Paris.[43]

At the 1855 exhibition Napoleon III announced the five-tier Bordeaux Classification of Growths which ushered in the first stage of the Frenchification of world wine over the subsequent century, as discussed in Chapter 1. Delightfully, in the heady climate of success for New South Wales wine in Paris, the *Times* predicted that, 'in a few years we hope to see the names of Camden Park, Irrawang, Tomago, Lochinvar, Cawarra, Tuteela, etc. rank as high in the wine-market as Lafite, Latour, Chateau-Margaux'. Wines, the *Times* effused, would surely soon equal 'wool, tallow, gold and coal' as export commodities from eastern Australia.[44]

Certificate of merit awarded to Maria Windeyer at the Paris Exhibition, 1855 for her Tomago wine. The certificate is signed by Napoleon III, architect of the Bordeaux Classifications which began the Frenchification of wine.

EXPOSITION UNIVERSELLE DE 1855

INDUSTRIE BEAUX-ARTS

LE JURY INTERNATIONAL

DÉCERNE

La Mention honorable

à M.me Windeyer — (Nouvelle-Galles-du-Sud),

pour ses vins de Tomago;

Exposant du Royaume uni de Grande-Bretagne & d'Irlande

Division de l'Industrie — 11.e Classe — N.o

Palais de l'Industrie

Paris le 15. Novembre 1855.

Le Président de la Commission Impériale

Napoléon Bonaparte

MITCHELL LIBRARY, STATE LIBRARY OF NSW, A 382

Sydney International Exhibition 1879–80,
Garden Palace. Wine prize winners included
Mudgee grower, Fred Bucholtz.

MITCHELL LIBRARY, STATE LIBRARY OF NSW, GOVERNMENT PRINTING OFFICE 1 — 35130

What in actual fact transpired from the showing in Paris was that growers and agricultural societies gained leverage to seek support from the British government and 'overseas learned societies' to promote colonial wine in Europe.[45]

New South Wales exhibitors commended for their wine at the next International Exhibition, in London in 1862, included experienced as well as new growers from a variety of districts in the colony; among them William Lawson's daughter Rebecca Bettington.[46] Exhibitions became a regular feature of wine quality testing. At the World's Columbian Exhibition in Chicago in 1893 more than fifty prizes were awarded to producers from throughout the colony's wine producing regions.[47] Most of the winners listed were from family enterprises and they represented the main areas of production in this period: the Hunter, the Riverina, the Central West and New England.

Exports

After success in Paris in 1855, producers from all of the Australian wine colonies received a rush of orders from Britain but the export of close to 25 000 gallons (from New South Wales, Victoria and South Australia combined) represented a clearing of stockpiles and would not be repeated again until a decade later.[48] One British exhibition official thought the Australian colonies scoring as high as Austrian wines and much higher than those from the Cape suggested Australian wines might serve as a replacement for dwindling supplies from Madeira and elsewhere due to the destruction of powdery mildew. 'At present there is scarcely a person in England (except those who have been to the colonies)', he said, 'who has tasted any of this wine, and there are also great numbers who do not even know that wine is made there at all; this, I think, ought not to be'.[49] There were critics, however. One correspondent to the *Times* sought to dispel any illusions about the potential for colonial wine. He said:

cultivation of the vine in Australia is as yet only the pursuit of a few wealthy landowners, who carry it on in the spirit of amateurs, as a branch of horticulture. It is more a fancy than an industry; and has not told with any appreciable effect on the taste or commerce of the colony. Hence, though we hear frequently of the wine of Australia, it is all sample and no bulk. It figures prominently in reports, as now in Paris, and in nearly all the books about the colony; but it has not yet found its way into the cellars and ledgers of 'the trade'.[50]

True, New South Wales producers needed a greater volume of wine to be able to translate symbolic value from international exhibitions into actual sales. But, to be fair, vine growing had only been pursued in New South Wales for seventy years.

> Fallon claimed that he held the largest store of first-class Australian wines in the world.

Fallon could later claim, as part of his marketing material for sales into Victoria that he held the largest store of first-class Australian wines in the world. His exports across the border into the neighbouring colony included Riesling, Verdelho, Shiraz and Cabernet (presumably Cabernet Sauvignon), which he guaranteed were of better quality and greater purity (free of spirits) than wines from outside of Australia. When Fallon headed a delegation of colonial representatives to visit British Chancellor of the Exchequer, Stafford Northcote, over the wine tariffs issue in 1876, the Chancellor asked 'whether there was much difference between the wines of Australia, whether there was a taste for those wines in this country, and where the demand for them was likely to arise – whether from the upper classes or from the general consumer'. Fallon said he thought Australian wines would appeal to the general consumer, 'as they possessed a peculiar flavour and quality of their own. They had some difficulty at first in getting these wines consumed in the Australian colonies themselves, but they were now generally consumed' though the export trade was 'but in its infancy'.[51]

How were New South Wales wines received in other colonies? Prior to Federation, Victoria had high tariffs to protect its wine industry against imports. This protectionism encouraged local production but also raised the costs of technology and New South Wales producers still exported to Victoria: Macarthur and Fallon among them. South Australian wines had more effective distribution structures, which gave them an advantage after 1901.[52] While wine growing seems to have made little impact on the New South Wales debate about Federation, South Australia's largest wine grower and distributer, Thomas Hardy, lobbied vigorously for the union of the Australian colonies and the removal of intercolonial trade barriers. The 'yes' vote for Federation was over 85 per cent in South Australian wine growing districts compared with an average of 66 per cent for the state as a whole.[53] Hardy sought wines from other colonies and in fact paid generous compliments to dry table wines from Dalwood estate in the Hunter, as described in Chapter 11.

Taste of *terroir* [54]

The word *terroir* appeared in colonial wine discourse from the 1840s as a means of distinguishing wines from each other; that is, as 'the natural *goût de terroir*, or that arising from the nature of the soil itself'.[55] But, in reference to colonial Australian wines, *goût de terroir* came to mean tasting *like* soil as opposed to *of the soil* and distinctive natural environment of its region, as we understand it now. In the second half of the nineteenth century, Australian colonial wine growers debated how to remove this flaw, which particularly afflicted red wines and probably resulted from inexperienced winemaking. Then, in 1908 there was a tremendous breakthrough in the long-fought effort to correct this taste *of* some wines and capture the British palate. At least three Australian newspapers on the same day reported that British merchants had tasted colonial Australian wines at the Franco-Britain Exhibition and declared a 'remarkable improvement ... There is a notable absence in the New South Wales wines ... of the unpleasant "terroir", or earthy taste, which is frequently present in Australian wine'.[56] The quest for this improvement underlines the challenge for wine makers to begin to find a market as they experimented with grape varieties and

MITCHELL LIBRARY, STATE LIBRARY OF NSW, CALL NUMBER: HOME AND AWAY - 7059

Woman drinking sparkling white wine c1930. Photograph by Sam Hood.

learned their craft, with little opportunity for formal training, and at the same time competing with established European wines being imported continuously into Australia and the wider British World.

Whereas the results of early Old World wine experimentation had been lost to memory, poor wine production could not be concealed in New South Wales in an era of emerging mass communication and competitive wine business. First director of the Department of Agriculture HCL Anderson recognised export might not succeed until Australian producers were not compelled to sell their wines to be made into blends of doubtful origin by Old World vintners *and* Australian consumers embraced their own wine over imported brands:

> When our upper classes will have ceased to consider it *infra dig* to place colonial wines on the table, and our lower classes will have learned to appreciate the light wines of this colony as the natural drink of this country, we shall be able to provide a home consumption for our own produce instead of sending it to England and France to be manipulated and returned to ourselves as Spanish port, German hock, and French clarets.[57]

This chimed with advice to producers and consumers on regionality in Muskett's *Art of Living*. In his chapter on wine, Muskett recommended how to taste imported wine as a refined art form as well as a means through which to improve Australian wines by encouraging imitation. He said that although champagne appears to be the 'highest type of wine ... an imperial drink', to be able to knowledgably discuss the great wines of Burgundy and Bordeaux constituted the higher expression of sophistication. This knowledge 'will do more to better the quality of our Australian wines than anything I know of'. He shared too the opinion of Victoria's Francois de Castella that wine growers should focus on regionality. By forming regional vineyard associations and within these associations developing particular grape varieties suited to their district, growers could assist merchants to talk more clearly with consumers about what to expect from their wines.[58]

A century later this is exactly what has happened.

10

The rise of regionality

Wines from New South Wales regions are the product of more than 200 years of risk, experimentation, co-operation and competition. Wine modernity means that very fine wines are made from multi-region grapes and excellent single varietals representing single regions may be crushed and fermented many kilometres from where the grapes were grown. Still, regionality represents nuanced and often historic connections between people, vines, wine and place. Of the wine growing districts discussed in this book, some – western Sydney, Camden and Albury – exist only in history. A few early locations have a continual story but many have links to a wine growing past which has vanished from national and sometimes even local memory. Although ebbs and flows of vineyard expansion, contraction and regrowth have shaped and reshaped the contours of New South Wales wine regionality, the state's wine story dates from 1788.

Beginning with the first wine grape plantings, the first Australian wine growers were looking for ideal vineyard sites in New South Wales but were limited in their choice compared with today. Experimental vineyard positions depended on broader forces such as access to land in a colony with no European-style roads, few large navigable rivers and strong resistance from traditional Aboriginal owners. As British settlement first crept then swept over Aboriginal land the colonial gentry carried grape vines to new areas. In this way, vine growing spread first across Cumberland County and south-west to Camden then accompanied the fanning out of settlers over the Great Dividing Range to Bathurst, up the coast to Newcastle and up river to the Hunter Valley; north to Port Macquarie; westward from Sydney to Mudgee, Orange, and Cowra on the Warwick Plains; north-westward to the Liverpool Plains and the New England; south to the Illawarra and further north to the Northern Rivers.

From the 1820s there was a small explosion of vine plantings at Bathurst and in the Hunter Valley region along the fertile flats of the Hunter, Paterson and William rivers. In the Hunter the relationship between wine growing and the land has been unbroken since 1830, in Mudgee since the 1850s, in the Riverina since the 1910s (or earlier if we take account of plantings at Wagga Wagga in the late 1840s and at Albury from the 1860s).[1] There were some vine plantings near Perricoota during the early flow of settlement but no wine was made until more recently. Wine was produced in the nineteenth century – in some cases substantial quantities within the context of limited colonial consumption and export – at Bathurst, the Canberra district, Cowra, Forbes, Gundagai, the Hastings, the Hawkesbury, Hilltops, the New England, Orange, the Shoalhaven Coast and the Southern Highlands. Several of these regions were reduced by changing social and economic circumstances from the late nineteenth century to the 1930s. In a few, wine growing ceased for several decades.

Just as the sweep of history influenced colonial wine growing, wider events in the twentieth century provided the backdrop against which vineyards in the new Australian national industry were planted and pulled out, then replanted; wine tastes made and changed. After the massive settlerist expansion of the nineteenth century, the world changed dramatically in the early twentieth century. European powers – who for a hundred years had focused their military might on snatching land, resources and trading rights from non-Europeans – were again at war with each other between 1914 and 1918 and then from 1939–45. Australian wines received imperial preference in Britain between the wars but greater consolidation of wine firms, high labour costs in Australia compared with its competitors in European wine countries, and stronger wine distribution from South Australia meant actual numbers of New South Wales vine growers were reduced.[2] Some vineyards survived as larger wine businesses bought up established properties across several Australian wine districts when small growers left the industry. Wine production focused on meeting British and Australian consumer demand for affordable port and sherry styles but Italian families began to influence the production of wines from the Riverina and Maurice O'Shea's Mount Pleasant (later McWilliam's Mount Pleasant) continued to produce small quantities of dry table wines.

"
Wine production focused on meeting British and Australian consumer demand for affordable port and sherry styles.

In the late 1950s and through the 1960s, the earliest signs of a renaissance in New World wine growing occurred in Australia. The 1970s saw a number of Sydney professionals undergo a vine change. They travelled on weekends to small farm acreages within driving distance; they built trellising and planted cuttings, or cared for young vineyards then returned to their offices each Monday. Some made a permanent move to the country.

From the mid-1980s vine plantings expanded more rapidly including in Tumbarumba, in the Snowy Mountains, a whole new region to wine growing. Across the state, and the nation, corporate investors hired a new generation of trained viticulturalists and wine science students to run vineyards and make wine. By the 1990s, most of the wine regions that had been dormant were reinvigorated. Wine enterprises ranged from boutique to multi-national. New South Wales, as Henry Lindeman had hoped, well and truly smiled with the vine.

Here we consider the origins of contemporary regions.

Bathurst

Given that the first wine made over the Blue Mountains by Fitzherbert Hawkins received its public debut in the advertisement office of the *Sydney Gazette* in 1831 (see Chapter 7), first plantings must have been at least three years earlier. Former Bordeaux wine merchant Thomas Scott, who had advised the Macarthurs on their first vineyard, very likely spoke with Hawkins about wine growing when he visited Bathurst in 1820.[3] Other key growers in these early years were George Ranken and possibly also George Suttor's son William. As James Busby's *Manual* fired new interest in vine growing in 1830, his brother George wrote from the district to say Bathurst settlers wanted more vine cuttings.[4] Ranken sponsored five vinedressers from Germany in the 1840s and counted among members of the New South Wales Vineyard Association in the 1850s.[5] Vineyards in Bathurst remained at least until the 1870s but by the late 1880s the region's handful of wine presses were based at Wellington.[6] Plantings have been revived since the 1980s and wineries include Vale Creek.

Hunter Valley

Irish settler William Buchanan observed in 1826 that his land grant on the banks of the Hunter River, about 80 miles (130 kilometres) from Newcastle, was too far from the sea or a market town to be fit for an 'agricultural farm, but it is well calculated for grazing or for vineyards'.[7] Whether Buchanan planted vines is not known but a list compiled by convict supervisor Frederick Hely (a friend of Busby) tells us that those settlers growing grapes in the region in 1832 were William Ogilvie at Merton and James Webber at Tocal, each with a 3 acre vineyard; George Wyndham at Dalwood and George Townshend at Trevallyn, each with 2 acres. Five one-acre plantings were the Kelman's Kirkton; Henry Dumaresq – Governor Ralph Darling's brother-in-law and private secretary – at St Helliers; Captain Pike at Pickering; Mr Pilcher at Maitland and Little (not listed as

'Uncle Dan' Tyrrell, second generation
Hunter wine grower

TYRRELL'S WINES

Mr Little, perhaps a freed convict?) at Invermien. Alexander Warren near Wighton had a half-acre vineyard.[8]

Hunter wine growing soon moved inland to Pokolbin, at the foot of the Brokenback Range. Edward Tyrrell had arrived in 1858, built a slab hut, planted vines from Kirkton and harvested his first vintage in 1864. His son Dan grew into the family business, and in 1885 made the first of his seventy-four consecutive vintages.[9] The Drayton family arrived in the valley in 1860, the Wilkinson family in 1866. In 1893, store-keeper and grazier John Younie Tulloch took over a vineyard of Shiraz vines as payment for a debt and went on to make his first wine with the advice of Blunno from the Department of Agriculture.[10] With more than 120 wine presses in operation in the Hunter in the late nineteenth century, the extent of plantings and many original family names have been lost in regional memorys.

Hastings Valley

The first boom in vine plantings in the 1830s extended to Port Macquarie in the Hastings. British migrants had moved into the region earlier, when the port became a site for secondary punishment, but Governor Lachlan Macquarie at first instituted tight controls to make it more of a prison than Sydney. Trade and alcohol were prohibited, shipping limited and cultivation permitted only in subsistence gardens; however, these regulations were gradually relaxed as settlers arrived. Sometime after 1836 Henry White planted vines on his property, which he sold to William Stokes in 1839. By 1847, the Stokes vineyard so impressed former commandant Archibald Innes that he purchased 10 acres of it as well as having an established vineyard at his estate at Lake Innes.[11]

In the late nineteenth century there were more than fifty vignerons in the Hastings and Manning river valleys and twelve wine presses, possibly including that of Margaret Wilson whose Douglas Vale vineyard is a key heritage site at Port Macquarie, though the Wilsons recorded their grape crush as treadings so they may not have used a press. Wilson's father George Francis trod out the first vintage in 1867 and her grandson completed the family's final crush in 1918.[12] Douglas Vale is now managed by volunteers and wine produced from vines on the historic site. John Cassegrain, a second generation French Australian from the region, reinvigorated the Hastings wine industry in 1980.

Mudgee

Mudgee's first British migrants, the Cox family, may have planted vines on Wiradjuri land from the 1820s but Cox properties closer to Sydney, such as Mulgoa, had some success with vineyards so production is more likely to have been focused at those sites.[13] The first known plantings at Mudgee occurred in the mid-century with the arrival of German settlers who had completed their sponsored migration labour contracts with wine squires of the period. Unlike British migrants from wealthy settler families who could afford to keep records of their achievements, much of the knowledge about the Mudgee Germans is held in memory rather than documents. Retired Mudgee wine grower and local historian Gil Wahlquist identified fifteen different German family groups who from 1860 created a strong culture of fruit growing, including grapes, to feed a rapidly growing community during the gold rushes and within the district's emerging grazing economy.[14] Fred Bucholtz is considered to be the region's first wine grower and he won prizes for wines at several international exhibitions: Paris in 1878; Sydney in 1879; Melbourne in 1880; Calcutta in 1883.[15] But Adam Roth and his family had by far the most extensive influence on Mudgee wine growing into the mid-twentieth century.

Valentin Rhineberger arrived in Sydney in the 1850s and his son Peter's diary later recorded exchanges of colonial wine with a local midwife, Mrs Schmid, and four other local families. Rheinberger's mother and sisters made their family's wine.

KEN HELM COLLECTION

Johann Frauenfelder, a first generation Albury wine grower, with vines he planted in the 1860s. Part of a magazine cover which claimed wine growing to be 'Albury's oldest and most beneficial industry'.

Margaret Wilson's wine ledger for Douglas Vale, Port Macquarie. The 1880 vintage produced 3000 gallons of wine from the property's old and new vineyards.

VICTOR PAYNE COLLECTION

Commenced t
the 9. Marc
first days work
2nd day 19 tre
worked late the two vai
to get it Cask and
done

March 11   1 7. tredines
do   12   5 tredings,
work raining
hard to Nig
March 2 h by tredings
March 13   16 tredings r
March 15   17 tredings fin
March 16   18 tredings f
March 17   16 tredings f
day on the l
March 19   8 tredings hea
dinner not n
March 22   11 tredings very
March 24   6 tredings

Sept 2/81 5 Galls
£ 115. Fu ma

Vintage on
1880
5 treding
ing felled
light Win
the big cask
d to bare off
raining very
ht
ining in morn
day
day
a day first
ll
Shower after
ing pickers
had to pick
~~H. T. Dang~~
Coach

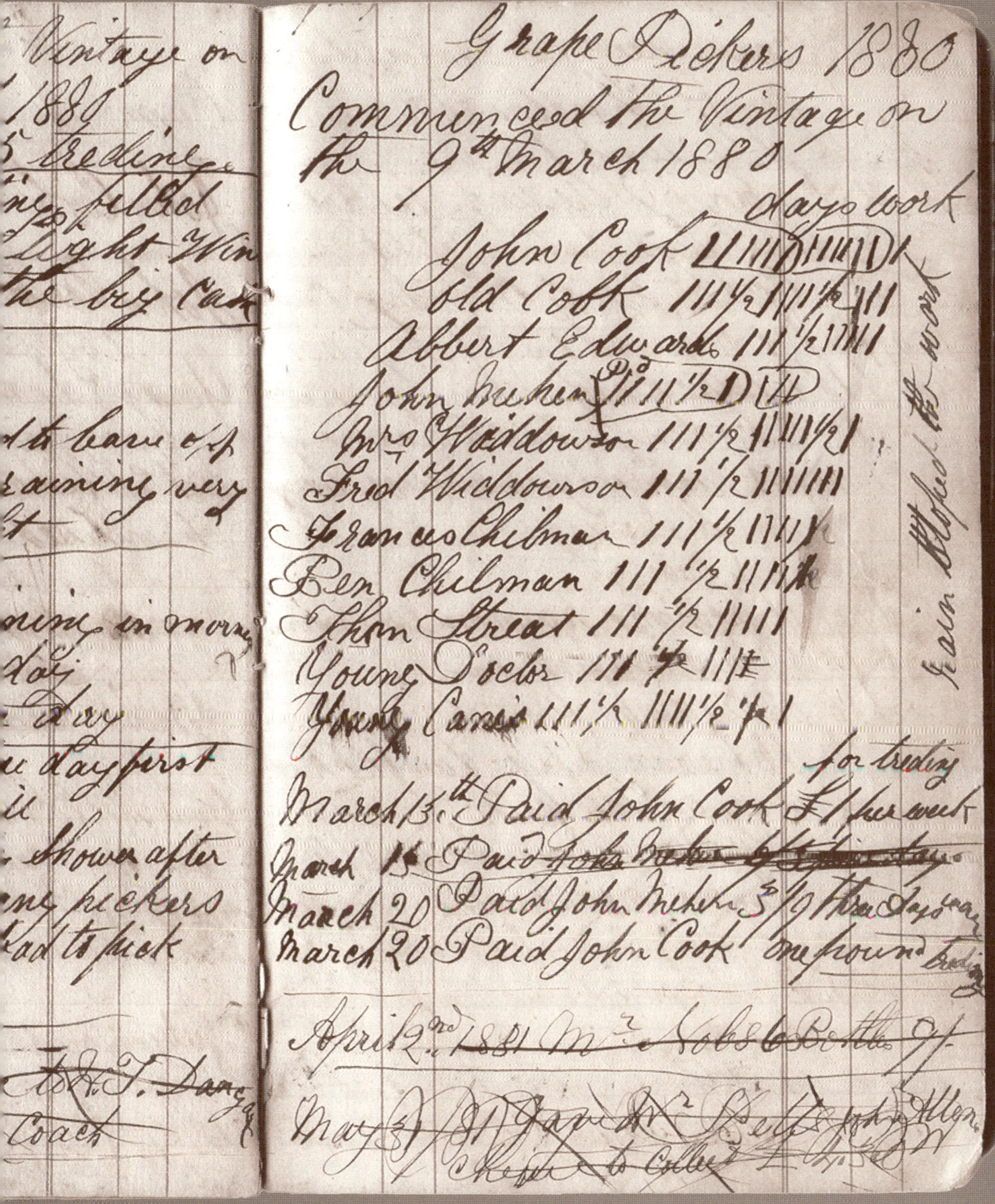

Grape Pickers 1880
Commenced the Vintage on
the 9th March 1880
days work
John Cook ||||||||||||
old Cook |||½ ||||½ |||
Albert Edwards |||½ |||||
John Meker 9d |||½ ||
Mrs Waddowson |||½ ||||½|
Fred Widdowson |||½ ||||||
Francis Chilman |||½ |||||
Ben Chilman ||| ½ |||||
Thom Streat ||| ½ |||||
Young Doctor ||| ½ |||
Young Cassie |||½ ||||½ ½|
Rain stopped the work
for treding
March 13th Paid John Cook £1 per week
March 13 Paid ~~John Meker~~ [illegible]
March 20 Paid John Meker 5/9 three days wages
March 20 Paid John Cook one pound treding
~~April 2nd 1881 Mr Nobbs Bottle 9/-~~
~~May [illegible]~~

Mudgee Wine Growers Association formed in the 1880s to oppose new licensing laws.[16] By this time there were six wine presses in the region. Craigmoor vineyard and winery, belonging to one of Roth's offspring (now owned by Oatley Wines) became the only surviving Mudgee wine

A wine label used by G David Kurtz (the author's great-great grandfather), who migrated from Germany in the 1850s with his parents. He was a second generation Mudgee wine grower

growing enterprise through the lean years of the mid-twentieth century.[17] My grandparents Alf and Laura Kurtz's Mudgee Wines began trading in the 1960s. From the early 1970s new investors like Bob and Wendy Roberts, Wahlquist and Pieter van Gent turned Mudgee to more extensive wine growing again. The Stein family, with links to early German vinedressers at Camden, established Robert Stein Wines in the 1970s.

Riverina

The Riverina story began in Wagga Wagga, with vines planted in the 1840s and then in Albury in the 1860s.[18] John Smith at Kyeamba and John Nixon of Gregadoo found a market for their wines on the goldfields in the 1850s and Elizabeth Vincent planted her Rock Cottage Vineyard about 1856, expending 'a great deal of time, trouble and money in bringing [it] to its present state of excellence and there can be no question that the wines she produces may rank with any other similar vintages in the world'.[19] Smith invested in skilled German labour during the wave of sponsored migrants in the late 1840s, bringing four vinedressers and their families to his station, including the three credited with beginning the Albury colonial wine industry: Sebastian Schubach, his brother-in-law Heinrich Rau and Johann Peter Frauenfelder.[20]

> **By the 1870s, Albury wine production was the highest of any district in the colony.**

In 1866, during a period of colonial vineyard expansion, Smith advertised 'a few thousands of strong rooted grape vines of best varieties for wine making, price, £4 per 1000'.[21] Nixon had presumably learned about wine growing as an overseer of convicts at Camden Park before moving his family to Kyeamba to raise cattle. Gregadoo wine was sent to Sydney wine merchants: a three to four month journey by bullock dray.[22] William Macleay owned a 40 acre vineyard near Wagga Wagga. His interest in viticulture comes as no surprise given his membership of the governing class of the colony.[23] Macleay's wines were produced by a German vinedresser and sold locally by an agent.[24]

By the 1870s, Albury wine production was the highest of any district in the colony.[25] The Riverina region is now centred on Griffith and Leeton and is again the state's largest wine producing area.

The McWilliam family has a deep history in the region, with Samuel McWilliam first based at Corowa from 1877. This provided second generation grower JJ McWilliam with the opportunity to gain experience

MCWILLIAM'S WINES

*McWilliam's Mark View Wines at Junee,
with pet kangaroos on barrels*

at home and with Henry Lindeman, who had a Corowa vineyard, so that when he established his Mark View vineyard and winery at Junee (in the Gundagai region) in 1896 he had been trained and working in wine growing all his life. His sisters Eliza, Rose and Mary also established their own vineyard, at Corowa, after the death of their father in the early 1900s. As land began to be offered for sale in the Murrumbidgee Irrigation Area, JJ moved his operation to just outside of Griffith. His confidence in the project led him to have vines planted in 1913, even before water began to flow. Remnants of these foundation vines, which produced their first vintage in 1917, are preserved at the McWilliam's company's Hanwood vineyard and winery.[26]

Just as Albury and Mudgee had German influence in the nineteenth century, Griffith and Leeton began to gain a strong Italian flavour after World War I. The De Bortoli family, the Calabrias of Westend Estate and the Bruno family of Toorak wines are among those who adapted their characteristic food culture to the region as well as innovating a range of contemporary wine styles. Frank Bruno first moved to Leeton after his brother Jim, a prisoner of war in New South Wales in the early 1940s, returned home to Italy with news of the opportunities in Australia. Frank's sons, Frank junior and Vince ran the family winery, which made its first commercial vintage in 1965. Frank junior's son Robert studied wine making and after working further afield now runs the family business on the same land his grandfather first purchased in the 1950s.[27]

> *"*
> *The De Bortolis, the Calabrias and the Bruno family adapted their characteristic food culture to the region.*

Canberra

Wine grapes were first planted at Gunning in the Canberra region in the 1840s by medical doctor Benjamin Clayton and his wife Fanny at Baltinglass. By 1847 the vineyard had an impressive array of vines including Verdelho, Riesling and the Cape varieties Steen and Hoenpoten (see Appendix 1), cuttings of which were advertised for sale from the property as a source of income.[28] In 1849, Dr Clayton's red wine won a gold medal at the Australian Botanic and Horticultural Exhibition. In 1878 Baltinglass wines were described as still excellent although the vineyard itself had gone out of production.[29] John Hardy planted vines at his Hardwicke property near Yass in 1853.[30] Sydney merchant Robert Campbell had vines at his Duntroon estate, which is now the site of Australia's military officer training college in Canberra, and Hamilton Hume trialled wine growing at Cooma Cottage in the 1860s. Campbell and Hume were both of the generation of wine squires. Hume had taken part in several missions to find pastoral and farming land for wine growing colonists John Macarthur and Alexander Berry, though he is best known for his travels with William Hovell.[31] The Colonial Wine Vaults at Yass sold Hardwicke wines in 1870 from 4 shillings a gallon. In the late colonial period there were more than 120 vignerons in the Canberra region and more than twenty wine presses.

CSIRO scientists Edgar Riek and John Kirk reinvigorated the region in the early 1970s at Cullarin and Clonakilla.

Forbes

Forbes' wine growing began when Joseph Reymond and Auguste Nicolas established Champsaur in 1866 on a 320 acre selection on the Lachlan River. Named for Reymond's home region in France, the property hosted a vineyard which at its peak produced up to 80 000 gallons of wine per year. Reymond expanded plantings during the 1880s economic boom and Champsaur remained in the family for many years. From 1999 it was operated by Dominic Williams (my father's cousin) and Pierre Dalle as Chateau Champsaur. The New South Wales Small Wine Growers Association began in Forbes in 1991. Sandhills Winery at Forbes maintains the district's connection with wine production.[32]

Gundagai

McWilliam's Mark View at Junee is considered to be the first Gundagai region vineyard and winery. Early Yass Plains plantings may also fall in this wine region. The region's twentieth century origins are due to the Paterson family of Paterson Gundagai Wines.

Orange

The efforts of Chinese market gardeners and British migrant farmers made Orange renowned for fruit production in the late nineteenth century. Settler John Hicks planted grapes at his orchard between 1857 and 1859 though these were probably table grapes.[33] Orange's wine growing has gone from strength to strength since the 1980s thanks to the initiative of the Doyle family at Bloodwood, the Swansons of Cargo Road Wines and Highland Heritage Estate.[34]

Cowra

Cowra dates its first vine planting to the 1860s. It had only one wine press in the late 1880s so we can assume the district's twenty-three vine growers were mainly producing table grapes. Of Cowra's wine growers, James Ousby's mixed farm on the Canowindra Road included a vineyard planted principally with Red Hermitage and Tokay which the local press declared to produce excellent wine. Robert Mankin's Bellview contained 3 acres of orchard and vineyard, with Muscatel, 'Baxter', sherry and Chassellas.[35] From 1891, farmers in the region were turning their land chiefly to wheat.[36] Wine growers returned to Cowra in the early 1970s but the region's boom began in the 1990s as new enterprises and established companies from other regions sought the particular qualities needed to make cool climate wines.[37] Second wave growers include Alan Mitchell, John Geber at Cowra Estate and the O'Dea's Windowrie Estate.

New England

Vineyards were planted and expanded in the New England and the Liverpool Plains districts of Inverell, Armidale and Tamworth from the mid-eighteenth century, including Wyndham's popular Bukkulla vineyard and winery (see Chapter 11). Before the 1890s Depression there were nearly thirty wine presses operating in the district and more than a hundred vignerons growing a combination of wine and table grapes.

To take advantage of the region's granite soils and cool climate, Thunder Ridge Wines near Armidale is one of several properties which have now turned a portion of grazing land to vines. In doing so, they have renewed the liaison between sheep, cattle and wine grapes in this district.

Hilltops

This region's first vines were planted as a result of the explosion of settlerist migration to New South Wales, land reforms and the frenzied internal migration of the gold rushes. In the 1860s, Croatian settler Nicholas Jasprizza planted vines near Young to supply diggers with grapes. Jasprizza later sponsored the migration of three nephews who brought Muscat cuttings with them. Growers from Boorowa were vocal about laws to force sulphuring of vines against powdery mildew in the 1860s; in the late 1880s there were several dozen grape growers in the region and six wine presses.

Peter Robertson at Barwang Wines began the regeneration of the district in 1969. McWilliam's Wines later purchased Barwang to take advantage of Hilltops ideal grape ripening conditions and granite soils. Twelve vineyards in the region produce a range of grape varieties for premium regional wines and cross-regional blends.[38]

MITCHELL LIBRARY, STATE LIBRARY OF NSW. GOVERNMENT PRINTING OFFICE 1-31058

Vine pruning at Clinton Estate soldier
settlement blocks, Inverell, post–World War I

Hawkesbury

Late in the nineteenth century, Thomas Fiaschi's Tizzana vineyard was a sole wine producer in a vast expanse of table grape vineyards on the outskirts of Sydney in the old colonial farming district of the Hawkesbury. Fiaschi epitomised wine business enterprise with a Sydney cellar door for his wines and cross-regional connections into Mudgee from the 1920s. The beauty and dignity of Tizzana was revived from the late 1960s by Peter and Carolyn Auld. Its restoration represents a twenty-first century realisation of the colonial vision for a Mediterranean lifestyle in Australia, exemplified in Muskett's *Art of Living* (see Chapter 9).

Shoalhaven Coast

Early Sydney merchant Alexander Berry, a great friend of James Busby – who originally promised Berry a good portion of his vines imported in 1832 – was among the early British migrants in this region.[39] In 1846, Anne Rees Jones visited Murramarang near Bawley Point and described seeing vines trellised high and along paths at an enormous garden some way from the house. 'The gardener was gathering grapes into a wheelbarrow', she said, 'telling us he was about to make wine'. When this wine making began, Jones and others were invited to the gardener's hut where the grapes were being crushed in a tub. 'I asked the gardener if sugar was used in the making of wine. It was afterwards told us that all the grapes they gathered were made into wine and then into brandy, and that the three, the gardener and the two young men drank all they made'. By the 1880s, there were ten vineyards and one wine press in the district; in 1892 champagne was being made at nearby Kiolo.[40]

The recent resurgence of Shoalhaven Coast began with the establishment of Coolangatta Estate by the Bishop family in 1988. Fern Gully Wines have operated in the region's maritime climate since the mid-1990s.

Southern Highlands

This region is thought to have been first planted with vines in the 1870s. Its first known vigneron, Joseph Vogt, migrated to New South Wales as part of the German diaspora of the mid-century, to work as a vinedresser at wine squire Charles Cowper's Wivenhoe, near Camden. He then bought land at Mandemar in the Southern Highlands. In 1886, a Berrima vintage produced 950 gallons of wine. Two presses were recorded in operation at Braidwood in the same era and one used by Vogt can still be seen at the Lambing Flat Museum. William Vogt became a second generation wine grower at Young.

Southern Highlands' wine growing renaissance came in 1983 with plantings by Joadja Vineyards and Winery. Brigadoon Vineyard was planted in 1988, followed by Eling Forest Vineyard, Howard's Vineyard in 1990 and the Old South Road vineyard in 1995.[41]

Perricoota

Named for the pastoral lease of former convict James Malden, vines were first planted in the Perricoota district on the Victorian side of the border in the 1850s. In the 1990s a small group of wine growers saw the potential for the soils and climate on the New South Wales side of this border district, on the threshold of Australia's wine export explosion. Its proximity to Melbourne was considered an advantage. The main varieties planted first were Shiraz, Cabernet Sauvignon and Chardonnay. These remain, along with other varieties identified as most suitable for the region: Pinot Gris, Sauvignon Blanc, and white Muscats to make increasingly popular Moscato. Small quantities of local wine were made in the mid-1990s but most of the harvest went to wineries outside the region. St Anne's winery was the first in the region in 1999.[42] Pericoota's production of fortified wines echoes the popularity of these styles in the nineteenth century.

Tumbarumba

Wine grape vines were first planted in this alpine region in 1981 by Frank and Christine Minutello at Tooma Vineyards in the Maragle Valley and Ian Cowell and Juliet Cullen on Courabyra Road. The 1990s wine boom and rise of Southcorp as a force in production resulted in expansion between 1992 and 1997. Tumbarumba has a small local winery, Tumbarumba Grape Processors, established by five local grape growers in 1999. Most of the region's grapes supply multi-regional companies based in the Hunter, Hastings and Riverina.[43]

11

A splendid bouquet ... of a similar character

Let's adjust the frame of our wine-focused lens on the past to zoom in and take a close view of one family. The story of this family wine business headed by, George Wyndham then his son John Wyndham, contains all of the elements of the history of wine in colonial New South Wales. From the first vintage of wine squire George to the success of wine businessman John; from George's classical revivalist farm house to John's proto-modern winery; through ampelographic confusion, the getting of intelligent industry, efforts to engineer a colonial wine culture – in the face of powdery mildew, phylloxera and economic depressions, the crystallisation of imperial vision into industry was lived out at the Wyndhams' Dalwood in the Hunter Valley, Australia's oldest surviving wine region.

George Wyndham signalled his intent to become a New South Wales wine grower even before his migration to the colony in the late 1820s by including wine regions in his early travels. He had first sailed to Canada

February —   1835.

Feb. 3.   Boy born at 5 P.M. Francis

S. 8.   Some rain in showers.

9. M.   Began my vintage. filled the pipe
with must of the Black Cluster.

10 T.   No appearance of fermentation.

11 W.   A.M. a froth rising — P.M. a head
foaming thick, and a vinous smell

12. T.   fermenting strongly. on the 10th
the temperature of ye must was
79°. the 11th was a fair hot day of 90°.
and I took the blankets off the
vat, to raise the temp.e of ye must.

13. F.   Very hot. 99° blankets on —

14 S.   very hot. — P.M. a much more violent
fermentation commenced, the froth
broke through the head. and filled
up to running over the 4 or 5 inches
to space. I took off blankets. but
keep the head covered.   56

15. Sun.   at 5. a.m. found the head had sunk
and sweet taste gone. and instead

MITCHELL LIBRARY, STATE LIBRARY OF NSW, ML B1313

*George Wyndham's first vintage, February
1835. Entry in his 1830–40 diary.*

then spent several months in Europe (where he met and married Margaret) and observed vine culture and wine making in France and Italy.[1] The only other colonists presently known to have arrived in New South Wales prepared to be wine growers were George Suttor, James Busby and the Wilkinson brothers, Fred and John. Many other colonists undertook wine study tours on their return to Europe and in Chapter 5 we saw how these tours become a valuable means of intelligence gathering and knowledge sharing. But why did Wyndham take an especial interest in wine growing so early? Although there are no clear links between Wyndham and colonial wine growing promoters such as Banks, for instance (see Chapter 4), as landed gentry George's father had a political career which connected him with British ruling class visions for empire. In the early 1820s London had been abuzz with what John Macarthur junior called a 'horticultural mania' about grapes and olives in the colonies, which would have reached George's ears.[2] It seems likely too that the library at the Wyndhams' English estate house, Dinton (newly built in the tradition of neo-classical country piles while George was in his early teens), contained impressions of New South Wales' early years and future prospects. A budding body of literature on the colony contained references to and recommendations for trials in wine growing.[3]

As the well-educated third son of a family of south-western English gentry, Wyndham caught the first small wave of the Settler Revolution to New South Wales. (This revolution is explained in Chapter 7.) George's father William had a position of respect as a land owner, 'a perfect country gentleman, a man of ancient family' as generous to the poor as to his associates in horse racing and fox hunting. William served as a magistrate, a role George would later take up alongside his rural pursuits in New South Wales.[4] As a result, the baggage George Wyndham brought with him to the colony comprised all-important financial capital, a small flock of sheep (reflecting the success of wool growing by this time), a desire to become a wine grower and *respectability*. In 1828 George purchased the property he named Dalwood, near present-day Branxton on the banks of the Hunter River. His civility and affability were very welcome with the crowd of elite Hunter colonists he fell in with, and among the ruling class

Dalwood Winery, 1886

MITCHELL LIBRARY, STATE LIBRARY OF NSW, PXD 740 P.16

of the colony more broadly. He went on to take part in colonial debates about the social and economic future of New South Wales but he did not, as many elites did, enter politics.[5]

At Dalwood, George and his assigned convict workers laid out his estate with a subsistence garden for the household and a combination of crops and grazing for income. In various years he sowed from 50 to 70 acres of wheat and his commercial orchard grew to comprise hundreds of fruit trees. Wyndham ran sheep and cattle, bred horses to work the farm (and later for racing), raised pigs, experimented with tobacco and hops, and used his own timber – sawn on site – for buildings and fences. The family properties grew to include, in addition to Dalwood, the 100 000 acre pastoral lease (and later vineyards) of Bukkulla at Inverell in the New England and Fernhill, George junior's subdivision where he planted vines in the 1850s.[6] Early on, a small number of grape vines were grown in Dalwood's garden, in keeping with usual colonial practice to this point. Wyndham then set about planning a more substantial vineyard with a wide variety of grapes as all growers did in this era before the varietal specialisation practiced today.

In mid-1830, Wyndham's diary (a day book of property tasks) tells us he 'began to clear the river bank for vines purchased from the Busby collection, on this side of the fence' at Dalwood. The first vines were planted on September first but within a few months he realised 'very few of my vines took, put out above 600. They were dead before I got them.'[7] These vines were part of the distribution of wine grape plant stock Busby made to around fifty colonists at this time, not the later plant material collected on his tour of Spain and France.[8] In late autumn of 1831 Wyndham returned to Sydney (slowly; the river route took him to Newcastle then along the coast to Port Jackson as there were not yet steamboats) to purchase stock from Thomas Shepherd's Darling Nursery: fruit trees such as nectarine, cherry, plum and peach. George called too at Blaxland's vineyard at Brush Farm to collect grape vine cuttings that

> *Wyndham's anticipation of this first vintage is palpable in the effusive telling of it.*

had been advertised both in Busby's *Manual of Plain Directions* and the *Sydney Gazette*.[9]

In January 1832, Wyndham's vines numbered 1400. He and his convict labourers worked to protect the young vines while preparing more land and a fence around a 'future vineyard'. Neighbours Captain Wright and Captain Pike delivered cuttings in early August, presumably pruned from their own vines. The lists of varieties from Wright and Pike indicate stocks mainly from the Cape, a principal source of wine grape plant stock to date. The first grapes were gathered from the garden in 1833 and by early winter that year Wyndham's vineyard comprised 4 acres. Planting continued in July from vines obtained from other growers in the district, including George Townshend (among them Shepherd's White, later called Shepherd's or Hunter Riesling before it was identified as Semillon).

When Wyndham planted acorns from Wright it may have been to establish a supply of oak wood for barrel making. In November 1834 a district cooper arrived at Dalwood – this skill was crucial in the early colony as barrels were used to store food as well as alcohol. In early February 1835 Wyndham began making wine by filling a barrel with the must of black cluster grapes. His anticipation of this first vintage is palpable in the effusive telling of it compared with every other entry in the ten-year span of his diary. A day after, on the tenth of February, Wyndham recorded no fermentation but twenty-four hours later a froth began rising and by that afternoon a head formed along with a 'vinous smell'; a day later still it was 'strongly' underway.

Wyndham constantly monitored the fermentation temperature. He used blankets to keep the ferment warm and removed them to cool it. Soon 'a more violent fermentation commenced, the froth broke through the head and filled up to running over the 4 or 5 inches to spare'. Within days 'the head had sunk and sweet taste gone … instead a harsh vinous taste. Drew it off and filled a hogshead' and another barrel. Fermentation continued violently: 'tried to stop it with sulphuring but too late. It is sharp and promises to make good vinegar.' This had to be most dispiriting; Wyndham had waited ten years to make his first colonial wine. However, he could not be deterred by a barrel of vinegar. Wyndham again fermented

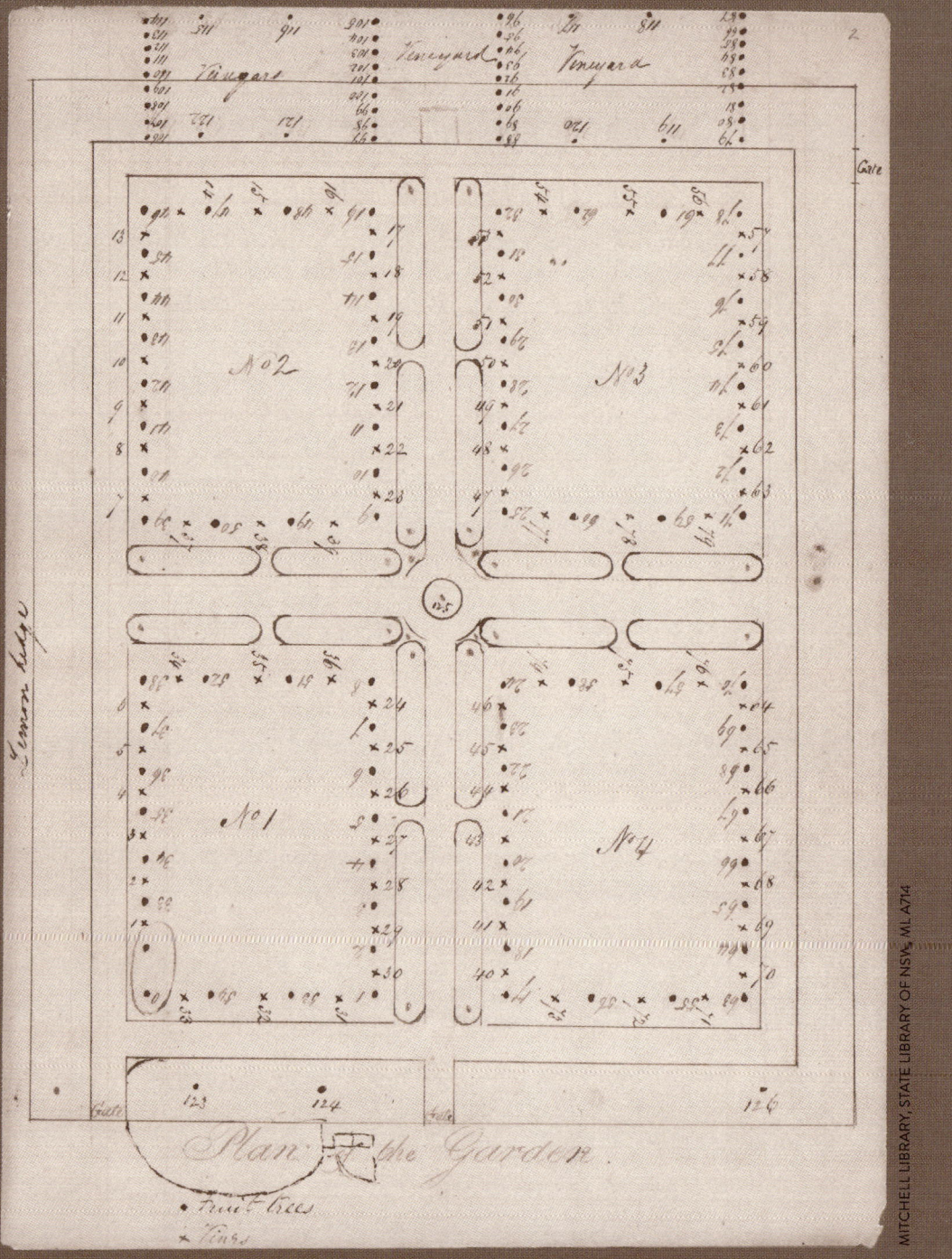

MITCHELL LIBRARY, STATE LIBRARY OF NSW, ML A714

*Vineyard in the garden from south end and no. 2 square,
c1844–48 from* Plans of Garden, Vineyard and
Orchard on Dalwood Estate *c1832–49*

Black Cluster grapes, with sugar and skins added. This time he 'over sulphured' (probably using bellows) to stop the fermentation and declared the result tasted of sulphur and 'a little sweet'. The experimentation continued with Muscatels, Gouais and the 'thick skinned white grape in the garden'. There might have been some success with one of the blends: 'discharged vat & chalked it, sweet taste being nearly gone. Vat had a splendid bouquet'. Such a frank account, intended perhaps only for Wyndham's own later reference, gives us a rare insight into early wine making when so much other material from the era on vine growing or wine making is less fulsome or polished for publication.

The following year's harvest and crush began at Dalwood almost the same time as the previous year but George did not share the same detail of the vintage as before. He made 1650 gallons of wine. In 1839 no wine production was recorded. That year he expressed greater concern about treating scab in his sheep.[10] And then the 1840s Depression hit the Wyndham enterprises hard, the family moved to Bukkulla for a time, and wine making had to wait.

The Hunter's style of settlement and proximity to Sydney and Maitland meant that prior to and following the retreat to Bukkulla, Wyndham lived in a close community compared with the social isolation of grazing properties further inland. His range of elite visitors included Townshend, Ogilvie, Webber, Glennie and Caswell; some of whom shared vine stock. Well-known colonial figures connected with wine growing also called at Dalwood: Samuel Marsden; AA Company head, Edward Parry; and former Port Macquarie commandant Archibald Innes. Wyndham in turn visited the Kelmans at Kirkton after vintage in 1836 and accompanied Dumaresq to James King's Irrawang which by then had a four-year-old vineyard. Of the Wyndhams' relationship with other key figures: they obtained wine and table grape vines from William Macarthur's plant nursery, 'repeatedly from 1828 up to 1862'.[11] John Wyndham also sold vine cuttings from his family's reinvigorated vineyards from the late 1860s. Glennie requested 1000 white Shiraz cuttings; second generation colonist Philip Gidley King wrote in 1870 to ask for sufficient vines to plant an acre of black Hermitage, an acre of white Pineau (Chardonnay?), an acre of

Vintage at Dalwood, 1886

MITCHELL LIBRARY, STATE LIBRARY OF NSW. PXD 740 P. 2

Verdelho and an acre of whatever Wyndham might select on his behalf.[12]

Margaret and George Wyndham had thirteen children and in the mid-1850s they decided to revive their wine growing enterprise with son John at the helm. Three to 4 acres were planted in 1854, a further 8 acres in 1856 and 2 acres of Shiraz in 1864.[13] When George died in 1870, John formally became the head of the family estate, which supported about seventy people. Not all first generation colonial wine enterprises survived the hand-over from father to son as the Wyndhams did. Other successful second generation growers in New South Wales included James Kelman, Dan Tyrrell, Audrey Wilkinson and JJ McWilliam. James Fallon at Albury was succeeded by his brother and Margaret Wilson succeeded her father at Douglas Vale in the Hastings district. Why did John become head of the family wine business? Because he shared his father's fascination for it. In the 1880s, John wrote that:

> Vine growing and wine making have been the work of my lifetime. It is
> now nearly fifty years since I first was allowed to tread out the grapes
> in my father's old wine press. The industry has been the work of my
> whole life, and of the deepest interest to me from earliest childhood.[14]

Many later generation wine growers would recognise how fermenting grape juice may creep into your blood flow when you grow up as John did among vines, wine, and talk of it as a valuable pursuit.

Like many colonial wine businesses, the Wyndhams used convict labourers and then German vinedressers.[15] These vinedressers, along with seasonal workers from the local community, received part payment in wine. This had been a controversial practice in the Hunter during the 1840s labour shortage but became common. In 1872, a Dalwood employee, P. Burke, received wages for twenty-four days work with a shilling of the pay deducted for wine consumed or taken home.[16]

While John handled the administration of the Wyndham enterprises, Bukkulla had an on-site manager, first Fred Wilkinson and then Wadham Wyndham. Fred's efficiency resulted in records which give a great deal of depth to the detail of the wine business. Bukkulla, in 1869, used two fermenting vats, four fermenting baskets, four wooden racking funnels and two pairs of sulphur bellows. Lists of iron and wooden buckets, hoes, ploughs and guns hint at the daily labour in an enterprise which had not existed a few decades earlier.[17] This inventory indicates the sort of stocktaking and general administrative work Fred did in the months after vintage and before pruning began in the vineyard. We know too that Wilkinson dealt swiftly with powdery mildew at Bukkulla.[18] As for grape phylloxera, that other vine threat of the century, Wyndham admitted it existed at Dalwood in 1885 but, as discussed in Chapter 8, was not surprised to find this was the case.[19]

> ❝
> *The industry has been the work of my whole life, and of the deepest interest to me from earliest childhood.*

Wines from Dalwood and Bukkulla won prizes at international exhibitions and were popular among a range of wine drinkers. Neighbour John Glennie, whose Orindinna wines were sold through Dalwood, believed competition for Hunter wines came mostly from the Fallons in Albury and from Adelaide producers.[20] In a congenial spirit of fellowship, however, South Australia's Thomas Hardy informed John Wyndham in the early 1870s that a Class 1 Dalwood blend from 1868 and 1869 had been sampled by the Adelaide Vigneron's Club, to great approbation.

> The best proof being, [Hardy told Wyndham] that the six bottles were empty before any others; the judges generally helping themselves to a glass of it to wind up with after each sitting. I am very much pleased to find that all your wines were of a similar character ... if it were not for the high [inter-colonial] duties there would be a ... demand for them here.[21]

Hardy went on to say that Wyndham's produced better quality light wines than Adelaide but the South Australians made superior full bodied wines.

What sort of wine did Wyndham's produce? They ranged from very fine to ordinary, to take account of a variety of colonial wallets and palates, and later export preferences. Grapes were discussed by Wilkinson in terms of their varietal types: Burgundy, Shiraz, Madeira, Pineau, Lambruscat, Verdot.[22] But Bukkulla wines were marketed by colour and quality: Australian Red; Bukkulla Reds and Whites, Classes 1 and 2. Dalwood wines were sold this way as well as, for a while, a *vin ordinaire*.[23] Later, Dalwood and Bukkulla wines were called dry Clarets, sweet, full-bodied reds and white wines; ordinary, fine and superfine; first, second or third class. A loyal customer wrote to John that when he had been bottling his latest Dalwood order from cask he found the wines differed so substantially from his favourite Bukkulla that he had to open a bottle of the northern Wyndham wine to satisfy himself that – yes – Bukkulla old was 'without exception the finest wine ever tasted and that has quite spoiled my taste for Dalwood'; if it were possible to buy such fine wine affordably, 'there would be little imported wine or spirits consumed in the colony'.[24] Here too was a nod to policies of substitution (see Chapter 6).

Cheque signed by Bukkulla manager Fred Wilkinson, 1869

KYLIE REES

Remarks by Wadham about the varied market for wine in the New England district demonstrate a relationship between wine quality, price and colonial culture. Wadham calculated he could sell his strong wines made in 1877 'to a chap at Goondimindi' who might be willing to take them: 'I think they are just the wines to please the shearer fellows'. But, the white 1876 would do better at Armidale, 'the fellows up there have money whereas there is no money in this neighbourhood. The fellows are all selectors with more land than they know what to do with – for which they have given all the cash they had – bad seasons come on top of it all so people are unable to pay their debts.'[25]

Dalwood wines had been sent to family and friends in England for some years and their style changed after George died. John's Aunt Charlotte wrote from England in the mid-1870s to say she was just drinking wines John had sent and fancied they were more like Claret than what her brother George used to call his Burgundy. But, she said, Uncle Charles liked the new wines much more than the old.[26] In the mid-1880s, James Kelman of Kirkton counted among the customers of John's wine.[27]

How were the wines sold? Two ways: wholesale direct from Dalwood by mail order, and retail by agents in Sydney and Newcastle. Orders were for casks or cases of bottled wine by the pint or quart. To provide these bottles, John ordered supplies from within the colony and abroad: in the 1870s, bottles from Singleton, cases from a Sydney timber merchant and at least one shipment of corks from London.[28] Advertisements for Dalwood and Bukkulla wines appeared in metropolitan newspapers. From the 1860s the Wyndham's depot in Pitt Street, Sydney served the public, including visiting ships.[29] The only other colonial wine with a substantial front page presence in this period, Fallon's, was distributed as Albury Colonial Wine. A Bathurst merchant mentioned to John that he could not sell Dalwood wines as readily as those from Albury as the latter were preferred by customers for being 'stronger'.[30]

In the late 1870s, as John conferred via mail with his brother Wadham at Bukkulla about whether to use a new sales agent in Sydney, Wadham pointed out that they should not release wines too early since Fallon guaranteed his to be seven years old. Wadham teased John that his wines needed at least four years to become full-bodied and reminded him that although he did not like to wait too long to sell, Bukkulla wines as old as eight years were fetching good prices.[31]

Dalwood and Bukkulla wines were sent in lots of ten- to fifteen-case loads on ships entering Newcastle harbour. Agent EH Timmins took charge of the Wyndham's Newcastle depot in the mid-1870s. He appears to have been a nervy individual but in his few short years on the payroll managed to ensure Wyndham wines travelled to Mauritius, Hong Kong, Adelaide, Calcutta, California, San Francisco and – much to his delight – the French Pacific colony of New Caledonia, which 'is thoroughly *French* and up to the present time *French* wines only have been introduced there' (Timmins' emphasis).[32]

In 1891 Dalwood wines were still being sent to French New Caledonia.[33] This same year, a principal exporter of Australian wine to Britain, PB Burgoyne & Co, sent instructions for the purchase of 1000 gallons of white wine from Dalwood. But sadly, after two generations of determined experimentation, the price the Wyndhams paid for exporting to Britain was that their wines had to be sent in barrels marked only with numbers not colonial wine names.[34] This arose from the British wine trade tradition of marketing blended wines with generic labels, which had created much confusion for early colonial wine growers. It also proved problematic that colonial producers used terms such as Madeira and Burgundy, which were place names themselves.

One colonial observer reported that:

> With reference to the question of the names of wines, it had often struck him that it was a great mistake on the part of Australian wine makers that they should call their wine after the names of known wines. Everybody tasting a wine so named judges it from the wines he had been accustomed to. English taste was so formed on port and sherry that there was scarcely another wine to which they could make

> *Wyndham wines travelled to Mauritius, Hong Kong, Adelaide, Calcutta, California, San Francisco and New Caledonia.*

MITCHELL LIBRARY, STATE LIBRARY OF NSW, PXD 640 P.25

John Wyndham, 1886

comparison, and they would ask if it was not like one of them, or per-haps sometimes it was like Claret or Burgundy. But Australian wines had an individuality of character of their own, which, if properly culti-vated and developed, was of great value … He liked to see wines named after the vineyards from which they were made. He should also like to see the design carried out of cultivating knowledge of the vines and of the grape best suited to the various localities.[35]

Knowledge of the best grapes for specific regions would of course come later. But in 1891, the manager of Dalwood had to brand his wine casks as Burgoyne's Australian Wine as 'we do not wish any other brand or mark of your vineyard to appear [for the British market]'.[36]

––––––

Due to financial strife caused by the 1890s Depression, Wyndham family ties with Hunter wine growing ended with the close of the nineteenth century but Dalwood came to be named Wyndham Estate and the site remains. Indeed, the property's twentieth century history, from a role in the interstate Penfold's corporation to ownership by former manager Perce McGuigan in the 1960s; from sale to a consortium including Brian McGuigan in 1970 to present ownership by multinational Premium Wine Brands, is a journey through the rise and rise of the Australian wine industry.

––––––

One early morning not so long ago, my neighbours Robin and Richard Little knocked on my door with a newspaper clipping reporting that an enormous collection of business documents, dated from the late 1860s to the early 1900s, had been donated to the State Library of New South Wales. It represented an extraordinary treasure trove: 3500 pieces of paper, mainly invoices and wine orders and a few letters, but amounting to a gold mine of material from a single company, the most significant colonial business archive in Australia, newly come to light – and on wine! What is more, the story of the papers themselves almost rivals the value of the information they contain. They had been thrown on a rubbish tip in the mid-twentieth century, rescued and kept safe for many years. Wyndham Estate manager Stephen Guilbaud-Oulton, on hearing of the papers, bought the lot from their careful custodian and bequeathed them to the State Library so they are available for ongoing public research.[37]

A selection of material from this new collection has been used here and so much more remains among its pages, yet to be discovered.

MITCHELL LIBRARY, STATE LIBRARY OF NSW. DG ON4/7066 HOME AND AWAY - 7066

*The elegant pose of this flapper, c1930s, picking
grapes, captures some of the romance of vine growing
in early New South Wales. Photograph by Sam Hood.*

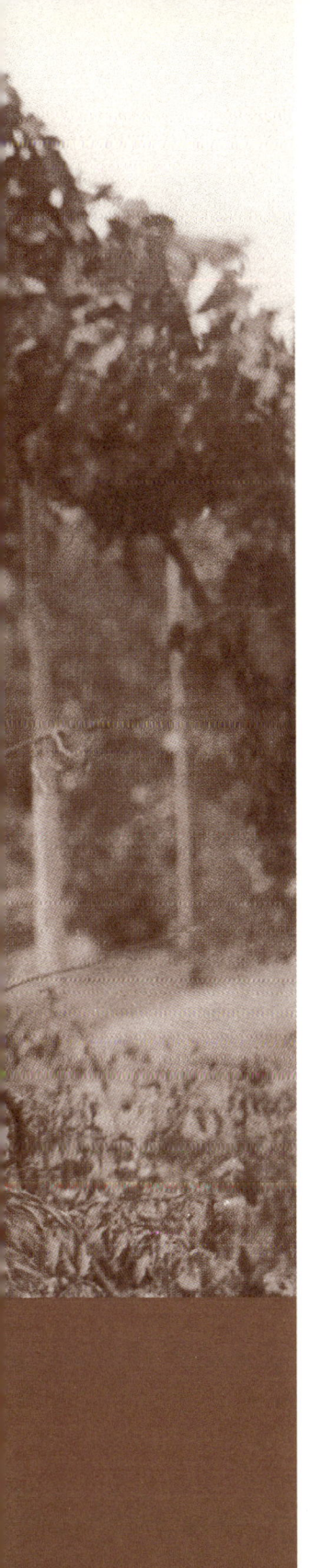

Conclusion

In a Max Dupain portrait of Maurice O'Shea (see page 222), we can see the twentieth century New South Wales vigneron holding a glass and scrutinising the wine in it for colour and body. O'Shea was famously short-sighted, so of course he had to peer very closely but in other respects he had a great far-sightedness. The French-Australian is revered for his original and long-lived red wines which were often blends from several vineyards.[1] When he began making wine in the Hunter Valley in the early 1920s, a range of suitable grape varieties had been established and identified. O'Shea applied his training in France and his family's experience as wine traders to discerning the distinctive qualities of grapes from particular vineyards, regions and other states and which qualities they could each bring to wine as it aged. By now Australia's idea of itself had matured into an egalitarian, pragmatic, irreverent, crackling dry wit which discouraged pretention, but O'Shea eloquently captured an echo of this earlier era of

Penfold's Wines display in a bar with bottle-lined shelves, 1939. Penfold's incorporated New South Wales sites into their South Australian based company, buying the Wyndham's Dalwood and establishing a winery at Griffith. Photograph by Sam Hood.

WINES

A good wor for Everybo

Penf

MITCHELL LIBRARY, STATE LIBRARY OF NSW. NCY30/437 HOME AND AWAY - 9791

classical revivalism, Romanticism and its links to ancient wine in a lecture he gave in 1951 in Sydney, which embodies the same spirit as Chapter 1 of this book.[2] As deftly as O'Shea blended his wines, he wove together the *idea* of wine with its place in history.

Another story linking wine and ideas of civilisation, which I think O'Shea might have enjoyed, occurred a century earlier when an admirer of a colonial wine, Kaludah Ruby, took a case of this Hunter red on a sightseeing tour of Egypt. The traveller, Professor Smith of the University of Sydney, later described it as his 'rare privilege to introduce the wine of Australia for the first time to the notice of the Pharaohs (at least of their mummies)' and to bring face to face the results of what he considered to be the newest and oldest civilisations of the globe. 'Wasn't that', Smith rhapsodised, 'a thought to fire ambition?'[3]

Smith's first bottle of Kaludah was 'broached' while sailing on the Nile, others once the boat arrived at the pyramids and he hoped to 'crack one in the lap of Rameses the Great'. A further bottle was cooled in the Nile then opened in Nubia after a camel ride.[4]

What Smith did not conceive of in his gleeful tale, but which shows what we can see with close scrutiny through a wine history lens, is that in the name of the wine Kaludah may be echoes of Aboriginal place. If so, in a very subtle way, an impression of the long-lived everyday of the oldest surviving culture in the world also came to be transported to the oldest civilisation of the Old World.

In contrast to this, we can see how the idea of wine culture soured in Australian thinking in the early1960s when the deceptively neat and tidy world of British Australia was shoved off its axis. The British Empire was in irreversible decline and an Australian way of life which had seemed natural under the immigration restrictions of the White Australia Policy began to appear threatened by the arrival of many more migrants from Europe, very many of whom drank wine. The implied threat of a wine culture was emphasised by the Scale of Australianism, twenty-eight questions devised by a psychologist in 1962 to encourage cultural assimilation of new migrants. These questions included the following (with preferred Australianist answers in parentheses). 'The Anglo-Saxon races owe their

ROSIE MARSON

Colonial wine lives on in the cellar at the
Macarthur family's Camden Park.

Maurice O'Shea. Photograph by Max Dupain, c1950.

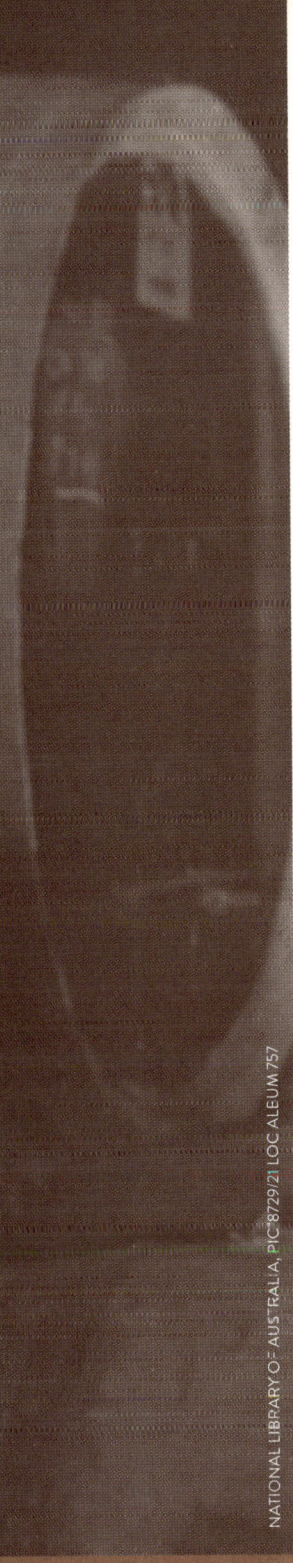

NATIONAL LIBRARY OF AUSTRALIA, PIC 8729/21 LOC ALEUM 757

leading position in the world to their outstanding qualities (agree) ... Wine is a good drink to offer to a friend who just drops in for a visit (disagree)'.[5] Presumably, an Australian should have offered their friend tea or beer. But the twentieth century renaissance of wine growing was already underway, and thanks to migration from wine countries, increased affluence, new laws, changing social conditions such as women being allowed into the front bars of pubs, and wines tailored more closely to consumer demand, there is no need for a narrow national vision of what we should drink.[6]

Maurice O'Shea did not live to see Australia become a wine drinking country but he and the glorious gallery of men and women who contributed to colonial wine experimentation would have toasted this transformation.

Let's take another look at O'Shea: holding the glass and seeing the wine. It puts me in mind of a Romantic poem on the love of nature which begins with the line: 'To see the world in a grain of sand'. I think O'Shea could see the world in a wine glass. And in the grand panorama of change in the nineteenth century, one of the most astonishing periods in human history, O'Shea's inheritance; the story of wine and wine growing in New South Wales, is a tiny bright thread to follow.

Appendix 1

Some grape variety importations into New South Wales, excluding the James Busby Collections from Spain and France

This table has been compiled from several sources interpreted with the assistance of George Kerridge and Angela Gackle (2005) *Vines for Wines, A wine lover's guide to the top wine grape varieties*, Melbourne: CSIRO Publishing and Jancis Robinson, ed. (2006) *The Oxford Companion to Wine*, Third edn, Oxford: Oxford University Press. The table contains some repetition due to the effort to extract a list from a range of material. It is by no means exhaustive and serves to emphasise the confusion about wine grape varieties which continued in the colony for much of the nineteenth century.

Year first imported, if known	Variety	Importer	Comments and other names
1800 & 1824	Madeira	In 1800: George Suttor per Joseph Banks. In 1824: for the Botanic Gardens, Sydney	These collections from 1800 and 1824 may also contain varieties purchased at the Cape of Good Hope for the First Fleet plant collection
"	Tokay	"	Muscadelle
"	White Frontignac	"	
"	White Muscardine	"	
"	Black Frontignac	"	
"	Constantia	"	Dessert wine: Muscat de Frontignan (Muscat Blanc à Petits Grains), Pontac, red and white Muscadel and a little Chenin Blanc
"	Muscat of Alexandria	"	
"	Pontac	"	Also known as Cape Pontac, resembled pinot noir when made into wine
"	Muscadel (red and white)	"	Muscadelle; known in early Australia as Tokay; see earlier listing for Tokay/Muscadelle
"	Steen (various descriptions)	"	Chenin Blanc or Semillon
"	Hoenpoten	"	If Hanepoot then Muscat Gordo Blanco, called Muscat of Alexandria in early Australia
"	Frontignac	"	Muscat à Petit Grains
"	Chrystal	"	Perhaps Crouchen which also came to be called Cape Riesling, whereas Rhine Riesling was known as Weisser at the Cape
"	Persian	"	Perhaps Shiraz, though in South Africa Shiraz was often called Hermitage, which presumably led to the practice in early Australia
"	Green grape	"	Semillon
1805	White Muscadelle	Mr Campbell	Vines imported from the Cape by Mr Campbell, sen. and long cultivated by him
1817	Burgundy	John Macarthur	As for above reference, James and Thomas Shepherd judged this to be generally but inaccurately called the Claret grape; source of most of the red wine in the colony. Cultivated by Gregory Blaxland. Could have actually been Cape Pontac
1817	Miller's Burgundy	John Macarthur, Samuel Marsden	Cultivated by Gregory Blaxland. Meunier, Pinot Meunier, Schwartzriesling
1817	Sweetwater	John Macarthur, Others, unidentified	The most common variety in the colony. Several sub-varieties available including Macarthur's from 1817 importation. William Macarthur made it into a 'pleasant light wine'. Possibly a grape used in sherries from the Spanish Xeres.
1817	French Gouais	John Macarthur	Poor eating grape and so far had made 'poor, insipid' wine
?	Black Muscadelle		Cultivated and liberally distributed by Robert Campbell. Robert Townson made a 'passable sweet wine' from this at Bunbury Curran near 'Campbell-Town'.

Year first imported, if known	Variety	Importer	Comments and other names
1817	Black Portugal or Oporto	John Macarthur	Some plants also at the Male Orphan School, Liverpool, also possibly at Robert Townson's vineyard. William Macarthur and James Busby agreed wine from it was insipid but worth more effort because it was used in 'port'.
1825	Red Muscadelle	AA Company	For sweet wines, seemed to be blight proof
1825	Tinta or Tintilla	AA Company	For making wine in hot climates but for colouring wine in cooler areas. Cultivated at Camden Park. Mr Fraser at the Botanic Gardens raised this variety, independently, from seed.
1825	Wantage Grape	AA Company	Also grown at Camden, but maybe not as a wine grape.
1829?	Black Hamburgh	William Macarthur	Cultivated for many years at the Botanic Gardens, Sydney, plus many cuttings distributed throughout the colony; an excellent eating grape, not a wine grape. Sent to Macarthur from England.
?	Black Cluster		Possibly a Burgundy grape, cultivated for many years in the colony, cultivated at the Botanic Gardens, not a good bearer.
1829?	Red Hamburgh	William Macarthur	Sent to Macarthur from England.
?	Unidentified black grape		A vine Busby could not identify grew at Mr Campbell's, Mr Johnston's of Annandale and the late Robert Townson's vineyard. It was a poor bearer but had recently been tried at Bayley Park by Mr Jones where it did better. Good for raisins.
1825	Verdelho, Verdelet (Madeira grape)	AA Company, George Townshend, Mr Park of Williams' River	Townshend and Park also reported other varieties from Madeira. Gouveio (Portugal).
1825	White Muscat of Alexandria	Lord Charles Somerset to Sir Thomas Brisbane	Somerset sent the vines to Brisbane from the Cape. Understood to be a variety from which Constantia was made; both William Macarthur and Mr Fraser believed them to be blighted as of the previous spring. Muscat Gordo Blanco.
[1825?]	Green Grape from the Cape	Somerset to Brisbane	Cultivated at Camden and at Botanic Gardens, said to be a delicious table grape. Semillon, Hunter River Riesling, Barnawatha Pinot.
1829?	Royal Muscadine	William Macarthur	Sent from England
1829?	White Frontignac	William Macarthur	Sent from England. Muscat a petits grains, Muscat d'Alsace, Moscato d'Asti.
1829?	White Corinth	William Macarthur	Sent from England
1829?	Red Corinth	William Macarthur	Sent from England
1829–30	Collares	Captain Wilson, Director of Public Works	Part of 'valuable collection' from Lisbon
1829–30	Bucellas	Captain Wilson	"
1829–30	'Port'	Captain Wilson	"
1829–30	Calcavella	Captain Wilson	"
1829–30	Muscatel	Captain Wilson	Part of valuable collection from Lisbon
1829–30	Muscatel	Alexander Riley	Riley, of London, sent vines to NSW
1829–30	Panse	Alexander Riley	"
1829–30	White Hermitage	Alexander Riley	Riley, of London, sent vines to NSW. Trebbiano.
1829–30	Black Hermitage	Alexander Riley	Riley, of London, sent vines to NSW. All of Riley's vines delivered by Mr Dutton who arrived on the Lady Blackwood. Shiraz
1820s?	Sherry	Alexander Baxter	Letter to the Maitland Mercury, 21 August 1850, claimed Baxter imported 'sherry' grapes into the colony from the vineyards of Duff, Gordon & Co of Xeres (Jerez de la Frontera), a famed Spanish sherry-producing region. Baxter, who died in the 1830s, was married to a Spanish heiress.
1838	Riesling	William Macarthur	Macarthur paid for cuttings to be imported and they were carried by a migrating vinedresser, Johann Stein who went on to be an independent wine grower.
1830s–1840s	Asmanhausen	William Macarthur	

Appendix 2

A selection of data on vines, wine presses, vignerons and wine regions

First returns of vineyards in New South Wales 1844–50

Year/ production	CROP (acres)	GRAPES (cwt)[1]	WINE (gallons)	BRANDY (gallons)
1843/4	483.5	408	29570	657
1845	559.25	5101	47856[2]	1018
1846	591.75	6045.5	51292[3]	1433
1847	743[4]	12988[5]	52337	1396
1848	897.5	20302.25 (1015 tons)	54035	1402
1849	895.5	6420	90300	1123
1850	956.5	No figures	97408	1266

Colonial Secretary Correspondence 1844-1851 Returns of Vineyards, SRNSW MS 4/7263

Number of wine presses in New South Wales 1888 and number of vignerons (wine and table grapes) in New South Wales 1891–92

ELECTORATE	Vignerons (all grapes)	Wine presses
Albury	93	48
Argyle	9	2
Balranald	6	1
Bogan	26	3
Boorowa	6	2
Bourke	10	...
Braidwood	6	2
Camden	83	7
Carcoar	19	...
Clarence	3	...
Cumberland	510	16
Durham	48	18
Eden	8	2
Forbes	23	3
Glen Innes	2	...
Gloucester	3	11
Goulburn	2	...
Grafton	24	7
Grenfell	14	1
Gundagai	15	7
Gunnedah	12	2
Gwydir	12	3
Hartley	3	2
Hastings & Manning	58	12
Hawkesbury	100	2
Hume	121	22
Hunter	157	52
Hunter (Upper)	40	13
Illawarra	10	1
Inverell	45	15
Kiama	...	...
Macleay	8	2
Macquarie, East		1
Macquarie, West		...
Maitland, East	8	...
Maitland, West	6	...
Molong	9	1
Monaro	1	...
Morpeth	5	6
Mudgee	55	6
Murray	19	...
Murrumbidgee	47	13
Namoi	36	2
Nepean	113	8
Newcastle	...	...
New England	5	...
Northumberland	17	3
Orange	12	...
Parramatta		...
Patrick's Plains	108	30
Queanbeyan	2	...
Richmond	54	2
Shoalhaven	3	...
Sturt	3	...
Tamworth	23	2
Tenterfield	5	2
Tumut	5	5
Wellington	23	3
Wentworth	2	...
Wilcannia	1	...
Wollombi	36	...
Yass Plains	3	1
Young	28	4
TOTAL	**2134**	**360**

Total of 3846 acres of land under wine grapes; 2148 acres under table grapes; 2287 acres not yet bearing. Total wine made equalled 913 107 gallons. Source: *Statistical Register of New South Wales*, Sydney: Charles Potter, Government Printer, 1889, pp. 244–45.

Regional groupings prior to 1890s Depression commensurate with twenty-first century New South Wales regions

NSW wine regions Geographical Indications (GI) (In alphabetical order)	Nineteenth century New South Wales grape growing districts	Number of vignerons (1891–92) (Wine and table grapes where wine grapes were approximately 60% of total colony-wide production)	Number of wine presses (1888)
Canberra District	Hume, Monaro, Queanbeyan, Yass (as well as Gundagai GI)	123	22
Cowra	Carcoar, Grenfell, Forbes	56	4
Gundagai	Gundagai, Tumut, Yass Plains	23	13
Hastings River	Hastings and Manning	58	12
Hilltops	Boorowa, Goulburn, Young	36	6
Hunter Valley	Durham, Hartley, Hunter, Maitland East Maitland West, Morpeth, Northumberland Patrick's Plains, Upper Hunter, Wollombi	428	124
Mudgee	Mudgee	55	6
New England	Inverell, New England, Glenn Innes, Grafton, Gwydir, Tenterfield, Tamworth	116	29
Orange	Molong, Orange	21	1
Perricoota	(First plantings 1860s then 1990s)		
Riverina	(Griffith from 1912)		
Shoalhaven Coast	Illawarra, Kiama	10	1
Southern Highlands	Braidwood	6	2
Tumbarumba	(First plantings 1982)		
GI areas across state borders			
Murray Darling	Balranald, Murray, Murrumbidgee, Wentworth	74	14
Swan Hill			
Non-GI areas			
Hawkesbury (Tizzana)	Hawkesbury	100	2
Bathurst (*Central Ranges Wine Zone*)	Wellington	23	3
Areas with no present plantings	Albury, Argyle, Bogan, Camden, Canterbury (Sydney), Central Cumberland (Sydney), Clarence (north coast), Eden Gloucester, Grafton, Gunnedah, Macleay (North Coast), Macquarie East, Namoi, Nepean, Richmond (North Coast), St Leonards (Sydney), Wilcannia	991	109

Notes

A note on style and measurements

1   Jan Todd, *For Good Measure, The making of Australia's measurement system*, Sydney: Allen & Unwin, 2004, p. 1.

2   Jancis Robinson, ed., *The Oxford Companion to Wine*, Third edn, Oxford: Oxford University Press, 2006, p. 532.

Introduction

1   Kolleen Guy, 'Wine, Champagne and the Making of French Identity in the Belle Epoque' in P. Scholliers ed., *Food, Drink and Identity: Cooking, eating and drinking in Europe since the Middle Ages*, Oxford: Berg, 2001, pp. 163–77; Robert C. Ulin, 'Invention and Representation as Cultural Capital: South west French winegrowing history', *American Anthropologist*, 97, 2, 1995, pp. 519–27.

2   A.E. Dingle, '"The Truly Magnificent Thirst": An historical survey of Australian drinking habits', *Historical Studies*, 19, 75, 1980, pp. 229–49; Diane Erica Kirkby, 'Drinking "The Good Life"', in *Alcohol: A social and cultural history*, Mack P. Holt, ed., New York: Berg, 2006, pp. 203–23. Australian academic works on wine include: David Dunstan, *Better Than Pommard!: A history of wine in Victoria*, Melbourne: Australian Scholarly Publishing, 1994, which makes some mention too of New South Wales wine growing; Barbara Santich, *McLaren Vale: Sea and vines*, Adelaide: Wakefield Press, 1998, pp. 122–71; Julie Holbrook Tolley, '"Gustav Got the Winery and Sophie Got the Soup Tureen", The contribution of women to the Barossa Valley wine industry 1836–2003', *History Australia*, 2, 3, 2005, pp. 86.81–86.88; W.P. Driscoll, *The Beginnings of the Wine Industry in the Hunter Valley*, Newcastle History Monographs No. 5, Newcastle: Newcastle Public Library, The Council of the City of Newcastle, 1969. Other work from 1940 and earlier plus additional publications in non-scholarly journals includes: J.H. Maiden, 'The Grape Vine. Notes on its introduction into New South Wales', *Agricultural Gazette of New South Wales*, 28, 1917, pp. 427–33; Eric Ramsden, 'James Busby, The prophet of Australian viticulture', *Journal of the Royal Australian Historical Society*, 26, 5, 1940, pp. 364–86; George Bell, 'The South Australian Wine Industry, 1858–1876', *Journal of Wine Research*, 4, 3, 1993, pp. 147–64; George Bell, 'The London Market for Australian Wines 1851–1901: A South Australian perspective', *Journal of Wine Research*, 5, 1, 1994, pp. 19–41; R. Dunphy and L. Lockshin, 'A History of the Australian Wine Show System', *Journal of Wine Research*, 9, 1998, pp. 87–105.

3   Australian Bureau of Statistics, *Apparent Consumption of Alcohol: Extended time series, 1944–45 to 2008–09*, 4307.0.55.002, <www.abs.gov.au>, accessed 14 February 2012. See James Simpson, *Creating Wine: The emergence of a world industry*, Princeton: Princeton University Press, 2011, pp. 220–39; Nicholas Faith, *Liquid Gold, The story of Australian wine and its makers*, Sydney: PanMacmillan, 2002; Kym Anderson and Robert Osmond, *Trends and Cycles in the Australian Wine Industry, 1850 to 2000*, Adelaide: Centre for International Economic Studies, University of Adelaide, 1998.

4   For example, James Halliday and Ray Jarratt, *The Wines and History of the Hunter Valley*, Melbourne: McGraw-Hill, 1979; John Beeston, *A Concise History of Australian Wine*, Sydney: Allen & Unwin, 1994. Surgeon, wine grower and wine writer Max Lake's wonderful books include *Hunter Wine*, Brisbane: Jacaranda Press, 1964. Medical doctor Philip Norrie revisited archives to correct errors he perceived in popular wine histories: Philip Norrie, 'A Study of the Original Documents on Viticulture in Early New South Wales and the Role of the Macleay Family 1788 to 1883', Master of Science, University of Sydney, 1992. See also Philip Norrie, *Vineyards of Sydney, Cradle of the Australian wine industry*, Sydney: Apollo Books, 1990. See too Charles Gent, *Mixed Dozen: The story of Australian winemaking from 1788*, Sydney: Duffy & Snellgrove, 2003. Among the best of the earlier encyclopedic Australian works by industry figures which incorporate research from secondary sources on wine are James Halliday, *Australian Wine Compendium*, Sydney: Angus & Robertson, 1985; Len Evans, *Australia and New Zealand Complete Book of Wine*, Sydney: Books for Pleasure, 1976. Wine company histories include Andrew Caillard, *Penfold's, The rewards of patience*, Sydney: Penfold's, 2004; Michael Harden, *Celebrazione! 75 Years of Eating and Drinking with the De Bortoli Family*, Melbourne: Hardie Grant, 2003; Fiona Sainty, *Nothing is Great Unless it is Good, The Tyrrell family wine story*, Sydney: Tyrrell's, 2008. An example of a varietal history produced in Australia is Ken Helm and Trish Burgess, *Riesling in Australia: The history, the regions, the legends, and the producers*, Adelaide: Winetitles, 2010. Valmai Hankel has played a vital role as a librarian and now as a columnist, for example, *Winestate Annual Edition*, 35, 1, 2012, p. 22.

5   Cited in H.E. Laffer, *The Wine Industry of Australia*, Adelaide: Australian Wine Board, 1949, p. 8.

6   Penny Russell, *Savage or Civilised, Manners in colonial Australia*, Sydney: New South, 2010.

7   Halliday, *Wine Compendium*, p. 7.

8   Richard Waterhouse, *The Vision Splendid, A social and cultural history of rural Australia*, Fremantle: Fremantle Arts Centre Press, 2005, p. 18.

9   Bill Gammage, *The Biggest Estate on Earth, How Aborigines made Australia*, Sydney: Allen & Unwin, 2011.

10 The efficiency and comprehensiveness of the New South Wales colonial project is argued in Alan Frost, *The First Fleet: The real story*, Melbourne: Black Inc, 2011; Alan Frost, *Botany Bay: The real story*, Melbourne: Black Inc, 2011.

Chapter 1

1 Barry Higman, *How Food Made History*, Oxford: Wiley-Blackwell, 2010.

2 Patrick McGovern, Stuart J. Fleming and Solomon H. Katz eds., *The Origins and Ancient History of Wine*, Amsterdam: Gordon and Breach, 1996, p. xii.

3 Daniel Zohary and Maria Hopf, *Domestication of Plants in the Old World, The origin and spread of cultivated plants in West Asia, Europe and the Nile Valley*, Third edn, Oxford: Oxford University Press, 2000, pp. 248–49, 156–57.

4 Tim Unwin, *Wine and the Vine, An historical geography of viticulture and the wine trade*, London: Routledge, 1991, p. 180.

5 Fernand Braudel, *The Structures of Everyday Life, Civilisation and Capitalism, 15th–18th Century*, trans. Sian Reynolds, Cambridge: Harper& Row, 1981, pp. 232–37.

6 William Hughes, *An Exact Abridgement of All Statutes in Force and Use*, London: Printed for J. Starkey and T. Bafset, 1662, p. 224.

7 Michael R. Best, 'The Mystery of Vintners', *Agricultural History*, 50, 2, 1976, pp. 365 and 370.

8 The colonial conception of the creation of 'civilisation' implied an ideological and racialised rising above or superiority to, rather than simple distinction from, the economic and cultural practices of Indigenous Australians. See John Gascoigne, *The Enlightenment and the Origins of European Australia*, Cambridge: Cambridge University Press, 2002, p. 149.

9 Maguelonne Toussaint-Samat, *A History of Food*, trans. Anthea Bell, Oxford: Blackwell, 1994, p. 261.

10 Cited in Unwin, *Wine and the Vine*: p. 102.

11 William Hughes, *The Compleat Vineyard: Or, an excellent way for the planting of vines, according to the German and French manner, and long practifed in England*, London: Printed by J.C. for Will. Creek, 1670, n.p.

12 Charles W. Bamforth, *Grape vs Grain, A historical, technological and social comparison of wine and beer*, New York: Cambridge University Press, 2008, p. xii.

13 John Burnett, *Liquid Pleasures, A social history of drinks in modern Britain*, London: Routledge, 1999, pp. 160–78.

14 Braudel, *Structures of Everyday Life*, pp. 241–49.

15 Toussaint-Samat, *History of Food*, p. 261; Henry Lindeman to the Editor, *Sydney Morning Herald*, 25 December 1867.

16 Norbert Elias, *The Civilising Process, The history of manners and state formation and civilisation*, Oxford: Blackwell, 1994

17 Russell, *Savage or Civilised?* pp. 9, 50, 99.

18 Louis E. Grivetti, 'Wine: The food with two faces' in McGovern et al., *Origins and Ancient History*, p. 9.

19 Author not stated, *Bibliotheca Biblia: Being a commentary upon the books Old and New Testament*, vol. 1, Oxford: n.p., 1720–1735, p. 251.

20 Genesis 9:20–25, *Holy Bible*, London: Eyre and Spottiswoode, year unknown. Subsequent references are from this copy of the King James Bible.

21 See for example Deuteronomy 18:3–4; II Chronicles 31:5.

22 Psalm 104.

23 Proverbs 9:2.

24 Proverbs 31:16.

25 See for example Isaiah 16:10.

26 Leviticus 10:9.

27 First Epistle of Saint Paul to Timothy 3:3 and 3:8.

28 Proverbs 20:1.

29 Psalm 75:8.

30 Psalm 60:3.

31 Psalm 65:17.

32 Revelation 18:3.

33 Matthew 20:1–16.

34 John 4:46.

35 Mark 15:23.

36 Virgil, cited in Clarence J. Glacken, *Traces on the Rhodian Shore, Nature and culture in western thought from ancient times to the end of the eighteenth century*, Berkeley: University of California Press, 1967, p. 143.

37 From Anonymous, 'Broadsides and ballads', Women Advising Women, Part 5, Fisher Library, University of Sydney, MF 305.405 10.

38 Hippocrates cited in McGovern et al., *Origins and Ancient History*, p. 3.

39 Plato cited in McGovern et al., *Origins and Ancient History*, p. 4.

40 Cited in Grivetti, 'Wine: The food with two faces', pp. 12–13.

41 Andre L. Simon, *The History of the Wine Trade in England*, vol. 1, London: The Holland Press, 1964, pp. 6–7. Simon's argument on this is persuasive despite being at odds with other sources, such as De Blij, *Wine: A geographic appreciation*, p. 45.

42 Unwin, *Wine and the Vine*, p. 147.

43 Simon, *Wine Trade in England*, pp. 42–43.

44 Unwin, *Wine and the Vine*, pp. 201–02.

45 Hugh Barty-King, *A Tradition of English Wine*, Oxford: Oxford Illustrated Press, 1977, p. 114.

46 Louis Salzmann, *English Trade in the Middle Ages*, London: H. Prodes, 1964, p. 376.

47 Hugh Johnson, *The World Atlas of Wine*, p. 15.

48 Sir Kenelme Digby, *The closet of the eminently learned Sir Kenelme Digby Kt*, London: Printed by E.C. & A.C. for H. Brome, 1671, includes traditional fermented wines such as mead (honey wine).

49 Thomas Short, *Vinum Britannicum: Or an essay on the properties and effects of malt liquor*, London: Printed for D. Midwinter and M. Bryson, 1727, pp. 44–61.

50 [JOURNAL] 1768 October 25: J. C. Beaglehole, ed., *The Endeavour Journal of Joseph Banks 1768–1771*, vol. 1, Sydney: Trustees of the Public Library of New South Wales in association with Angus & Robertson, 1963, pp. 176–77.

51 Pierre Spahni, *The International Wine Trade*, Cambridge: Woodhead, 1998, p. ix.

52 A.D. Francis, *The Wine Trade*, London: Adam & Charles Black, 1972, p. 244.

53 Burnett, *Liquid Pleasures*, pp. 145–46.

54 Charles Cameron Ludington, 'Politics and the Taste for Wine in England and Scotland, 1660–1860', PhD thesis, Columbia University, 2003, pp. 37–38, 48, 405, 447.

55 Charles Ludington, '"Claret is the Liquor for Boys; Port for Men": How port became the "Englishman's Wine"', *Journal of British Studies*, 48, 2, 2009, pp. 370, 383, 386.

56 See John Gascoigne, *The Enlightenment and the Origins of European Australia*, Cambridge: Cambridge University Press, 2002, p. 10.

57 ibid.

58 Michèle Cohen, 'The Grand Tour: Constructing the English gentleman in eighteenth century France', *History of Education*, 21, 1992: p. 241.

59 Julia Horne, *The Pursuit of Wonder: How Australia's landscape was explored, nature discovered and tourism unleashed*, Melbourne: Miegunyah Press, 2005, p. 7.

60 Peter Watson, *Ideas: A history from Freud to fire*, London: Weidenfeld & Nicholson, 2005, p. 610.

61 Andre Simon quoted in the frontispiece of Simpson, *Creating Wine*.

62 James Halliday and Hugh Johnson, *The Art and Science of Wine, The winemaker's options in the vineyard and the cellar*, London: Mitchell Beazley, 1992.

63 Unwin, *Wine and the Vine*, p. 258.

64 Chateau Mouton-Rothschild received a promotion from second to first growth in the 1970s. The later Burgundy system of *grand cru* and *premier cru* vineyards is distinct from Bordeaux Classifications.

65 Ulin, 'Invention and Representation', pp. 519–27.

66 A detailed argument about this is given in Julie McIntyre, 'Resisting Ages-old Fixity as a Factor in Wine Quality: Colonial wine tours and Australia's early wine industry', *Locale: The Australasian–Pacific Journal of Regional Food Studies* 1, 1, 2011: pp. 1–19.

67 Ulin, 'South west French Winegrowing

History', pp. 519–27.

68 Pierre Bourdieu, *Distinction: A social critique of the judgement of taste*, trans. Richard Nice, London: Routledge & Kegan Paul, 1984, p. 7. See also Michael Patrick Allen and John Germov, 'Judging Taste and Creating Value: The cultural consecration of Australian wines', *Journal of Sociology*, 47, 35, 2011, pp. 35–51.

69 Bourdieu, *Distinction*, p. 53.

70 Ulin, 'Cultural capital', pp. 519–27.

71 Phillip McIntyre, *Creativity and Cultural Production, Issues for media practice*, London, Palgrave Macmillan, 2012, p. 204.

Chapter 2

1 Watkin Tench, *Sydney's First Four Years, Being a reprint of a narrative of the expedition to Botany Bay and a complete account of the settlement at Port Jackson*, first published 1789 and 1793, Sydney: Angus & Robertson, 1963, p. 18.

2 *Edinburgh Review or Critical Journal*, vol. 45 December 1826–March 1827, p. 22.

3 'A new universal history of arts and sciences, vol. 2, 1759', *Eighteenth Century Collections Online (ECCO)*, accessed 30 August 2005, pp. 550 and 551.

4 Ludington, 'The "Englishman's Wine"', p. 371–78.

5 ibid., pp. 214–15.

6 Alan Frost, *The First Fleet, The real story*, Melbourne: Black Inc, 2011, pp. 145–53.

7 ibid., pp. 136–39; Arthur Phillip to Evan Nepean, 2 December 1786, *HRNSW*, vol. 2, p. 30; Secretary Stephens to Arthur Phillip, 23 February 1787, *HRNSW*, vol. 2, p. 49; Arthur Phillip to Evan Nepean, 1 March 1787, *HRNSW*, vol. 2, p. 54.

8 Arthur Phillip to Evan Nepean, 8 May 1787, *HRNSW*, vol. 2, p. 101; Lord Sydney to Arthur Phillip, 5 May 1787, *HRNSW*, vol. 2, p. 91.

9 Frost, *First Fleet*, p. 139.

10 Arthur Phillip to Evan Nepean, 10 June 1787, *HRNSW*, vol. 2, p. 108.

11 Arthur Phillip to Evan Nepean, 2 September 1787, *HRNSW*, vol. 1, p. 112.

12 Ludington, 'The "Englishman's Wine"', p.379.

13 See for example, Robert Ross, 'The Rise of the Cape Gentry', *Journal of Southern African Studies*, 9, 2, 1983, pp. 199 and 205–06.

14 John Easty, *Memorandum of Transactions of a Voyage from England to Botany Bay: 1787–1793: A First Fleet journal*, Sydney: Trustees of the Public Library of New South Wales in association with Angus & Robertson, 1965, p. 49.

15 According to Stephen Greenblatt, Europeans had a 'stockpile of representations' from which they drew and in turn contributed to

through expression of these representations in texts such as travel literature, Stephen Greenblatt, *Marvellous Possessions, the Wonder of the New World*, Oxford: Oxford University Press, 1991, p. 6.

16 Alan Frost, *Arthur Phillip 1738–1814, His Voyaging*, Melbourne: Oxford University Press, 1987, pp. 59 and 132.

17 Frost, *The First Fleet*, p. 167.

18 'The Original Arthur Bowes Smyth Manuscript of His Voyage to Australia', University of Newcastle MF 3799.

19 John White, *Journal of a Voyage to New South Wales*, Facsimile edn, Sydney: Angus & Robertson, 1962, p. 83.

20 Stockdale, *The Voyage of Governor Phillip to Botany Bay*, p. 39.

21 David Collins, *An Account of the English Colony in New South Wales* (Facsimile edition), Adelaide: Libraries Board of South Australia, 1971 p. xxvii.

Chapter 3

1 Henry Hobhouse, *Seeds of Wealth: Four plants that made men rich*, London: Macmillan, 2003, p. 101.

2 Unwin, *Wine and the Vine*, pp. 216–18.

3 De Blij, *Wine*, p. 57.

4 Marie Kimball, 'Some Genial Old Drinking Customs', *The William and Mary Quarterly*, 2, 1945, p. 354; Edward Williams, *Virginia's Discovery of Silke-worms ... also the dressing and keeping of vines, for the rich trade of making wines there*, London: Printed by T.H. for John Stephenson, 1650, p. 32.

5 Arthur H. Hirsch, 'French Influence on American Agriculture in the Colonial Period with Special Reference to Southern Provinces', *Agricultural History*, 4, 1, 1930: pp. 1–3.

6 Joyce Chaplin, *An Anxious Pursuit, Agricultural Innovation and Modernity in the Lower South, 1730–1815*, Chapel Hill: University of North Carolina Press, 1993, p. 131.

7 Louis De Saint Pierre, *The Art of Planting and Cultivating the Vine*, London: Printed by J. Wilkie and J. Walter, 1772, pp. xiv–xv.

8 James Maria Matra, 'A Proposal for Establishing a Settlement in New South Wales' in *HRNSW* vol.1, pp. 265–66.

9 See for example Philip Norrie, *Vineyards of Sydney, Cradle of the Australian wine industry*, Sydney: Apollo Books, pp. 14–16; H. E. Laffer, *The Wine Industry of Australia*, Adelaide: Australian Wine Board, 1949, pp. 1–2; Arthur Phillip to Joseph Banks, 22 August 1790, Banks Papers, Botanical and Horticultural 1789–1796, Mitchell Library, State Library of New South Wales (ML) CY3005/68.

10 Beaglehole (ed) *Endeavour Journal*, vol. 1,

pp. 193–205.

11 David Collins, *An Account of the English Colony in New South Wales*, Facsimile edition, Adelaide: Libraries Board of South Australia, 1971, p. xxviii.

12 ibid., p. xxvii.

13 Beaglehole (ed.), *Banks' Endeavour Journal*, vol. 2, p. 409.

14 George Suttor to Joseph Banks, 10 December 1800, ML A79–3, p. 272.

15 *Sydney Gazette*, 16 December 1824.

16 Smyth, *Journal*, pp. 53–54.

17 Hakluyt, 'The First English Voyage', p. 89.

18 Beaglehole, *Banks' Endeavour Journal*, vol. 1, p. 218.

19 George Worgan, *Journal of a First Fleet Surgeon* (1788), <http://gutenberg.net.au> accessed 21 January 2012.

20 Paul Fidlon and R.J. Ryan (eds), *The Journal of Philip Gidley King: Lieutenant, R.N. 1787–1790*, Sydney: Australian Documents Library, 1980, p. 34.

21 Worgan, *Journal*

22 Arthur Phillip's Orders, Frederick Watson (ed.), *Historical Records of Australia (HRA)* I, vol. 1, Sydney: Library Committee of the Commonwealth Parliament, 1914, pp. 13–14.

23 Seminal works on the complexities of early cultural contact in Australia include Henry Reynolds, *The Other Side of the Frontier, Aboriginal resistance to the European invasion of Australia*, Melbourne: Penguin, 1981; Inga Clendinnen, *Dancing with Strangers*, Melbourne: Text Publishing, 2003; Grace Karskens, *The Colony, A history of early Sydney*, Sydney: Allen & Unwin, 2009; Richard Broome, *Aboriginal Australians: A history since 1788* (Revised edition), Sydney: Allen & Unwin, 2010.

24 Worgan, *Journal*.

25 Maggie Brady, 'Alcohol Policy Issues for Indigenous People in the United States, Canada, Australia and New Zealand', *Contemporary Drug Problems*, 27, 3, 2000, p. 438.

26 Reynolds, *Other Side of the Frontier*, p. 2.

27 Tench, *Sydney's First Four Years*, p. 140.

28 ibid., p. 143.

29 Bennelong was known by several names: 'Bannelon, Wollewarre, Boinba, Bundebunda, Woge trowey', King in *Hunter, An Historical Journal*, p. 405.

30 Tench, *Sydney's First Four Years*, p. 160.

31 Clendinnen, *Dancing with Strangers*, p. 178. In another example of Bennelong's initiative, he established the terms of his relationship with Phillip by including the governor in the burial of his baby, as described in Alan Atkinson, *The Europeans in Australia, A History: Volume One, The Beginning*, Melbourne: Oxford University Press, 1997, p. 157.

32 Tench, *Sydney's First Four Years*, p. 160.

33 King in *Hunter, An Historical Journal*, p. 405.

34 Clendinnen, *Dancing with Strangers*, p. 124.

35 Tench, *Sydney's First Four Years*, pp. 178–79.

36 Dixon, *The Course of Empire*, p. 8, shows the problem of determining true authorship due to editing, with particular reference to Arthur Phillip's published account of the colonisation of New South Wales.

37 Other versions are Tench, *Sydney's First Four Years*, p. 160; *Hunter, An Historical Journal*, p. 207.

38 Clendinnen, *Dancing with Strangers*, pp. 110–32.

39 See, for example, L. R. Hiatt, 'Bennelong and Omai', *Australian Aboriginal Studies*, 2, 2004: pp. 87–89.

40 Jeff Power, 'Sniffing Petrol, Reclaiming Story and Valuing Kin: An interview with Craig San Roque', *Australia and New Zealand Journal of Family Therapy*, 24, 4, 2003: p. 206. San Roque stressed his story telling was not a clinical trial. Thanks to Ben Ewald for the reference.

41 *Sydney Morning Herald*, 27 February 2012.

Chapter 4

1 This interpretation is given in Michael Lehany, 'First Government House, Grounds and Garden History', *Report to Historic Houses Trust of New South Wales*, Sydney, 1994 cited in Tim McCormick (with Robert Irving, Elizabeth Imashev, Judy Nelson, Gordon Bull), *First Views of Australia 1788–1825, An early history of Sydney*, Sydney: David Ell Press, 1987, p. 44–45.

2 I am indebted to Joy Hughes, Museum of Sydney, for the definition of the garden as 'subsistence' rather than a 'kitchen' garden which implies a separate 'pleasure' garden also existed. Email correspondence, 23 December 2008.

3 G. Karskens, *The Colony, A history of early Sydney*, Sydney: Allen & Unwin, 2009, p. 106.

4 Baron Charles von Hugel, *New Holland Journal, November 1833–October 1834*, Dymphna Clark, trans. and ed., 1994, pp.263–264, <www.collection.hht.net.au/>.

5 John Stockdale, *The Voyage of Governor Phillip to Botany Bay with an Account of the Establishment of the Colonies of Port Jackson and Norfolk Island*, London: Printed by John Stockdale, 1789, p. 129.

6 Richard Johnson to Henry Fricker, 21 August 1790, Letters of Reverend Richard Johnson to Henry Fricker, ML Z SAFE 1/121. Watkin Tench (Tim Flannery, ed.), *1788*, Melbourne: Text Publishing, 1996, p. 153.

7 Arthur Phillip to Joseph Banks, 22 August 1790, ML CY3005/68.

8 A. J. Gray, 'Dodd, Henry Edward (?–1791)', *ADB*, <www.adb.anu.edu.au/biography/dodd-henry-edward-1984/text2411>, accessed 30 March 2012.

9 Robert Hughes, *The Fatal Shore, A History of Transportation of Convicts to Australia, 1787–1868*, London: Collins Harvill, 1987, p. 460–70; Frost, *Botany Bay*, p. 202–03; Karskens, *The Colony*, p. 63–64.

10 Philip Gidley King to Evan Nepean, 5 January 1791, *HRNSW*, vol. 1, p. 419.

11 Robert Ross to Arthur Phillip, 11 February 1791, *HRNSW*, vol. 1, p. 438.

12 Tench, *1788*, p. 179.

13 Tench is the only writer to record this occasion: *Sydney's First Four Years*, p. 321n.

14 Arthur Phillip to Joseph Banks, 3 December 1791, ML A81, pp. 39–40.

15 Tench, *Sydney's First Four Years*, p. 247.

16 The material here on Philip Schaeffer has been published in Julie McIntyre, 'Not rich and not British: Philip Schaeffer, "failed" farmer', *Journal of Australian Colonial History*, 11, 2009, pp. 1–20.

17 Deed of Land Grant to Philip Schaeffer, 22 February 1792, ML Safe 1/86; Arthur Phillip to William Grenville, 5 November 1791, *HRA* I, vol. 1, p. 271.

18 Arthur Phillip to William Grenville, 5 November 1791, *HRA* I, vol. 1, p. 279; on Governor Phillip's vision for agriculture using Rio de Janeiro as a model, see Angus McGillivery, 'Convict Settlers, Seamen's Greens, and Imperial Designs at Port Jackson: A maritime perspective of British settler agriculture', *Agricultural History*, 78, 3, 2004, pp. 261–70.

19 Enclosure No. 5, 'Return of Lands Granted in His Majesty's Territory of New South Wales and it's Dependences', Arthur Phillip to William Grenville, 5 November 1791, Bigge Appendix, ML A1213, p. 58.

20 Collins, *An Account of the English Colony*, p. 132; Tench, *Sydney's First Four Years*, p. 254.

21 Arthur Phillip to Henry Dundas, 19 March 1792, *HRA* I, vol. 1, p. 341.

22 Mrs Dashwood to Joseph Banks, 20 August 1792, Banks Papers, 1789–1796, ML A81.

23 Arthur Phillip to Henry Dundas, 2 October 1792, *HRA* I, vol. 1, p. 375.

24 William Paterson to Joseph Banks, 17 March 1795, ML A81.

25 Johann Frederich Blumenbach to Joseph Banks, 28 December 1794, pp. 222–23, Banks Papers, Mitchell Library Manuscript M1192, State Library of New South Wales.

26 Acting Governor Philip Gidley King to the Duke of Portland, 1 March 1802, *HRA* I, vol. 1, pp. 405–06.

27 Michael Flynn, *The Second Fleet, Britain's Grim Convict Armada of 1790*, Sydney: Library of Australian History, 2001, p. 522.

28 William Paterson to Joseph Banks, 20 February 1800, Banks Papers, ML A82, p. 125.

29 See Colleen Morris, *Lost Gardens of Sydney*, Sydney: Historic Houses Trust, 2008, p. 47.

30 Banks to Hunter, *The Letters of Sir Joseph Banks: A selection, 1768–1820*, pp. 201–02.

31 George Suttor to Joseph Banks, 16 May 1799, ML A79–3, p. 237; George Suttor to Joseph Banks, 25 August 1799, ML A79–3, p. 242; Letter from George Suttor (to unnamed correspondent), 8 November 1799, ML A79–3, p. 244.

32 George Suttor to Joseph Banks, 10 December 1800, ML A79–3, p. 272.

33 The Duke of Portland to the Governor of New South Wales, 22 April 1800, *HRA* I, vol. 2, p. 493.

34 Philip Gidley King to the Duke of Portland, 10 March 1801, *HRA* I, vol. 3, p. 6.

35 Philip Gidley King to Joseph Foveaux, 19 December 1800, Philip Gidley King's Letterbook 1797–1806, ML 2015, p. 169.

36 George Suttor, *The Culture of the Grape-Vine and the Orange in Australia and New Zealand*, London: Smith, Elder, 1843, p. 37.

37 The Frenchmen were promised an annual salary of £60 for three years' work in New South Wales, Philip Gidley King to the Duke of Portland, 10 March 1801, *HRA* I, vol. 3, p. 6.

38 J.B. Laideau, 'Method of Preparing a Piece of Land for the Purpose of Forming a Vineyard', Enclosure No. 1, Duke of Portland to the Governor of New South Wales, 22 April 1800, *HRA* I, vol. 2, pp. 494–96.

39 Philip Gidley King to Lord Hobart, 9 May 1803, *HRA* I, vol. 4, p. 78; *Sydney Gazette and New South Wales Advertiser*, 5 March 1803, 12 March 1803, 2 April 1803; Philip Gidley King to Lord Hobart, 9 May 1803, *HRA* I, vol. 4, p. 78.

40 Philip Gidley King to Joseph Foveaux, 19 December 1800, Philip Gidley King's Letterbook, ML 2015, p. 169.

41 Lord Hobart to Philip Gidley King, 30 January 1802, *HRA* I, vol. 3, p. 368.

42 Suttor, *Culture of the Grape-Vine*, p. 37.

43 *Australian Agricultural Act 1824*, 5 Geo. IV c. 86.

44 Elizabeth Macarthur to an unnamed friend, 22 August 1794, *HRNSW*, vol. 2, pp. 508–09.

45 V.W.E. Goodin, 'Townson, Robert (1762(?)–1827)', *ADB*, vol. 2, pp. 537–38.

46 Robert Townson, *Travels in Hungary with a Short Account of Vienna in the Year 1793*, London, printed for GG and J Robinson, 1797, pp. 262–74.

Chapter 5

1 Ambrose Serle to Samuel Marsden, 15 April 1805, Marsden Papers, vol. 1, MLMSS A1992, p. 27.
2 James Busby, *A Manual of Plain Directions for Planting and Cultivating a Vineyard and for Making Wine in New South Wales*, Sydney: Printed by R. Mansfield, for the executors of R. Howe, 1830, p. 39.
3 Unwin, *Wine and the Vine*, p. 300.
4 Henry Swinburne, *Travels Through Spain, in the Years 1775 and 1776*, vol. 2, London: n.p., 1787, p. 279.
5 Grace Karskens and Richard Waterhouse, '"too sacred to be taken away": Property, liberty, tyranny and the "Rum Rebellion"', *Journal of Australian Colonial History*, 12: pp. 1–22.
6 Gregory Blaxland to John Thomas Bigge, 28 November 1815, ML Bigge Appendix BT Box 15, p. 1473.
7 Thomas Pinney, *A History of Wine in America: From the beginnings to prohibition*, Berkeley: University of California Press, 1989, pp. 121–22.
8 John Macarthur (senior) to John Macarthur (junior), 9 April 1815, ML A2899, p. 1; James Macarthur, Unpublished Journal, 12 March 1815 to 28 April 1816, ML A2929.
9 James Macarthur, Unpublished journal dated 12 March 1815 to 28 April 1816, in Macarthur Family Papers, ML A2929.
10 Maro (William Macarthur), *Letters on the Culture of the Vine, Fermentation, and the Management of Wine in the Cellar*, Sydney: Statham and Forster, 1844, pp. v–vii.
11 T. H. Scott to John Macarthur (junior), 22 March 1822, Macarthur Papers, ML A2955.
12 ibid.
13 Maro (William Macarthur), *Letters on the Culture of the Vine*, p. vii.
14 (Edward Macarthur and William Macarthur), *Some Account of the Vineyards at Camden on the Nepean River, Forty Miles South West of Sydney, the Property of James and William Macarthur*, London: Printed by John Nichols, Milton Press, 1849, p. 3.
15 James Macarthur, Journal, ML A2929.
16 Jill Conway, 'Blaxland, Gregory (1778–1853)', *ADB*, vol. 1, pp. 115–17.
17 Gregory Blaxland to Earl Bathurst, August 1816, Bigge Appendix, BT Box 15, p. 1470.
18 Conway, 'Blaxland', pp. 115–17.
19 Gregory Blaxland to Earl Bathurst, August 1816, Bigge Appendix, BT Box 15, p. 1470.
20 Gregory Blaxland to Lachlan Macquarie, August 1816, Bigge Appendix, BT Box 15, pp. 1466–69.
21 Gregory Blaxland, 'A Statement on the Progress of the Culture of the Vine', Bigge Appendix, BT Box 17, pp. 2266–67; James Busby, *A Manual of Plain Directions*, pp. 37–38.
22 Society for the Encouragement of Arts Manufactures and Commerce, Transactions of the Society, vol. 50, London: The Society, 1823, p. xiv.
23 John Thomas Bigge to George Wilmot MP, 18 November 1822, Bigge Appendix, BT Box 28.
24 Society for the Encouragement of Arts Manufactures and Commerce, 'Wine from New South Wales', *Transactions*. vol. 46, in Bigge's Appendix BT Box 61, pp. 104–05.
25 Society for the Encouragement of Arts Manufactures and Commerce, *Transactions*, vol. 50, pp. xxxi–xxxii.
26 Laffer, *Wine Industry of Australia*, p. 118.
27 Louis Isidore Duperrey cited in Norrie, *Vineyards of Sydney*, p. 95.
28 Edward Ford, 'Redfern, William (1774?–1833)', *ADB*, vol. 2, pp. 368–71.
29 Sarah Redfern on behalf of William Redfern to Earl Bathurst, 1824, *HRA* I, vol. 11, p. 203.
30 Driscoll, *The Beginnings of the Wine Industry*, p. 25.
31 John Thomas Bigge, *Report of the Commissioner of Inquiry on the State of Agriculture and Trade in the Colony of New South Wales*, London: Printed by order of the British House of Commons, 1823, p. 87.
32 James Busby, *A Treatise on the Culture of the Vine and the Art of Making Wine; Compiled from the works of Chaptal, and other French writers; and from the notes of the compiler, during a residence in some of the wine provinces of France*, Facsimile edition, 1979, Sydney: David Ell Press, pp. xix, xxvi.
33 E. Ramsden, 'James Busby, the Prophet of Australian Viticulture', *Journal of the Royal Australian Historical Society*, 26, 1940, p. 369.
34 Busby, *A Treatise*, pp. 109–10 and 137.
35 ibid., pp. 38–39.
36 Busby, *A Treatise*, pp. 41 and 48.
37 Thomas Brisbane to Earl Bathurst, 14 May 1825, *HRA* I, vol. 11, pp. 574 and 586; James Busby to Sir George Murray, Secretary of State for the Colonies, 10 January 1831, *HRA* I, vol. 16, p. 41.
38 Ramsden, 'James Busby', p. 364.
39 Ramsden, 'James Busby'. p. 370.
40 ibid., p. 371.
41 *The Colonist*, 3 September 1835.
42 *Sydney Gazette*, 5 March 1831.
43 *The Colonist*, 3 September 1835.
44 James Busby to Viscount Goderich, 6 January 1832, *HRA* I, vol. 11, p. 508.
45 Busby, *Journal of a Tour*, pp. 2–5.
46 Francis Forbes, Alexander McLeay, John Jamison, William Macarthur, Thomas Shepherd, 'Report on the Vines, Introduced into the Colony of New South Wales, in the Year 1832, by James Busby, 1834', Macarthur Papers, MI. A4298.
47 Maro (Macarthur), *Letters on the Culture of the Vine*, p. 18.
48 William Macarthur to Thomas Holt, 15 July 1844, Macarthur Papers, Volume 37B, Sir William Macarthur, Letterbooks 1844–1874, ML A2933, p. 56.
49 No author, *The Murray Valley Vineyard and Australian Vines and Wines*, Melbourne: Azzopardi, Hildreth, 1874, Ken Helm Collection, pp. 22–23.
50 Bigge, *Report*, pp. 13, 80.
51 On Jamison's vineyard see Colleen Morris, *Lost Gardens of Sydney*, Sydney: Historic Houses Trust, 2009, pp. 51–52.
52 Busby, *Manual of Plain Directions*, pp. 30 and 42.
53 *Sydney Gazette*, 6 February 1834.
54 Ramsden, 'James Busby', p. 371.
55 Suttor, *The Culture of the Grape-Vine*, p. 83.
56 ibid., pp. 71–72.
57 ibid., pp. 50–56 and 130–34.
58 M. Roe, *Quest for Authority in Eastern Australia, 1835–1851*, Melbourne: Melbourne University Press, 1965, p.48.
59 These members were: Alexander Berry, William Bland, Charles Cowper, Edward Cox, John Dunmore Lang, William Lawson, Hannibal Macarthur, William Macarthur, Thomas Mitchell, Alexander Park and William Charles Wentworth.
60 *Maitland Mercury*, 25 January 1853.
61 Suttor, *The Culture of the Grape-Vine*, p. 18.
62 Liz Thach and Lillian Bynum, 'Managing Human Resources in the Wine Industry', in Liz Thach and Tim Matz (eds), *Wine, a Global Business*, New York: Miranda Press, 2004, pp. 170–71.
63 Letter from Ellen Ogilvie cited in Allan Wood, *Dawn in the Valley, The story of settlement in the Hunter River Valley to 1833*, Sydney: Wentworth Books, 1972, p. 188.
64 Journal of Thomas Mitchell, Sir Thomas Livingstone Mitchell Papers, ML A295 3, p. 273; <www.records.nsw.gov.au> Archives-in-brief-83, accessed 20 February 2012.
65 J.D. Lang, *An Historical and Statistical Account of New South Wales*, London: Sampson, Low, Marston, Low & Searle, 1875, p. 106.
66 Lang, *Historical and Statistical Account*, pp. 106, 271–72.
67 Ambrose Serle to Samuel Marsden, 15 April 1805, Marsden Papers, vol. 1, ML A1992, p. 27.
68 Frederick Hely, superintendent of convicts, 1832 cited in Driscoll, *Beginnings of the Wine Industry*, p. 11–12.
69 Richard Bourke, 'Proclamation on Emigration (1835)', *HRA* I, vol. 18, p. 828.
70 Edward Macarthur to George Grey, 15

March 1837, *HRA* I, vol. 18, pp. 717–718.

71 Lord Glenelg to Governor Bourke, 29 March 1837, *HRA* I, vol. 18, pp. 716–717.

72 David Blackbourn, *The Long Nineteenth Century, A History of Germany 1780–1918*, New York: Oxford University Press, 1997, p. 113.

73 Edward Macarthur to Henry Laboucher, 15 July 1839, New South Wales Governor's Despatches, May to August 1839, ML A1280, p. 451. Macarthur anglicised the Germans' first names in this record.

74 'Copy of the Agreement', Macarthur Papers, ML A2918, p. 155.

75 Alan Atkinson, *Camden: Farm and Village Life in Early New South Wales*, Melbourne: Oxford University Press, 1988, pp. 36–38.

76 William Macarthur to Captain O'Halloran, 1 October 1844, ML A2933, p. 82; Clements Lester to William Macarthur, 19 May 1845, ML A2918, pp. 293–295; William Macarthur to Clements Lester, 19 May 1845, ML A2918, pp. 297–298.

77 See D. F. Branigan, T. G. Vallance, 'Keene, William (1798–1872)', *ADB*, vol. 5, p. 6.

78 'List of persons to whom permission has been given to import Labourers from the Continent of Europe under the Notice of the 7th April 1847', Enclosure in Governor FitzRoy's Despatch No. 232 to George Grey, 1847, NSW Governor's Despatches, 1846–1848, ML A1267–23.

79 The migration figures include Germans to colonies other than New South Wales and are from R.F. Haines, *Nineteenth Century Government Assisted Immigrants from the United Kingdom to Australia: Schemes, regulations and arrivals, 1831–1900 and some vital statistics 1834–1860 (Occasional Papers in Economic History No. 3)*, Adelaide: Flinders University, 1995, pp. 51. By contrast, more than a million Germans migrated to North America between 1830 and 1860: E.J. Passant, *A Short History of Germany 1815–1945*, Cambridge: Cambridge University Press, 1959, p. 81. See also James Jupp and Barry York, *Birthplaces of the Australian People: Colonial and Commonwealth Censuses, 1828–1991*, Canberra: Centre for Immigration and Multicultural Studies, 1995, p. 14.

80 Driscoll, *The Beginnings of the Wine Industry*, p. 25.

81 William Macarthur to Thomas Mitchell, 26 July 1844, Macarthur Papers, ML A2933, p. 70; James King to Thomas Mitchell, Sir Thomas Livingstone Mitchell Papers, 31 July 1848, ML A293. William Macarthur to 'Mr Lawson', 7 August 1846, ML A2933, p. 98.

82 Journal of Sir Thomas Mitchell, ML A295–2, pp. 179–80.

83 Macarthur communicated these details to Alex Kelly, *The Vine in Australia*,

Melbourne: Red Dog 2008 (first published 1861), p. 34.

84 *Australian Town and Country Journal*, 22 September 1883, p. 32.

85 *Murray Valley Vineyard*, p. 21.

86 Thomas Hardy, *Notes on Vineyards in America and Europe*, Adelaide: L. Henn & Co., 1885; Thomas Hardy, *A Vigneron Abroad: Trip to South Africa*, Adelaide: s.n., 1899.

87 Quotes are from *The Argus* (Melbourne), 10 March 1897.

88 Michael Godley, 'Bacchus of the East: The Chinese grape wine industry 1892–1938', *Business History Review*, 60, no. 3, 1986: pp. 383–409.

Chapter 6

1 Karskens and Waterhouse, 'Property, Liberty, Tyranny', p. 2.

2 Karskens, *The Colony*, p. 126. See also McIntyre, 'Philip Schaeffer', p. 4.

3 A.E. Dingle, '"The Truly Magnificent Thirst": An historical survey of Australian drinking habits', *Historical Studies*, 19, 1980, pp. 228–29.

4 Karskens, *The Colony*, p. 78.

5 George Caley to Joseph Banks, 7 July 1808, ML A79–1, p. 185.

6 Vivienne Parsons, 'Hayes, Michael (1767–1825)', *ADB*, <www.adb.anu.edu.au/biography/hayes-michael–2174/text2791>, accessed 25 January 2012.

7 On price, see Hori, 'Wine and Conspicuous Consumption', pp. 1457–69.

8 *Sydney Gazette*, 10 August 1811.

9 ibid., 26 October 1811.

10 Hannibal Macarthur to John Macarthur, 4 July 1813, ML MSS 2901.

11 Hannibal Macarthur to John Macarthur, 16 August 1813, ML MSS 2901.

12 Hannibal Macarthur to John Macarthur, 16 May 1814, ML MSS 2901.

13 *The Australian*, 16 June 1825.

14 *The Sydney Herald*, 28 December 1840.

15 Colin Dyer, 'The Indigenous Australians in Sydney and Its Environs as Seen by French Explorers, 1802–1831', *Journal of the Royal Australian Historical Society*, 88, 2, 2002: p. 157.

16 Roe, *Quest for Authority*, pp. 69, 165,166.

17 ibid., p. 168.

18 *The Teetotaller, and General Newspaper*, 8 January 1842.

19 7 Vict. No. 7. See also George Gipps to Lord Stanley, New South Wales Governors' Despatches to the Secretary of State for the Colonies, vol. 44, January–April 1844, ML A1233, pp. 24–25.

20 Roe, *Quest for Authority*, p. 174.

21 George Gipps to Lord Stanley, ML A1233, p. 25.

22 George Gipps to Lord Stanley, ML A1233,

pp. 26–30.

23 Lord Russell to Governor George Gipps, 4 July 1841, Secretary of State for the Colonies' Despatches to the Governor of New South Wales, April–July 1841, ML A1285, pp. 609–11.

24 Lord Russell to Governor George Gipps, 28 March 1841, ML A1284, pp. 763–71.

25 James King, *Australia may be an Extensive Wine-Producing Country*, Edinburgh: Printed for private circulation, 1857, p. 3.

26 A. Lynn Martin, 'National Reputations for Drinking in Traditional Europe', *Parergon* 17, 2, 1999: pp. 175–6.

27 Smith, *Wealth of Nations*, vol. 1, p. 518.

28 Julie McIntyre, 'Adam Smith and faith in the transformative qualities of wine in colonial New South Wales', *Australian Historical Studies*, 42, no. 2, 2011: pp. 194–211.

29 *Sydney Morning Herald*, 5 October 1859.

30 *New South Wales Medical Gazette*, July 1872, in Lindeman (Holdings) Ltd Papers, Z418/Box 157, NBAC.

31 *Sydney Morning Herald*, 6 September 1862.

32 Unwin, *Wine and the Vine*, p. 333.

33 *Sydney Morning Herald*, 6 September 1862.

34 ibid., 6 September 1862.

35 ibid., 6 September 1862.

36 ibid., 1 November 1862.

37 ibid., 1 November 1862.

38 ibid., 17 December 1862; *Sydney Morning Herald*, 22 December 1863.

39 *New South Wales Medical Gazette*, July 1872.

40 *The Brisbane Courier*, 21 June 1873.

41 Henry Lindeman to the Editor, *Sydney Morning Herald*, 25 December 1867, in Lindeman (Holdings) Ltd Papers, Z418/Box 157, NBAC.

42 L. Holden to 'Bertie', Z418/Box 148, NBAC.

43 *New South Wales Medical Gazette*, July 1872.

44 Burnett, *Liquid Pleasures*, pp. 148–49.

45 D. Dunstan, *Better than Pommard!: A history of wine in Victoria*, Melbourne: Australian Scholarly Publishing, 1994, pp. 158–59.

46 Penny Russell (ed.), *This Errant Lady: Jane Franklin's overland journey to Port Phillip and Sydney, 1839*, Canberra: National Library of Australia, 2002, p. 135.

47 Busby, *Manual of Plain Directions*, pp. 10 and 27.

48 Suttor, *Culture of the Grape-Vine*, p. i.

49 Kate Hassall to Reverend James Hassall, 15 & 16 February 1846, Hassall Family Correspondence, ML A1667–3, p. 3011.

50 Eliza Hassall to Reverend James Hassall, 23 February 1848, ML A1677–1, p. 315.

51 Thomas Mitchell to Roderick Mitchell, 12 March 1846, Sir Thomas Livingstone Mitchell Papers, ML 295–2, p. 106.

52 *Sydney Morning Herald*, 25 December 1867.

53 See for example, Hubert De Castella to Henry Parkes, 29 October 1881, Parkes Correspondence, vol. 50, MLMSS A920, pp. 614–19.

Chapter 7

1 James Belich, *Replenishing the Earth: The settler revolution and the rise of the Anglo-world*, Oxford: Oxford University Press, 2009.
2 ibid., pp. 1–25.
3 ibid., pp. 145–79.
4 H. Mortimer Franklyn, *A Glance at Australia in 1880: Or, Food from the South: Showing the Present Condition and Production of Some of Its Leading Industries, namely, wool, wine, grain, dressed meat, etc etc*, Melbourne: The Victorian Review Publishing Company, 1881, pp. 160–61.
5 H.C.L. Anderson, *New South Wales Statistical Register for 1906 and Previous Years. Compiled from Official Returns*, Sydney: The Government of the State of New South Wales, 1908, pp. 920–21.
6 Tench, *Sydney's First Four Years*, p. 75.
7 Erica Hannickel, 'Cultivation and Control: Grape growing as expansion in nineteenth-century United States and Australia', *Comparative American Studies*, 8, 4, 2010: p. 296.
8 Ernest Seyd, *California and its Resources, A work for the Merchant, the Capitalist and the Emigrant*, London: Trübner & Co, 1858, p. 135.
9 Belich, *Replenishing the Earth*, pp. 85–89; Kym Anderson and Robert Osmond, *Trends and Cycles in the Australian Wine Industry, 1850 to 2000*, Adelaide: Centre for International Economic Studies, University of Adelaide, 1998, p. 38. Note that the first boom in booster literature on wine growing occurred only in New South Wales due to timing of settlement.
10 T. Pinney, *A History of Wine in America: From the Beginnings to Prohibition*, Berkeley: University of California Press, 1989, pp. 221–22.
11 See for example, *New South Wales Magazine*, 1 September 1833.
12 Driscoll, *Beginnings of the Wine Industry*, p. 37.
13 George McEwin, *The South Australian Vigneron and Gardeners' Manual Containing Plain Practical Directions for the Cultivation of the Vine ... Etc Etc*, Adelaide: James Allen, 1843.
14 Maro (Macarthur), *Letters on the Culture of the Vine*, p. i.
15 Driscoll, *Beginnings of the Wine Industry*, p. 37.
16 David Mossenson, 'Nash, Richard West (1808–1850)', *ADB*, vol. 2, p. 278.

17 John Belperroud and David Pettavel, *The Vine: With instructions for its cultivation, for a period of six years: The treatment of the soil, and how to make wine from Victorian grapes*, Geelong: Heath and Cordell, 1859; John Bleasdale, *On Colonial Wines: A paper read before the Royal Society of Victoria, 13th May 1867*, Melbourne: Printed by Stillwell and Knight, 1867; Kelly, *The Vine in Australia*; Alex Kelly, *Wine Growing in Australia* (1867), Sydney: David Ell Press, 1980.
18 Alan Atkinson, *The Europeans in Australia, Vol. 2, Democracy*, Melbourne: Oxford University Press, 2004, p. 245.
19 *Sydney Gazette*, 3 December 1831.
20 *Sydney Morning Herald*, 12 November 1912; early Bathurst settlers were all known wine growers.
21 *Maitland Mercury*, 13 November 1850.
22 Comparison from Beverley Kingston, *A History of New South Wales*, Melbourne: Cambridge University Press, 2006, p. 61.
23 Details from notes in Dominic Williams Collection.
24 Anderson and Osmond, *Trends and Cycles*, p. 4.
25 A. Kelly, *The Vine in Australia*, Facsimile of 1861 edn, Sydney: David Ell Press, 1980, p. 2.
26 Hubert De Castella, *John Bull's Vineyard*, Melbourne: Sands & McDougall, 1886.
27 Simpson, *Creating Wine Business*, pp. 235–39.
28 G. Bell, 'The South Australian Wine Industry, 1858–1876', *Journal of Wine Research*, 4, 1993, pp. 147–64.
29 W.P. Driscoll, 'Fallon, James Thomas (1823–1886)', *ADB*, vol 4, p. 151.
30 J.T. Fallon, The Wines of Australia: A Paper Read before the Royal Colonial Institute on the 20th of June 1876, London: Unwin Brothers, 1876, pp. 5, 7 and 17.
31 John Barleycorn, *A Glass of Ale*, Melbourne: Printed by McCarron, Bird and Co, 1873, p. 7, DSM/042/P41, SLNSW.
32 Waterhouse, *The Vision Splendid*, pp. 130–31.
33 Dingle, 'The Truly Magnificent Thirst', pp. 243 and 248.
34 Waterhouse, *The Vision Splendid*, p. 130.
35 Cited in Gerald Walsh, 'The Wine Industry of Australia 1778–1979', paper presented at the Wine Talk symposium, Canberra, September 1979, p. 12.
36 *Statistical Register of New South Wales for the Year 1888*, Sydney: Charles Potter, Government Printer, 1889, p. 293. A thorough account of such licences was given for the years 1887 and 1888.
37 *The New York Times*, 7 July 1889.
38 Cecily Joan Mitchell, *Hunter's River, A history of early families and the homes they built in the lower Hunter Valley*

between 1830 and 1860, Sydney: The Family of Cecily Joan Mitchell, 1984, p. 72.
39 *Wagga Wagga Express*, 9 January 1892.
40 Beatrice Davis and Jamie Grant (eds) *Australian Verse, An illustrated treasury*, Sydney: State Library of New South Wales Press, 1996, p. 21.
41 Cited in Richard White, *Inventing Australia, Images and Identity, 1688–1980*, Sydney: Allen & Unwin, 1981, p. 100.
42 R.F. Brissenden, 'Wine and Poetry', paper presented at the Wine Talk symposium, Canberra, September 1979: pp. 32–33.
43 Philip Muskett, *The Art of Living in Australia*, London: Eyre & Spottiswoode, 1893, ch. 12.
44 'The Romance of Wine Making in Australia', Z418/Box 148, NBAC.
45 Kenneth D. Boyer, 'Is There a Principle for Defining Industries? Reply', *Southern Economic Journal*, 52, no. 2, 1985, p. 542.
46 *Times of London*, 27 November 1855.

Chapter 8

1 The way in which demand for fresh food out of season drove industrial farming and related technologies in the United States is discussed in Higman, *How Food Made History*, p. 71.
2 G. Raby, *Making Rural Australia: An economic history of technical and institutional creativity 1788–1860*, Melbourne: Oxford University Press, 1996, p. 153.
3 Captain Baudin to A. de Jussieu, 20 Brumaire, XI (1803), BT Biography, vol. 1, ML 2000–1, pp. 236–37.
4 John Thomas Bigge to Robert Wilmot (on behalf of Gregory Blaxland), 18 November 1822, Bigge's Appendix, BT ML BT28, pp. 6990–92.
5 See for example, *Sydney Gazette*, 5 March 1831; *Sydney Gazette*, 25 June 1831.
6 Maro [Macarthur], *Letters on the Culture of the Vine*, pp. 30–34.
7 Laffer, *Wine Industry of Australia*, p. 18; Charles James King, 'The First Fifty Years of Agriculture in New South Wales', in *Extracts from Review of Marketing and Agricultural Economic, August 1948–December 1949*, Sydney: Department of Agriculture, 1950, pp. 569–70.
8 Maro (Macarthur), *Letters on the Culture of the Vine*, pp. 30–34.
9 *Maitland Mercury*, 8 March 1851.
10 Paul D. Peterson, Clay S. Griffith and C. Lee Campbell, 'Frank Lamson-Scribner and American Plant Pathology, 1885–1888', *Agricultural History*, 70, 1, 1996, p. 33.
11 Alfred Crosby, *Ecological Imperialism: The biological expansion of Europe, 900–1900*, Cambridge: Cambridge University Press, 1986.

12 Unwin, *Wine and the Vine*, pp. 203–92.

13 Robinson, *Oxford Companion to Wine*, pp. 543–44.

14 De Castella, *John Bull's Vineyard*, p. 137.

15 *Sydney Morning Herald*, 4 December 1867.

16 ibid., 5 December 1867.

17 ibid., 10 December 1867.

18 ibid., 4 February 1869; 6 February 1869; 10 February 1869.

19 ibid., 13 February 1869.

20 ibid., 19 February 1869; 20 February 1869; 21 February 1869.

21 ibid., 23 January 1869; 30 January 1869. Petitions about the Diseases in Grapes Vines Bill were also received from other regions but it is not clear whether they were for or against. The districts represented were Wagga Wagga, Goulburn and Campbelltown.

22 ibid., 23 January 1869.

23 ibid., 23 January 1869.

24 *The Albury Banner*, 10 April 1869.

25 ibid., 10 April 1869.

26 Christy Campbell, *Phylloxera, How Wine Was Saved for the World*, London: Harper Perennial, 2004, p. 31.

27 Diary of George Wyndham, ML B1313.

28 Peterson et al., 'Frank Lamson-Scribner', pp. 42–45.

29 *The Albury Banner*, 11 March 1871.

30 *The Brisbane Courier*, 21 June 1873.

31 *The Albury Banner*, 29 May 1872.

32 David Randall to Henry Parkes, 11 March 1874, Parkes Correspondence, ML A903.

33 George Ordish, *The Great Wine Blight*, London: Dent, 1972, p. 168.

34 *Sydney Morning Herald*, 14 January 1886.

35 Campbell, *Phylloxera*, p. 221.

36 H.C. Anderson, *New South Wales Statistical Register for 1906 and Previous Years*, Sydney: the Government of the State of New South Wales, 1908, p. 920.

37 Ordish, *Great Wine Blight*, pp. 168–77.

38 *Australian Town and Country Magazine*, 22 June 1895, p. 20. The history and consequences of Victoria's vine pull policy have been best explored in Dunstan, *Better than Pommard!*, ch. 7.

39 *New South Wales Government Gazette* (*NSW Gov. Gazette*), vol. 1, 1878, p. 465.

40 *The [ ] Argus*, 10 January 1911.

41 *Sydney Morning Herald*, 10 October 1878.

42 ibid., 27 May 1885.

43 Hardy, *Notes on Vineyards*, p. 16.

44 *Maitland Mercury*, 21 June 1892.

45 ibid., 20 November 1886.

46 Henry Bonnard, Progress Report to the Director of the Botanic Gardens, 22 August 1885 and final Report to the Director of the Botanic Gardens Sydney, 1 September 1885, ML A2970.

47 *Maitland Mercury*, 7 December 1886.

48 ibid., 2 June 1887.

49 *Australian Town and Country Journal*, 22 June 1895, p. 20.

50 D. Gillies to the Colonial Secretary of New South Wales, January 1888, Colonial Secretary of New South Wales Correspondence, Phylloxera Papers 1888–9, SRNSW 4/890.2.

51 E Burney Young to the Chief Secretary (Adelaide), 7 August 1888, SRNSW 4/890.2; Chief Secretary (Adelaide) to New South Wales Colonial Secretary, 17 August 1888, SRNSW 4/890.2.

52 Charles Moore to the Colonial Secretary, 3 September 1888, SRNSW 4/890.2.

53 *NSW Gov. Gazette*, vol. 1, 1887, p. 1069.

54 *NSW Gov. Gazette*, vol. 1, 1888, p. 489; *NSW Gov. Gazette*, vol. 3, 1888, p. 6287.

55 Charles Moore to the Colonial Secretary, 21 September 1888, SRNSW 4/890.2.

56 Charles Moore to the Colonial Secretary, 2 October 1888, SRNSW 4/890.2.

57 Charles Moore to the Colonial Secretary, 28 September 1888; Office of the New South Wales Colonial Secretary to the Premier of Victoria, Duncan Gillies, 29 September 1888, Charles Moore to Colonial Secretary, 26 March 1889; 15 October 1888; SRNSW 4/890.2.

58 *Australian Town and Country Journal*, 13 March 1886, p. 21.

59 *Clarence and Richmond Examiner*, 3 January 1882, 1 April 1882, 15 September 1885.

60 Ordish, *Great Wine Blight*, pp. 208–11.

61 *Maitland Mercury*, 12 June 1883; Dr Nolz to the New South Wales Colonial Secretary, undated, SRNSW 4/890.2; Charles Moore to the Colonial Secretary, 17 October 1888; Premier of Victoria to New South Wales Colonial Secretary, 22 October 1888; Charles Moore to the Colonial Secretary, 25 October 1888; Charles Moore to the Colonial Secretary, 29 October 1888; Charles Moore to the Colonial Secretary, 26 November 1888; John Kidd to the Colonial Secretary, 15 December 1888, SRNSW 4/890.2.

62 Charles Moore to the Colonial Secretary, 26 February 1889, SRNSW 4/890.2.

63 Honorary Secretary of the Corowa Vine and Fruit Growers' Association to the Colonial Secretary, 20 April 1889, SRNSW 4/890.2.

64 *Daily Telegraph*, 16 March 1889.

65 Charles Moore to the Colonial Secretary, 26 March 1889, SRNSW 4/890.2.

66 *Clarence and Richmond Examiner*, 12 January 1889; 30 March 1889.

67 *NSW Gov. Gazette*, vol. 3, 1890: p. 4999; *Agricultural Gazette of New South Wales*, vol. 1, 1890. p. 353, *NSW Gov. Gazette*, vol. 4, 1892: p. 5332; *NSW Gov. Gazette*, vol. 5, 1893: pp. 6922, 7180, 8390; *NSW Gov. Gazette*, vol. 1, 1894: pp. 59, 653, 711, 1033, 1044; *NSW Gov. Gazette*, vol. 2, 1894: pp. 2277, 2278, 2539; *NSW Gov. Gazette*, vol. 2, 1894: p. 1478.

68 *Maitland Mercury*, 21 June 1892.

69 *The Brisbane Courier*, 19 January 1897.

70 Louis L. Smith to Victorian Minister for Agriculture, 27 December 1882, Miscellaneous Reports, Victoria Phylloxera 1876–1890; W.T. Thiselton-Dyer to Saul Samuel, 1 November 1895; Saul Samuel to W. T. Thiselton-Dyer, 5 January 1897; W.T. Thiselton-Dyer to Saul Samuel, 6 February 1897; Saul Samuel to W. T. Thiselton-Dyer, 9 February 1897, Kew MR/400.

71 Department of Agriculture expert, Michele Blunno had recommended this action from 1897, see P. J. Mylrea, *In the Service of Agriculture: A Centennial History of the New South Wales Department of Agriculture, 1890–1990*, Sydney: NSW Agriculture and Fisheries, 1990, p. 58.

72 *The Brisbane Courier*, 2 November 1898. See also T.A. Coghlan, *Wealth and Progress 1898–1899*, Twelfth issue, Sydney: Printed by William Applegate Gullick for the NSW Government, 1900, p. 785.

73 Mylrea, *In the Service of Agriculture*, pp. 55–56.

74 *Agricultural Gazette of New South Wales*, vol. 1, 1890: pp. 1–2.

75 Mylrea, *In the Service of Agriculture*, pp. 57–59 and 269.

76 J.A. Despessis, 'Choice Italian Grapes', *Agricultural Gazette of New South Wales*, vol. 2, December 1891, pp.804–06.

77 Everard Digby (ed.), 'John A. Wilkinson, Esquire, Coolalta', *Australian Men of Mark*, vol. 2, series 4, Sydney: Charles Maxwell, 1889, pp. 274–76. Thanks to Don Seton-Wilkinson.

78 W.P. Driscoll, 'Wilkinson, Audrey Harold (1877–1962)', *ADB*, <www.adb.anu.edu.au>, accessed 29 February 2012.

79 A.R. Callaghan and A.J. Millington, *The Wheat Industry in Australia*, Sydney: Angus and Robertson, 1956, p. 4.

80 *Maitland Mercury*, 12 May 1849, in James King Papers, 1826, 1839–1920, ML 682/3x, frame 47.

81 'Regulations of the Hunter River Vineyard Association, instituted 19th May, 1847, for the Purpose of Promoting the Culture of the Vine, and Turning its Products to the Most Profitable Account' in *Historical Summary of the Proceedings and Reports of the Hunter River Vineyard Association, from its Origination to its First Annual Meeting in the Year 1853*, Sydney: W. R. Piddington, 1854, p. 40.

82 Cited in Mitchell, *Hunter's River*, pp. 41–42.

83 Cited in James T. Fallon, *The Wines of Australia: A paper read before the Royal Colonial Institute on the 20th of June 1876*, London: Unwin Brothers, 1876, p. 5.

84 Fallon, *The Wines of Australia*, p. 34.

85 ibid., p. 35.

86 Driscoll, 'Fallon, James Thomas', p. 151.
87 Busby, *A Manual*, p. 81.
88 J. Thompson, 'A Continuous Wine Press', *Agricultural Gazette of New South Wales*, vol. 10, August 1899, p. 837.
89 See Appendix 2.
90 *Statistical Register of New South Wales, for the Year 1888*, Sydney: Charles Potter, Government Printer, 1889, pp. 244–45.
91 *Sydney Morning Herald*, 22 February 1890.
92 *Maitland Mercury*, 26 June 1883.
93 Leonce Frere, 'Report on Colonial Timbers to be Used as Wine Casks', *Agricultural Gazette of New South Wales*, vol. 10, 1899, pp. 1260–63.
94 See for example, *Maitland Mercury*, 25 January 1851.
95 *Australian Brewer's Journal*, 20 November 1888; P.F. Adams, 'Directions for Bottling Wine for Private Use', *Agricultural Gazette of New South Wales*, vol. 6, March 1895, p. 188.
96 *Maitland Mercury*, 26 June 1883.
97 *Sydney Morning Herald*, 16 December 2011.

Chapter 9

1 Society for the Arts, 'Wine from New South Wales', pp. 104–05.
2 This approximation has been devised using details from Robinson, *Oxford Companion*, pp. 76, 172–73.
3 R. Montgomery Martin, *History of Southern Africa*, London: John Mortimer, 1836, p. 240.
4 John Macarthur (junior) to James Macarthur, 24 March 1822, ML A2911, pp. 139–40.
5 John Macarthur (senior) to John Macarthur (junior), 24 January 1824, ML A2911, pp. 94–95.
6 Vineyard dates from Macarthur, *Some Account*, p. 3; quote and brandy details from William Macarthur to Edward Macarthur, 5 June 1832, ML A2935, pp. 21–22.
7 Busby, *Journal of a Tour*, p. 2.
8 *Sydney Morning Herald*, 6 September 1862.
9 Penny Russell, *This Errant Lady: Jane Franklin's overland journey to Port Phillip and Sydney, 1839*, Canberra: National Library of Australia, 2002, p.140 and 149; Jane Franklin to James King, undated, James King Papers, ML 682/1, pp. 237–38. On the emergence of the Tasmanian industry see Tony Walker, 'The History of the Wine Industry in Tasmania', Masters thesis, History, University of Tasmania, 2012.
10 *The Weekly Register*, 7 December 1844.
11 A label from the Camden Park archives for an 1876 Muscat uses exactly the same design, Macarthur Family Private Collection.
12 Joubert & Murphy to James and William Macarthur, 5 August 1847, ML A2968.
13 C.L. [unreadable] to James and William Macarthur, 14 January 1846, ML 2968.
14 Letter to Reverend [indecipherable] from William Macarthur, 26 July 1844, ML A2933, pp. 6, 23–6 and 69.
15 *Sydney Morning Herald* article reprinted in *Maitland Mercury*, 20 October 1849.
16 The imitation of Camden wine is referred to in Atkinson, *Camden*, p. 90.
17 Norrie, *Vineyards of Sydney*, p. 127.
18 R. Dunphy and L. Lockshin, 'A History of the Australian Wine Show System', *Journal of Wine Research*, 9, 1998, p. 89.
19 Brian H. Fletcher, *The Grand Parade, A history of the Royal Agricultural Society of New South Wales*, Sydney: The Royal Agricultural Society of New South Wales, 1988, p. 28.
20 Dunphy and Lockshin, 'A History of the Australian Wine Show System', p. 89.
21 Merab Harris Tauman, 'Lochee, Francis (1811–1893)', *ADB*, vol. 2, pp. 121–22.
22 Fletcher, *Grand Parade*, p. 35.
23 Driscoll, *The Beginnings of the Wine Industry*, p. 50.
24 'Regulations of the Hunter River Vineyard Association, instituted 19th May, 1847, for the Purpose of Promoting the Culture of the Vine, and Turning its Products to the Most Profitable Account' in *Historical Summary of the Proceedings and Reports of the Hunter River Vineyard Association, from its Origination to its First Annual Meeting in the Year 1853*, Sydney: W.R. Piddington, 1854, pp. 3–4.
25 *The Perth Gazette*, 29 March 1850.
26 *Maitland Mercury*, 21 April 1855.
27 *Annual Report of the New South Wales Vineyard Association (NSWVA)*, Sydney: Printed by D.L. Welch, c1851, pp. 7, 13–15.
28 Fletcher believed the NSWVA members were more dispersed on the Cumberland Plain than the Hunter, which had a greater 'identity of interest' in wine growing: Fletcher, *Grand Parade*, pp. 41–42; office bearers are listed by Fletcher at pp. 313–22.
29 *Maitland Mercury*, 4 January 1851.
30 Pinney, *Wine in America*, p. 217. The first group was the Gasconade Grape Growing Society of Hermann, Missouri.
31 Hoffenberg, *An Empire on Display*, pp. 5–8.
32 Handwritten draft entitled 'Wines from Camden', ML A2869; Macarthur, *Some Account*, p. 11.
33 Maro [William Macarthur], *Letter on the Culture of the Vine*, p. 27.
34 Macarthur, *Some Account*, p. 4. This booklet appeared to be published in 1849 but a note on the cover of the copy in the Macarthur archive has the date changed to '51' and a note 'June 1851' In the top right-hand corner of the cover; Macarthur Papers, ML A2969.
35 Macarthur, *Some Account*, p. 5.
36 King related this story, including the report on the Macarthurs, in Hunter River Vineyard Association (HRVA), 'Historical Summary of Proceedings and Reports', Sydney: HRVA, 1854, p. 31.
37 HRVA, 'Historical Summary', p. 35.
38 William Macarthur's role at the Paris Exhibition is discussed in Julie McIntyre, 'Camden to London and Paris: The role of the Macarthur family in the early New South Wales wine industry', *History Compass*, 5, no. 2, 2007, pp. 434–35.
39 William Macarthur's emphasis.
40 All direct quotes on the Paris Exhibition wine judging to this point are from William Macarthur to James Macarthur, 12 August 1855, Macarthur Papers, ML A2934, pp. 98–104.
41 William Macarthur to James Macarthur, 1 September 1855, ML A2934, pp. 120–22.
42 *The Times of London*, 27 August 1855. The detail about Macarthur's modesty was reprinted in the colony: *Maitland Mercury*, 5 December 1855.
43 See Hoffenberg, *Empire on Display*, p. 108; David S. McMillan, 'King, James (1800–1857), *ADB*, vol. 2, pp. 54–55 and 'Certificate of Merit to Maria Windeyer of Tomago Wines', ML A3812.
44 *Times of London*, 20 July 1857.
45 Hoffenberg, *Empire on Display*, p. 108.
46 Knight, *Australasian Colonies*, pp. 59–60.
47 Cyril Renwick, *A Study of Wine in the Hunter Region of N.S.W.*, Hunter Valley Research Foundation Monograph No.39, Newcastle: Hunter Valley Research Foundation, 1977, pp. 48–50.
48 Laffer, *Wine Industry of Australia*, p. 123.
49 *The Times of London*, 22 November 1855.
50 ibid., 27 November 1855.
51 *Morning Advertiser*, 28 July 1876 and *The Wine Trade Review*, cited in Fallon, *The Wines of Australia*, pp. 40 and 45.
52 The comparison of trade policies is made in George Bossy, 'Effects of Tariff Protection on Economic Development in Australia: Victoria and New South Wales from 1871 to 1900', PhD thesis, University of Columbia, 1964, p. 370. {Bossy, 1964 458}
53 Faith, *Liquid Gold*, pp. 74 and 105.
54 This section has been published as McIntyre, 'Colonial wine tours', pp. 13–19.
55 *The Australian*, 30 April 1842.
56 *The [Adelaide] Advertiser*, 20 November 1908; *Sydney Morning Herald*, 20 November 1908; *The Brisbane Courier*, 20 November 1908.
57 H.C.L. Anderson cited in Mylrea, *In the Service of Agriculture: A centennial history of the New South Wales Department of Agriculture, 1890–1990*, Sydney: NSW Agriculture & Fisheries, 1990, p. 55. *Infra dig* is 'below one's dignity'.
58 Muskett, *Art of Living*, chapter 12.

Chapter 10

1 Wagga Wagga plantings listed in Return Vineyards, SRNSW 4/7263. Wine expert John Beeston completed the enormous task of briefly mapping each of Australia's wine regions in the late 1990s, which I found after my initial research with historical societies. His efforts, published in *Wine Regions of Australia*, Sydney: Allen & Unwin, 1999 have been invaluable here.

2 Laffer, *Wine Industry of Australia*, pp. 95–136.

3 *Sydney Gazette*, 11 November 1820.

4 Ramsden, 'James Busby', p. 372.

5 Bernard Greaves ed., *The Story of Bathurst*, Third edn, Sydney: Angus & Robertson, 1976, p 148

6 *Bathurst Times*, 14 May 1870. Statistics for numbers of vignerons and wine presses used throughout this chapter are listed in Appendix 2.

7 William Buchanan to his mother, 28 March 1826 cited in W. Allan Wood, *Dawn in the Valley, The story of settlement in the Hunter River Valley to 1833*, Sydney: Wentworth Books, 1972, p. 98.

8 Hely cited in Driscoll, *Beginnings of the Wine Industry*, pp. 11–12.

9 Gil Wahlquist, 'Tyrrell, Edward George Young (Dan) (1871–1959)', *ADB*, vol. 16, p. 426.

10 Some of the information in this section comes from notes in the Tulloch Family File, Local Studies, Cessnock Council Library, as well as Halliday, *Australian Wine Compendium*, p. 64.

11 W. Howell, 'Vineyards and Vignerons of Port Macquarie', *Hastings District Historical Society*, 12, 1978: p. 4.

12 Norrie Doyle, *Chronicle, Margaret Wilson*, Port Macquarie: Douglas Vale Conservation Group, 2006, pp. 19–20, 41–42.

13 Gil Wahlquist, *Some of My Best Friends Are Winemakers and Other Tales, A history of the wine industry of Mudgee, N.S.W.*, Sydney: the author, 2008, p. 7.

14 Wahlquist, *Wine Industry of Mudgee*, p. 17.

15 *The Muse*, July 1972, p. 7. Thanks to Margaret Rhodes.

16 Rheinberger details from short entries in The Diary of Peter Joseph Rheinberger, Willow Vale, Eurunderee; Statement from the Mudgee District Wine Growers Association, Eurunderee, 20 March 1881, Rheinberger Papers, Mudgee Museum.

17 Wahlquist 'Roth Adam', *ADB*, p 46

18 Keith Swan, *A History of Wagga Wagga*, Wagga Wagga: City of Wagga Wagga, 1970, pp. 138–39.

19 Swan, *Wagga Wagga*, pp. 45 and 67. Quote cited in Sherry Morris, 'The Wine Industry in Wagga Wagga', Unpublished manuscript, Albury & District Historical Society Archives, p. 6.

20 Morris, 'Wine Industry in Wagga Wagga', p. 5.

21 *Wagga Wagga Express*, 4 August 1866.

22 Tracy Sinclair, 'Robert Nixon: Aspects of Robert Nixon's involvement in the development of Wagga Wagga, 1840–1900', Wagga Wagga Local Studies, 1980, p. 2.

23 Michael Hoare and Martha Rutledge, 'Macleay, Sir William John (1820–1891)', *ADB*, vol. 5, pp. 185–87.

24 *Wagga Wagga Advertiser*, 20 December 1879.

25 *Australian Town and Country Journal*, 25 July 1874, p. 14.

26 Details from Lloyd Evans, 'McWilliam Wine Growers a Centenary Wine History 1877 to 1977', kindly provided by Doug McWilliam from his collection of family papers; also State Library of South Australia, PRG 1453/9/10.

27 Email correspondence, Robert Bruno, 26 March 2012.

28 *Sydney Morning Herald*, 2 June 1847, also cited in Brian Johnston and Janet Johnson, *Wines of the Canberra District: Coming of Age*, Canberra: the authors, 2011, p. 4.

29 *Australian Town and Country Journal*, 12 January 1878, p. 23.

30 D. Mulholland, *Far and Away Days, A history of the Murrumbateman, Jeir and Nanima districts*, Canberra: Murrumbateman Old School Grounds Committee, 1992, pp. 207–08. Thanks to Rob Howell.

31 Stuart Hume, 'Hume, Hamilton (1797–1873)', *ADB*, <**Error! Hyperlink reference not valid.**accessed 28 February 2012.

32 *Forbes History Book*, details in documents in Dominic Williams Collection.

33 David Holmes, Andrew Honey and John Miller, *Orange, A vision splendid*, Orange: Orange City Council, 2001, pp. 60–62.

34 Beeston, *Wine Regions*, p. 431.

35 D. Croft, 'Agriculture', in Joan Marriott ed., *Cowra on the Lachlan*, Cowra: Cowra Shire Council, 1988, pp. 66–68.

36 *Australian Town and Country Journal*, 26 October 1901, p. 29.

37 Beeston, *Wine Regions*, pp. 414–15.

38 ibid., p. 492. Email correspondence with Brian Freeman, 29 May 2012.

39 James Busby to Alexander Berry, 11 January 1833, James Busby Correspondence, ML 1319, p. 23.

40 Wine making story and champagne details from B.V. Hamon, *They Came to Murramarang: A history of Murramarang, Kioloa and Bawley Point*, Canberra: Centre for Resource and Environmental Studies, Australian National University, 1994, pp. 17–18 and 60. Thanks to Max Staniford.

41 Email correspondence with Mark Bourne, 28 May 2012.

42 Email correspondence with Richard McLean, 29 May 2012.

43 Email correspondence with Cathy Gairn, 29 May 2012.

Chapter 11

1 Text accompanying H.B. Ballard, Photographs of the Dalwood Vineyards, 1886, ML PXD 740.

2 John Macarthur (junior) to James Macarthur, 21 March 1822, ML A2911, pp. 139–40.

3 See chapter 4.

4 *The Gentleman's Magazine*, vol. 16, 1841.

5 Judith Wright McKinney, 'Wyndham, George (1801–1870)', *ADB*, vol. 2, pp. 630–31.

6 ibid.; Don Seton-Wilkinson, *Dalwood House: Its importance and its associations*, Sydney: the author, 1986, n.p.

7 Diary of George Wyndham, ML B1313. The figure of '600' was not written clearly.

8 Don Seton-Wilkinson, *Photographs of the Dalwood Vineyards near Branxton, New South Wales, Australia*, Sydney: Dalwood Restoration Association, 2010.

9 Diary of George Wyndham, ML B1313.

10 ibid..

11 *Maitland Mercury*, 16 May 1872.

12 John Glennie to John Wyndham, 17 May 1869; Philip Gidley King to John Wyndham, 29 June 1870, ML 8051, Box 1.

13 *Maitland Mercury*, 16 December 1865.

14 ibid., 20 November 1886.

15 *Sydney Morning Herald*, 8 May 1869.

16 A cheque signed by John Wyndham dated Dalwood, 22 June 1872 in Stan Parkes Collection, Box 2, Cessnock City Local Studies Collection (CCLSC).

17 Inventory of plant at Bukkulla by Fred Wilkinson, 1 June 1869, ML 8051, Box 1.

18 Fred Wilkinson to John Wyndham, 4 January 1868, ML 8051, Box 1.

19 *Maitland Mercury*, 20 November 1886.

20 John Glennie to John Wyndham, 17 May 1869, ML 8051, Box 1.

21 Thomas Hardy to John Wyndham, 19 January 1872, ML 8051, Box 1.

22 Inventory of wines at Bukkulla by Fred Wilkinson, 1 June 1869, ML 8051, Box 1.

23 Order from Newcastle, 22 December 1874, ML 8051, Box 1.

24 Henry White to George or John Wyndham, 3 May 1869 ML 8051, Box 2.

25 Wadham Wyndham to John Wyndham, 14 October 1878, ML 8051, Box 1.

26 Charlotte Starky to John Wyndham, 1875, ML 8051 Box 1.

27 James Kelman to John Wyndham, 28 September 1885, ML 8051, Box 2.

28 Stephen Cosgrove to John Wyndham, 25 February 1870; John Taylor & Co to John Wyndham, 1 September 1875; London merchant [illegible name] to John Wyndham,

24 March 1871, ML 8051, Box 1.
29 *Sydney Morning Herald*, 15 June 1870.
30 James Fitzpatrick to John Wyndham, 10 January 1877, Ml 8051, Box 1.
31 Wadham Wyndham to John Wyndham, 14 October 1878, ML 8051, Box 1.
32 E.H. Timmins to John Wyndham, 24 October 1871, ML 8051, Box 2.
33 O.L. Montefiore to Manager, Dalwood, 23 May 1891, Ml 8051, Box 1.
34 A.H. Nicholson (for P. B. Burgoyne & Co London) to the Manager, Dalwood Vineyards, 24 December 1891, ML 8051, Box 1.
35 Fallon, *The Wines of Australia*, pp. 23–24.
36 A.H. Nicholson (for P. B. Burgoyne & Co London) to the Manager, Dalwood Vineyards, 24 December 1891, ML 8051, Box 1.
37 *Sydney Morning Herald*, 5 January 2011.

Conclusion

1 Campbell Mattinson, *The Wine Hunter, Maurice O'Shea: The man who changed Australian wine*, Sydney: McWilliam's

Wines, 2005.
2 Maurice O'Shea, 'The Use of Wine in Ancient Times', Presentation for the Seventh Annual J. K. Walker Lecture Series, Maurice O'Shea Papers, A3040, Newcastle Region Library Archives.
3 *Maitland Mercury*, 24 June 1861
4 Reprinted in *Sydney Morning Herald*, 8 July 1861.
5 Janis Wilton and Richard Bosworth, *Old Worlds and New Australia, The post–war migrant experience*, Melbourne: Penguin, 1984, pp. 23–24. Thanks to Richard White.
6 Australian Bureau of Statistics, Apparent Consumption of Alcohol: Extended Time Series, 1944–45 to 2008–09, 4307.0.55.002,<www.abs.gov.au>, accessed 14 February 2012.

Appendix 2

1 So many counties recorded 'unknown' for the weight of grapes harvested that these figures cannot be used to determined yields (harvest quantity/ acreage). The best use that can be made

of this part of the returns is to conclude that record-keeping in grape growing was very rudimentary; even more so than in wine making, where at least some record was kept of the quantity of production.
2 Includes 40 gallons of wine reported for Bathurst in 1846 returns but for 1845 because too late for that year.
3 This figure includes 12.000 gallons which was the previous year's Camden production; James Macarthur gave 1845 figures for 1846 because of drought, which creates confusion in attempting to arrive at reliable data. The 29 pipes of wine made at Port Macquarie equalled approximately 3390 gallons.
4 This figure has been rounded up from 742.91 as some of the reported vine acreages were in fractions of an acre.
5 Includes the figure 240 cwt converted from 12 tons in the returns (on the basis of 20 cwt equals one ton).

Select bibliography

PRIMARY SOURCES

Archives accessed

Albury & District Historical Society Archives
Cessnock City Library Local Studies
   Collection
Dominic Williams Collection
Ken Helm Collection
Royal Botanic Gardens, Kew
Macarthur Private Collection
McWilliam's Family Collection
Mudgee Museum
National Library of Australia
Newwcastle region Library Archives
Noel Butlin Archives Centre, Australian
   National University
Rhodes–Kurtz Family Collection
State Library of New South Wales
State Library of South Australia
State Records Office of New South Wales
Wagga Wagga Riverina Archives

Published material

Anderson, HC (1908) *New South Wales
   Statistical Register for 1906 and Previous
   Years*, Sydney: the Government of the
   State of New South Wales.
Beaglehole, JC ed. (1963) *The Endeavour
   Journal of Joseph Banks 1768–1771*, vol.
   1, 2nd edn, Sydney: Angus & Robertson.
Belperroud, J and D Pettavel (1859) *The Vine:
   With instructions for its cultivation, for
   a period of six years: The treatment of
   the soil, and how to make wine from
   Victorian grapes*, Geelong: Heath and
   Cordell.
Bigge, JT (1823) *Report of the Commissioner
   of Inquiry on the State of Agriculture
   and Trade in the Colony of New South
   Wales*, London: Printed by order of the
   British House of Commons.
Bleasdale, JI (1867) *On Colonial Wines: A
   paper read before the Royal Society
   of Victoria, 13th May 1867/ by J.I.
   Bleasdale, Together with the report of
   the late Intercolonial Exhibition Jury in*

Class 3, Section Ix, Wines, Melbourne:
   Printed by Stillwell and Knight.
Britton, A, ed. (1892) *Historical Records of
   New South Wales*, vols. 1 & 2, Sydney:
   Charles Potter.
Busby, J (1825) *A Treatise on the Culture of
   the Vine and the Art of Making Wine;
   Compiled from the works of Chaptal,
   and other French writers; and from the
   notes of the compiler, during a residence
   in some of the wine provinces of France*,
   Facsimile edition, 1979, Sydney: David
   Ell Press.
— (1830) *A Manual of Plain Directions for
   Planting and Cultivating a Vineyard
   and for Making Wine in New South
   Wales*, Sydney: Printed by R. Mansfield,
   for the executors of R. Howe.
— (1833) *Journal of a Tour through Some
   of the Vineyards of Spain and France*,
   Facsimile edition, 1979, Sydney: David
   Ell Press.
Coghlan, TA (1900) *Wealth and Progress
   of New South Wales 1898–1899*,
   Twelfth issue, Sydney: Printed by
   William Applegate Gullick for the NSW
   Government.
Collins, D (1798; Facsimile edition 1971) *An
   Account of the English Colony in New
   South Wales*, Adelaide: Libraries Board of
   South Australia.
De Castella, H (1886) *John Bull's Vineyard*,
   Melbourne: Sands & McDougall.
De Saint Pierre, L (1772) *The Art of Planting
   and Cultivating the Vine*, London:
   Printed by J. Wilkie and J. Walter.
Despessis, JA (1891) 'Choice Italian Grapes',
   *Agricultural Gazette of New South
   Wales*, vol. 2, December, pp. 804–06.
Digby, Sir K (1671) *The Closet of the
   Eminently Learned Sir Kenelme Digby
   Kt*, London: Printed by E.C. & A.C. for
   H. Brome.
Easty, J (1965) *Memorandum of Transactions of
   a Voyage from England to Botany Bay:
   1787–1793: A First Fleet journal*, Sydney:
   Trustees of the Public Library of New
   South Wales in association with Angus &
   Robertson.

Fallon, JT (1876) *The Wines of Australia: A
   paper read before the Royal Colonial
   Institute on the 20th of June 1876*,
   London: Unwin Brothers.
Fidlon, PG and RJ Ryan, eds (1980) *The Journal
   of Philip Gidley King: Lieutenant,
   R.N. 1787–1790*, Sydney: Australian
   Documents Library.
— (1981) *The Journal and Letters of Lt. Ralph
   Clark 1787–1792*, Sydney: Australian
   Documents Library.
Franklyn, HM (1881) *A Glance at Australia in
   1880: Or, food from the south: Showing
   the present condition and production of
   some of its leading industries, namely,
   wool, wine, grain, dressed meat, etc
   etc*, Melbourne: The Victorian Review
   Publishing Company.
Hakluyt, R (c2004) 'The First English Voyage
   Made to the Coasts of America, 1589'
   in Newton K and R Bucholz, eds,
   *Sources and Debates in English History
   1485–1714*, Malden: Blackwell.
Hardy, T (1885) *Notes on Vineyards in America
   and Europe*, Adelaide: Printed by L.
   Henn.
— (1899) *A Vigneron Abroad: Trip to South
   Africa*, Adelaide: s.n.
*Historical Summary of the Proceedings and
   Reports of the Hunter River Vineyard
   Association, from its Origination to its
   First Annual Meeting in the Year 1853*,
   Sydney: W. R. Piddington, 1854.
Holy Bible (n.y.), London: Eyre and
   Spottiswoode.
Hughes, W (1670) *The Compleat Vineyard:
   Or, an excellent way for the planting
   of vines, according to the German and
   French manner, and long practised in
   England*, London: Printed by J.C. for Will
   Creek.
Hunter, J (1793) *An Historical Journal of the
   Transaction at Port Jackson and Norfolk
   Island, with the Discoveries Which Have
   Been Made in New South Wales and in
   the Southern Ocean since the Publication
   of Phillip's Voyage, Compiled from the
   official papers; including the journals
   of Governors Phillip and King, and of*

Lieut. Ball, and the voyages from the first sailing of the Sirius in 1787 to the return of that ship's company to England in 1792, London: Printed for John Stockdale.

Kelly, A (1861; Facsimile edn 1980) *The Vine in Australia*, Sydney: David Ell Press.

— (1867; Facsimile edn 1980) *Wine-Growing in Australia*, Sydney: David Ell Press.

King, J (1857) *Australia May Be an Extensive Wine-Producing Country*, Edinburgh: the author.

Lang, JD (1875) *An Historical and Statistical Account of New South Wales*, vols. 1 & 2, London: Sampson, Low, Marston, Low & Searle.

Liebig, J (1843) *Chemistry in its Application to Agriculture and Physiology*, trans. Lyon Playfair, Philadelphia: James M. Campbell & Co.

Maro (William Macarthur) (1844) *Letters on the Culture of the Vine, Fermentation, and the Management of Wine in the Cellar*, Sydney: Statham and Forster.

McEwin, G (1843) *The South Australian Vigneron and Gardeners' Manual Containing Plain Practical Directions for the Cultivation of the Vine; the propagation of fruit-trees, with catalogue and directions for cultivation; and the management of the kitchen garden, with catalogue of culinary vegetable*, Adelaide: James Allen.

Mitchell, T (1849) *Notes on the Cultivation of the Vine and the Olive; and on the methods of making wine and oil...in southern parts of Spain, taken during a tour through Andalusia in...1847*, Sydney: D.L. Welch.

Muskett, P (1893) *The Art of Living in Australia*, London: Eyre & Spottiswoode.

New South Wales Government Gazette, Sydney: Government Printer, 1878, 1887, 1888, 1890, 1892, 1893 and 1894.

Russell, P, ed. (2002) *This Errant Lady: Jane Franklin's overland journey to Port Phillip and Sydney, 1839*, Canberra: National Library of Australia.

Seyd, E (1858) *California and its Resources, A work for the merchant, the capitalist and the emigrant*, London: Trübner & Co.

Short, T (1727) *Vinum Britannicum: Or an essay on the properties and effects of malt liquor*, London: Printed for D. Midwinter and M. Bryson.

Smith, A (1961) *An Inquiry into the Causes of the Wealth of Nations*, first published 1776, vols. 1 & 2, London: Methuen.

Society for the Encouragement of Arts Manufactures and Commerce, *Transactions of the Society (1823, 1828)*, vols. 46 and 50, London: The Society for the Encouragement of Arts Manufactures and Commerce.

Suttor, G (1843) *The Culture of the Grape-Vine and the Orange in Australia and New Zealand*, London: Smith, Elder.

Swinburne, H (1787) *Travels Through Spain, in the Years 1775 and 1776*, vol. 2, London: n.p., accessed on Eighteenth Century Collections Online <http://find.galegroup.com.ezproxy2.library.usyd.edu.au/ecco/>, 27 January 2012.

Tench, W (1961) *Sydney's First Four Years, Being a reprint of a narrative of the expedition to Botany Bay and a complete account of the settlement at Port Jackson*, first published 1788 and 1793, Sydney: Angus & Robertson. ¾ (1996) *1788*, T Flannery, ed., Melbourne: Text Publishing.

Townson, R (1797) *Travels in Hungary with a Short Account of Vienna in the Year 1793*, London: Printed for G.G. and J. Robinson.

Watson, F, ed. (from 1914) *Historical Records of Australia*, Series I, vols 1, 2, 3, 4, 11, 16, 18, Sydney: Library Committee of the Commonwealth Parliament, 1914–48.

White, J (1962) *Journal of a Voyage to New South Wales*, Facsimile edn, Sydney: Angus & Robertson.

Williams, E (1650) *Virginia's Discovery of Silke-worms ... also the dressing and keeping of vines, for the rich trade of making wines there*, London: Printed by T.H. for John Stephenson.

Worgan, G (1788) *Journal of a First Fleet Surgeon*, <http://gutenberg.net.au>, accessed 21 January 2012.

Young, A (1794) *Travels During the Years 1787, 1788, and 1789. Undertaken more particularly with a view of ascertaining the cultivation, wealth, resources, and national prosperity of the Kingdom of France*, second edn, vol. 2, London: Bury St. Edmund's.

SECONDARY SOURCES

Published material

Adas, M (1989) *Machines as the Measure of Men: Science, technology, and ideologies of Western dominance*, New York: Cornell University Press.

Allen, MP & J Germov (2011) 'Judging taste and creating value: The cultural consecration of Australia wines', *Journal of Sociology*, 47, 35, pp. 35–51.

Anderson, K and R Osmond (1998) *Trends and Cycles in the Australian Wine Industry, 1850 to 2000*, Adelaide: Centre for International Economic Studies, University of Adelaide.

Atkinson, A (1988) *Camden: Farm and village life in early New South Wales*, Melbourne: Oxford University Press.

— (1997) *The Europeans in Australia, A history: Vol. 1, The beginning*, Melbourne: Oxford University Press.

— (2004) *The Europeans in Australia, A history, Vol. 2: Democracy*, Melbourne: Oxford University Press.

Barty-King, H (1977) *A Tradition of English Wine*, Oxford: Oxford Illustrated Press.

Beeston, J (1994) *A Concise History of Australian Wine*, Sydney: Allen & Unwin.

— (1999) *Wine Regions of Australia*, Sydney: Allen & Unwin.

Belich, J (2011) *Replenishing the Earth, The settler revolution and the rise of the Anglo-world*, Oxford: Oxford University Press.

Bell, G (1993) 'The South Australian Wine Industry, 1858–1876', *Journal of Wine Research*, 4, pp. 147–64.

— (1994) 'The London Market for Australian Wines 1851–1901: A South Australian perspective', *Journal of Wine Research*, 5, pp. 19–41.

Best, MR (1976) 'The Mystery of Vintners', *Agricultural History*, 50, no. 2, pp. 362–76.

Blackbourn, D (1997) *The Long Nineteenth Century, A history of Germany 1789–1918*, New York: Oxford University Press.

Bolton, G (1981) *Spoils and Spoilers, Australians make their environment 1788–1980*, Sydney: George Allen & Unwin.

— (1999) 'Rediscovering Australia: Hancock and the wool seminar', *Journal of Australian Studies*, 62, pp. 159–70.

Bourdieu, P (1984) *Distinction: A social critique of the judgement of taste*, trans. Richard Nice, London: Routledge & Kegan Paul.

Boyden, S (2004) *The Biology of Civilization, Understanding human culture as a force in nature*, Sydney: UNSW Press.

Boyer, KD (1985) 'Is There a Principle for Defining Industries? Reply', *Southern Economic Journal*, 52, pp. 542–46.

Brady, M (2000) 'Alcohol Policy Issues for Indigenous People in the United States, Canada, Australia and New Zealand', *Contemporary Drug Problems*, 27, pp. 435–509.

Braudel, F (1981) *Civilization and Capitalism 15th–18th Century: The structures of everyday life, the limits of the possible*, trans. Sian Reynolds, London: Harper & Row.

— (1982) *Civilization and Capitalism, 15th–18th Century: The wheels of commerce*, trans. Sian Reynolds, London: Harper Row.

— (1984) *Civilization and Capitalism, 15th–18th Century: The perspective of the world*, trans. Sian Reynolds, London: Harper & Row.

Brissenden, RF (1979) 'Wine and Poetry', Paper presented at the Wine Talk Symposium, Canberra.

Brook, J (2001) 'The Forlorn Hope: Bennelong and Yemmerrawannie go to England', *Australian Aboriginal Studies*, 36, 12, pp. 36–47.

Broome, R (2010) *Aboriginal Australians: A history since 1788* (Revised edn), Sydney: Allen & Unwin.

Brown, EA (2002) 'Eleanor of Aquitaine Reconsidered: The woman and her seasons', in B Wheeler and JC Parsons, eds, *Eleanor of Aquitaine, Lord and Lady*, New York: Palgrave Macmillan.

Burnett, J (1999) *Liquid Pleasures, A social history of drinks in modern Britain*, London: Routledge.

Callaghan, AR and AJ Millington (1956) *The Wheat Industry in Australia*, Sydney: Angus and Robertson.

Campbell, C (2004) *Phylloxera, How wine was saved for the world*, London: Harper Perennial.

Canny, N (1976) *The Elizabethan Conquest of Ireland: A pattern established 1565–76*, Sussex: Harrister Press.

Carman, HJ and RG Tugwell (1938) 'The Significance of American Agricultural History', *Agricultural History*, 12, 2, pp. 99–106.

Chaplin, JE (1993) *An Anxious Pursuit, Agricultural innovation and modernity in the lower south, 1730–1815*, Chapel Hill, NC: University of North Carolina Press.

Clendinnen, I (2003) *Dancing with Strangers*, Melbourne: Text Publishing.

Cobley, J (1980) *Sydney Cove 1788–1792, Australia's first five years*, Sydney: Angus & Robertson.

Cohen, M (1992) 'The Grand Tour: Constructing the English gentleman in eighteenth century France', *History of Education*, 21, 3, pp. 241–57. Croft, D (1988) 'Agriculture', in J Marriott, ed., *Cowra on the Lachlan*, Cowra: Cowra Shire Council.

Crosby, A (1986) *Ecological Imperialism: The biological expansion of Europe, 900–1900*, Cambridge: Cambridge University Press.

Darian-Smith, K (2002) 'Up the Country, Histories and Communities', *Australian Historical Studies*, 32, 118, pp. 90–99.

Davis, B and J Grant, eds (1996) *Australian Verse, An illustrated treasury*, Sydney: State Library of New South Wales Press.

Davison, G, J Hirst and S MacIntyre, eds (2001) *The Oxford Companion to Australian History*, Melbourne: Oxford University Press.

De Blij, HJ (1983) *Wine: A geographic appreciatio*, Totowa, NJ: Rowman & Allanheld.

Digby, E, ed. (1889) 'John A. Wilkinson, Esquire, Coolalta', *Australian Men of Mark*, vol. 2, series 4, Sydney: Charles Maxwell.

Dingle, AE (1980) '"The Truly Magnificent Thirst": An historical survey of Australian drinking habits', *Historical Studies*, 19, pp. 227–49.

Dixon, R (1986) *The Course of Empire, Neo-Classical culture in New South Wales 1788–1860*, Oxford: Oxford University Press.

Doyle, N (2006) *Chronicle, Margaret Wilson*, Port Macquarie: Douglas Vale Conservation Group.

Driscoll, WP (1969) *The Beginnings of the Wine Industry in the Hunter Valley*, Newcastle History Monographs No. 5, Newcastle: Newcastle Public Library, The Council of the City of Newcastle.

Dunphy, R and L Lockshin (1998) 'A History of the Australian Wine Show System', *Journal of Wine Research*, 9, pp. 87–105.

Dunstan, D (1994) *Better Than Pommard!: A history of wine in Victoria*, Melbourne: Australian Scholarly Publishing.

— (2002) 'The Wine Press (Essay)', *Meanjin*, 61, 4, pp. 34–43.

Dupre, P (1993) 'Thudichum and Dupre – Brothers-in-Law', *Journal of the Royal Society of Medicine*, 86, pp. 417–20.

Dyer, C (2002) 'The Indigenous Australians in Sydney and its Environs as Seen by French Explorers, 1802–1831', *Journal of the Royal Australian Historical Society*, 88, pp. 147–62.

Edwards, EE (1939) 'Agricultural Records: Their nature and value for research', *Agricultural History*, 13, 1, pp. 1–12.

Evans, L (1976) *Australia and New Zealand Complete Book of Wine*, Sydney: Books for Pleasure.

Faith, N (2002) *Liquid Gold, The story of Australian wine and its makers*, Sydney: PanMacmillan.

Fletcher, BH (1969) 'Agriculture', in GJ Abbot and NB Nairn, eds, *Economic Growth of Australia 1788–1821*, Melbourne: Melbourne University Press.

— (2001) *The Grand Parade, A history of the Royal Agricultural Society of New South Wales*, Sydney: The Royal Agricultural Society of New South Wales.

Flynn, M (2001) *The Second Fleet, Britain's grim convict armada of 1790*, Sydney: Library of Australian History.

Francis, AD (1972) *The Wine Trade*, London: Adam & Charles Black.

Frost, A (1987) *Arthur Phillip 1738–1814, His voyaging*, Melbourne: Oxford University Press.

— (2011) *Botany Bay, The real story*, Melbourne: Black Inc.

— (2011) *The First Fleet, The real story*, Melbourne: Black Inc.

Fussell, GE (1969) 'Science and Practice in Eighteenth Century British Agriculture', *Agricultural History*, 43, 1: pp. 7–17.

Gascoigne, J (2002) *The Enlightenment and the Origins of European Australia*, Cambridge: Cambridge University Press.

Gent, C (2003) *Mixed Dozen: The story of Australian winemaking from 1788*, Sydney: Duffy & Snellgrove.

Geraci, VW (2000) 'The Family Wine-Farm: Vintibusiness style', *Agricultural History*, 74, 2, pp. 419–32.

— (2004) 'Fermenting a Twenty-First Century California Wine Industry', *Agricultural History*, 78, 4, pp. 438–65.

Glacken, CJ (1967) *Traces on the Rhodian Shore, Nature and Culture in Western Thought from Ancient Times to the End of the Eighteenth Century*, Berkeley: University of California Press.

Godley, M (1986) 'Bacchus of the East: The Chinese grape wine industry 1892–1938', *Business History Review*, 60, 3, pp. 383–409.

Goodall, H (1996) *Invasion to Embassy: Land in Aboriginal politics in New South Wales, 1770–1972*, Sydney: Allen & Unwin

Greaves, B (1976) *The Story of Bathurst*, Third edn, Sydney: Angus & Robertson.

Greenblatt, S (1991), *Marvelous Possessions, The wonder of the New World*, Oxford: Oxford University Press.

Guy, K (2001) 'Wine, Champagne and the Making of French Identity in the Belle Epoque' in P Scholliers, ed., *Food, Drink and Identity: Cooking, eating and drinking in Europe since the Middle Ages*, Oxford: Berg, pp. 163–77.

Haines, RF (1995) *Nineteenth Century Government Assisted Immigrants from the United Kingdom to Australia: Schemes, regulations and arrivals, 1831–1900 and some vital statistics 1834–1860 (Occasional Papers in Economic History No. 3)*, Adelaide: Flinders University.

Halliday, J (2004) *Australian Wine Compendium*, Sydney: Angus & Robertson.

Halliday, J and H Johnson (1992) *Art and Science of Wine, The wine maker's options in the vineyard and the cellar*, London: Mitchell Beazley. Hancock, D (1998) 'Commerce and Conversation in the Eighteenth-Century Atlantic: The invention of Madeira wine', *Journal of Interdisciplinary History*, 26, 2, pp. 197–219.

Hamon, BV (1994) *They Came to Murramarang: A history of Murramarang, Kioloa and Bawley Point*, Canberra: Centre for Resource and Environmental Studies, Australian National University.

Hannickel, E (2010) 'Cultivation and Control: Grape growing as expansion in nineteenth-century United States and Australia',

Comparative American Studies, 8, 4, pp. 283–99.

Hiatt, LR (2004) 'Bennelong and Omai', Australian Aboriginal Studies, 2, pp. 87–89.

Higman, BW (2012) How Food Made History, Oxford: Blackwell/Wiley.

Hirsch, AH (1930) 'French Influence on American Agriculture in the Colonial Period with Special Reference to Southern Provinces', Agricultural History, 4, 1, pp. 1–9.

Hobhouse, H (2003) Seeds of Wealth: Four plants that made men rich, London: Macmillan.

Hobsbawm, E (1968) Industry and Empire, An economic history of Britain since 1750, London: Weidenfeld and Nicolson.

Hoffenberg, PH (2001) An Empire on Display: English, Indian and Australian exhibitions from the Crystal Palace to the Great War, London: University of California Press.

Holmes, D, A Honey and J Miller (2001) Orange, A Vision Splendid, Orange: Orange City Council.

Hori, M (2008) 'The Price and Quality of Wine and Conspicuous Consumption in England 1646–1759', English Historical Review, 73, 505, pp. 1457–69.

Horne, J (2005) The Pursuit of Wonder: How Australia's landscape was explored, nature discovered and tourism unleashed, Melbourne: Miegunyah Press.

Howell, W (1978) 'Vineyards and Vignerons of Port Macquarie', Occasional Paper 1978/12, Hastings District Historical Society Bulletin.

Hughes, R (1987) The Fatal Shore, A history of transportation of convicts to Australia, 1787–1868, London: Collins Harvill.

Hyams, E (1952) Soil and Civilization, London: Thames and Hudson.

Jackson, RV (1998) 'The Colonial Economies: An introduction', Australian Economic History Review, 38, pp. 1 15.

Johnson, H (1971) The World Atlas of Wine, London: Mitchell Beazley.

Johnston, BG and JE Johnson (2011) Wines of the Canberra District, Canberra: The authors.

Jupp, J and B York, Birthplaces of the Australian People: Colonial and Commonwealth Censuses, 1828–1991, Canberra: Centre for Immigration and Multicultural Studies.

Karskens, G (2009) The Colony, A history of early Sydney, Sydney: Allen & Unwin.

Karskens, G and R Waterhouse (2010) '"Too sacred to be taken away": Property, liberty, tyranny and the "Rum Rebellion"', Journal of Australian Colonial History, 12, pp. 1–22.

Kerridge, G and A Gackle, Vines for Wines, A wine lover's guide to the top wine grape varieties, Melbourne: CSIRO Publishing.

Kett, JF (1981) 'Temperance and Intemperance as Historical Problems', Journal of American History, 67, pp. 878–85.

Kimball, M (1945) 'Some Genial Old Drinking Customs', The William and Mary Quarterly, 2, pp. 349–58.

King, CJ (1950) 'The First Fifty Years of Agriculture in New South Wales', in Extracts from Review of Marketing and Agricultural Economics, August 1948 –December 1949, Sydney: Department of Agriculture, p. 574.

Kingston, B (2006) A History of New South Wales, Melbourne: Cambridge University Press.

Kirkby, DE (2006) 'Drinking "The Good Life"', in MP Holt, ed., Alcohol: A social and cultural history, New York: Berg, pp. 203–23.

Laffer, HE (1949) The Wine Industry of Australia, Adelaide: Australian Wine Board.

Lake, M (1964) Hunter Wine, Brisbane: Jacaranda Press.

— (1979) 'The Wine', in Mines, Wine and People: A history of greater Cessnock, Cessnock: Council of the City of Greater Cessnock.

Lake, M and H Reynolds (2008) Drawing the Global Colour Line, White men's countries and the question of racial equality, Melbourne: Melbourne University Press.

McCormick, T (with R Irving, E Imashev, J Nelson and G Bull) (1987) First Views of Australia 1788–1825, An early history of Sydney, Sydney: David Ell Press.

McGillivery, AR (2004) 'Convict Settlers, Seamen's Greens, and Imperial Designs at Port Jackson: A maritime perspective of British settler agriculture', Agricultural History, 78, 3, pp. 261–88.

— (2004), 'From Sods to Seed-Beds: Cultivating a familiar field at Port Jackson', Journal of Australian Colonial History, 5, pp. 1–29.

McGovern, P, SJ Fleming and SH Katz, eds (1996) The Origins and Ancient History of Wine, Amsterdam: Gordon and Breach.

McGrath, A (1990) 'The White Man's Looking Glass: Aboriginal–colonial gender relations at Port Jackson', Australian Historical Studies, 24, pp. 189–206.

McIntyre, J (2007) 'Camden to London and Paris: The role of the Macarthur family in the early New South Wales wine industry', History Compass, 5, pp. 427–38.

— (2008) '"Bannelong Sat Down to Dinner with Governor Phillip, and Drank His Wine and Coffee as Usual": Aborigines and wine in early New South Wales', History Australia, 5, 2, pp. 39.1–39.14.

— (2009) 'Not Rich and Not British: Philip Schaeffer, "failed" farmer', Journal of Australian Colonial History, 11, pp. 1–20.

— (2011) 'Adam Smith and Faith in the Transformative Qualities of Wine in Colonial New South Wales', Australian Historical Studies, 42, 2, pp. 194–211.

— (2011) 'Resisting Ages-old Fixity as a Factor in Wine Quality: Colonial wine tours and Australia's early wine industry', Locale: The Australasian–Pacific Journal of Regional Food Studies, 1, 1, pp. 1–19.

McIntyre, P (2012) Creativity and Cultural Production, Issues for media practice, London: Palgrave Macmillan.

Maiden, JH (1917) 'The Grape Vine, Notes on its introduction into New South Wales', Agricultural Gazette of New South Wales, 28, pp. 427–33.

Martin, AL (1999) 'National Reputations for Drinking in Traditional Europe', Parergon, 17, 2, pp. 163–86.

Matasar, AB (2006) Women of Wine, The rise of women in the global wine industry, Berkeley: University of California Press.

Mattinson, C (2005) The Wine Hunter, Maurice O'Shea: The man who changed Australian wine, Sydney: McWilliam's Wines.

Mitchell, CJ (1984) Hunter's River, A history of early families and the homes they built in the lower Hunter Valley Between 1830 and 1860, Sydney: The Family of Cecily Joan Mitchell.

Morgan, R (1994) The History of Bathurst, Sydney: Runciman Press.

Morris, C (2008) Lost Gardens of Sydney, Sydney: Historic Houses Trust.

Morris, S (1999) Wagga Wagga, A history, Wagga Wagga: The Council of the City of Wagga Wagga.

Mulholland, D (1992) Far and Away Days, A history of the Murrumbateman, Jeir and Nanima districts, Canberra: Murrumbateman Old School Grounds Committee.

Murphy, K (2009) '"The Modern Idea is to Bring the Country into the City": Australian urban reformers and the ideal of rurality, 1900–1918', Rural History, 20, 1, pp. 119–36.

Mylrea, PJ (1990) In the Service of Agriculture: A centennial history of the New South Wales Department of Agriculture, 1890-1990, Sydney: NSW Agriculture & Fisheries.

Norrie, P (1990) Vineyards of Sydney, Cradle of the Australian wine industry, Sydney: Apollo Books.

Ordish, G (1972) The Great Wine Blight, London: Dent.

Oxford Dictionary of National Biography, <www.oxforddnb.com>, accessed 30 April 2008.

Passant, EJ (1959) A Short History of Germany 1815–1945, Cambridge: Cambridge

University Press.

Pemberton, PA (1986) *Pure Merinos and Others: The "shipping lists" of the Australian Agricultural Company*, Canberra: Australian National University Archives of Business and Labour.

Peterson, PD, CS Griffith and CL Campbell (1996) 'Frank Lamson-Scribner and American Plant Pathology, 1885–1888', *Agricultural History*, 70, 1, p. 33–56.

Phillips, R (2000) *A Short History of Wine*, London: Allen Lane Penguin Press.

Pike, D, ed. (1967–2006) *Australian Dictionary of Biography*, vol.1 to suppl. vol., Melbourne: Melbourne University Press, <www.adb.anu.edu.au/>.

Pinney, T (1989) *A History of Wine in America: From the beginnings to Prohibition*, Berkeley: University of California Press.

Porter, R (1990) *English Society in the Eighteenth Century*, Revised edn, London: Penguin.

Raby, G (1996) *Making Rural Australia: An economic history of technical and institutional creativity 1788–1860*, Melbourne: Oxford University Press.

Power, J (2003) 'Sniffing Petrol, Reclaiming Story and Valuing Kin: An interview with Craig San Roque', *Australia and New Zealand Journal of Family Therapy*, 24, 4, pp. 206–10.

Ramsden, E (1940) 'James Busby, the Prophet of Australian Viticulture', *Journal of the Royal Australian Historical Society*, 26, pp. 364–86.

Reece, R (1974) *Aboriginals and Colonists: Aborigines and colonial society in New South Wales in the 1830s and 1840s*, Sydney: Sydney University Press.

Renwick, C (1977) *A Study of Wine in the Hunter Region of N.S.W.*, Hunter Valley Research Foundation Monograph No.39, Newcastle, NSW: Hunter Valley Research Foundation.

Reynolds, H (1981) *The Other Side of the Frontier*, Melbourne: Penguin.

Robinson, J, ed. (2006) *The Oxford Companion to Wine*, Third edn, Oxford: Oxford University Press.

Roe, M (1965) *Quest for Authority in Eastern Australia, 1835–1851*, Melbourne: Melbourne University Press.

Ross, R (1983) 'The Rise of the Cape Gentry', *Journal of Southern African Studies*, 9, pp. 199–206.

Russell, P (2010) *Savage or Civilised? Manners in colonial Australia*, Sydney: New South.

Salzmann, L (1964) *English Trade in the Middle Ages*, London: H. Prodes.

Seton-Wilkinson, D (1986) *Dalwood House: Its importance and its associations*, Sydney: the author.

Sherington, G (1980) *Australia's Immigrants, 1788–1978*, Sydney: Allen & Unwin.

Simon, AL (1964) *The History of the Wine Trade in England*, vol. 1, London: The Holland Press.

Simpson, J (2011) *Creating Wine: The emergence of a world industry*, Princeton: Princeton University Press.

Spahni, P (1998) *The International Wine Trade*, Cambridge: Woodhead.

Steckley, GF (1980) 'The Wine Economy of Tenerife in the Seventeenth Century: Anglo–Spanish partnership in a luxury trade', *Economic History Review*, 33, pp. 335–50.

Stockdale, J, ed. (1789) *The Voyage of Governor Phillip to Botany Bay with an Account of the Establishment of the Colonies of Port Jackson and Norfolk Island*, London: Printed by John Stockdale.

Stoler, AL (c2002) *Carnal Knowledge and Imperial Power, Race and the intimate in colonial rule*, Berkeley: University of California Press.

Sullivan, J (1999) *Charles Boydell 1800–1869 and Camyr Allyn, Allyn River, Gresford*, Paterson, NSW: Paterson Historical Society.

— (2006) *Patch and Glennie of Orindinna*, Gresford, Paterson, NSW: Paterson Historical Society.

Swan, K (1970) *A History of Wagga Wagga*, Wagga Wagga, NSW: City of Wagga Wagga.

Tampke, J (2006) *The Germans in Australia*, Melbourne: Cambridge University Press.

Thach, L and L Bynum (2004) 'Managing Human Resources in the Wine Industry', in Thach, L, D Gastin, M Schwing and A Gilinsky, *Wine, A global business*, New York: Miranda Press.

Tolley, JH (2005) '"Gustav Got the Winery and Sophie Got the Soup Tureen", The contribution of women to the Barossa Valley wine industry 1836–2003', *History Australia*, 2, pp. 86.81–86.88.

Toussaint Samat, M (1994) *A History of Food*, trans. A Bell, Oxford: Blackwell.

Tyrrell, I (1999) *True Gardens of the Gods, Californian–Australian Environmental Reform, 1860–1930*, Berkeley: University of California Press.

Ulin, RC (1995) 'Invention and Representation as Cultural Capital: South west French winegrowing history', *American Anthropologist*, 97, 2, pp. 519–27.

Unwin, T (1991) *Wine and the Vine: An historical geography of viticulture and the wine trade*, London: Routledge.

Wahlquist, G (2008) *Some of My Best Friends Are Winemakers and Other Tales, A history of the wine industry of Mudgee, N.S.W.*, Sydney: The author.

Walsh, G (1979) 'The Wine Industry of Australia 1778–1979', Paper presented at the Wine Talk Symposium, Canberra, September.

Waterhouse, R (1995) *Private Pleasures, Public Leisure: A history of Australian popular culture since 1788*, Melbourne: Longman.

— (2005) *The Vision Splendid, A social and cultural history of rural Australia*, Fremantle: Fremantle Arts Centre Press.

Webb, J, T Schirato and G Danaher (2002) *Understanding Bourdieu*, Sydney: Allen & Unwin.

White, R (1981) *Inventing Australia, Images and identity, 1688–1980*, Sydney: Allen & Unwin.

Wilkinson, D (1986) *Dalwood House: Its importance and its associations*, Sydney: The author.

Wilton, J and R Bosworth (1984) *Old Worlds and New Australia, The post–war migrant experience*, Melbourne: Penguin.

Wood, WA (1972) *Dawn in the Valley, The Story of Settlement in the Hunter River Valley to 1833*, Sydney: Wentworth Books.

Zohary, D and M Hopf (2000) *Domestication of Plants in the Old World, The origin and spread of cultivated plants in west Asia, Europe and the Nile Valley*, Third edn, Oxford: Oxford University Press.

Theses

Bossy, G 'Effects of Tariff Protection on Economic Development in Australia: Victoria and New South Wales from 1871 to 1900', PhD thesis, University of Columbia, 1964, p. 370.

Ludington, CC 'Politics and the Taste for Wine in England and Scotland, 1660–1860', PhD thesis, University of Columbia, 2003.

Norrie, P 'A Study of the Original Documents on Viticulture in Early New South Wales and the Role of the Macleay Family 1788 to 1883', Master of Science thesis, University of Sydney, 1992.

Walker, T 'The History of the Wine Industry in Tasmania', Masters thesis, History, University of Tasmania, 2012.

Newspapers, trade journals and magazines

Agricultural Gazette of New South Wales
Albury Banner
Australian Brewer's Journal
Australian Town & Country Journal
Clarence and Richmond Examiner and New England Advertiser
Maitland Mercury
Perth Gazette
Sydney Gazette
Sydney Morning Herald
The Australian
The Gentleman's Magazine
The Times of London
Wagga Wagga Express

Index